A Mourne Townland

The History and People

of

Aughnaloopy

by

Fiona Doyle Jones

with research by Sheila Phillips

Mourne Miners

Publications

This work is dedicated to the memory of two special women – both residents of Newcastle Street, Kilkeel and both beloved grandmothers to the researchers of this work.

Granny Doyle - Ellen Doyle nee Murray (1897–1975)

&

Grandma Doyle - Sarah Elizabeth Doyle nee Rogers (1898–1982)

FRONT COVER
Mr. Peter Flanagan outside his family home in Aughnaloopy, Summer 2008 Copyright Ciera E. Jones.

Copyright 2012 by Fiona Doyle Jones (author)
All rights reserved.
No part of this publication may be reproduced, stored in a retrieval system or transmitted in any form or by any means without written permission of the author.

About the Researchers

Sheila Phillips from Ballymartin, Co. Down and Fiona Doyle Jones, who resides in New Jersey, USA, first made contact in 2006 via the Internet and quickly discovered they shared an interest in researching the Doyle family of Kilkeel. It wasn't long before Fiona asked Sheila if she knew anything about James Doyle's wife Ann Quinn who was born c.1840. Quinn is a common name throughout the Kilkeel area and it was difficult to know where to begin to learn more about Ann. After a couple of trips to the Public Records Office of Northern Ireland (PRONI), Sheila discovered that Fiona's Great-Grandmother Ann Quinn was in fact the daughter of James 'Hamilton' Quinn from Aughnaloopy. Further research revealed more ties between the researchers, including that their paternal grandmothers had been neighbours on Newcastle Street in Kilkeel town for over fifty years. As a result of weekly trips to PRONI over the next five years and a scouring of all available online resources, a detailed picture of the Quinn family emerged, including information that Ann had several brothers who had settled in New Zealand.

Fiona and Sheila discovered that the lives of the families of this small townland were so intermingled that it was impossible to understand the history of one family without understanding the personal and business interactions that they had with their neighbours and so their investigation expanded to include all residents of Aughnaloopy. This book is the result of that research.

Sheila passed away on January 12, 2012 while working on the Moore family chapter of this book. It was her wish that the work was published with the reminder to all that family research is never complete and that we have an obligation to share our knowledge with others.

Acknowledgments

So many people have contributed to this project and where possible names have been included in the individual family chapters. Many thanks go to Brenda Anderson and Peter Meaney for their painstaking work transcribing the 1901 census for Kilkeel Poor Law Union; to Raymond Kelly and Ros Davies for the wealth of information they have made available on the Internet; to Catherine Hudson, John and Nora Newell, for their inspiration and local knowledge; to Vincey Quinn and Bill Quinn, for sharing their knowledge of family history.

Thank you Deirdre McEvoy for your expertise knowledge of the Hamilton family and for your wiliness to check resources at the General Register Office and The National Archives of Ireland.

Special thanks David and Jonathon at www.emeraldancestors.com for granting us access to your wonderful website.

We are especially indebted to Terence (self-professed Style Guru) and Stephen Patton - past and present editors at the Mourne Observer Newspaper. Also to Eddie McGlue and Peter Flanagan for providing great assistance in locating family homesteads and to Dennis Cunningham who did a wonderful job of driving Ciera Jones around Aughnaloopy and the surrounding townlands so that she could take photographs for the book.

Shelley Crawford Maskery also deserves a special mention for her beautiful sketches of Aughnaloopy that are presented in this book.

This project would not have been possible without the tremendous support and encouragement of all members of the Yahoo County Down Genealogy Group
http://groups.yahoo.com/group/CountyDownGenealogy/

Thank you to Nan Brennan for believing that this project would eventually become a reality. Also to Peter Dillon and Murray Lynn for their invaluable assistance in researching the families from Aughnaloopy that settled to New Zealand.

And of course, a special thank you to our families for their patience and encouragement while we spent hours engrossed in ancient texts, staring at a computer screen or peering through a microfiche reader.

Fiona Doyle Jones & Sheila Phillips

Author's Preface

Why a study of the people of Aughnaloopy? What interest could the history of this small townland, sheltered within the ancient Kingdom of Mourne have to people today? Aughnaloopy is a townland, with a population of just 119 residents in 1911; there was no church, no school, and no major commerce or industry. Some might argue that there is nothing special about Aughnaloopy, but that is exactly what makes it so special. Aughnaloopy represents so many rural townlands across Ireland. The story of the people of Aughnaloopy, their lives, their turmoil, their contribution to the local and global community throughout history, mirrors those of the Irish across the 32 counties living in more than 64,000 townlands.

This book is not intended as a definitive study of the geography, history or politics of the townland and the authors claim no expertise in any of these subject matters. This project merely aims to offer some insight into the families that made Aughnaloopy their home and share their contribution to the world around them.

Aughnaloopy townland consists of a little over 382 acres, in the Civil Parish and Poor Law Union of Kilkeel, in the Barony of Mourne, in the County of Down, in the Province of Ulster. It lies just to the north of Kilkeel town (Ballymageough townland). To the southwest is Drumcro townland, to the east is Aughnahorey, to the northeast is Leitrim and to the north is Ballinran. The far southwestern tip borders Aughrim townland and the southeastern tip borders Kilkeel townland. Just as the residents of Aughnaloopy strayed across these borders, so too does the research that is presented in this book. Aughnaloopy is chosen as a starting point to study these families, it is not meant to be restrictive.

Traditionally, it was accepted that the townland name came from the Irish *Achadh na Lúibe* meaning 'field of the loop/bend'. An examination of the topography of the land makes it difficult to say what this 'loop' actually refers to. One explanation is that Aughnaloopy derives its name from a meandering river which either curves its way through the townland or forms part of the boundaries, but the only river running near Aughnaloopy never meanders to form a loop or bend. An alternative explanation is that the name could be derived from the shape of the townland itself. One reference records *lub talmhan* - a V-shaped piece of land - and it is true that part of the townland boundaries could be described as V-shaped. The authors will leave the readers to make up their own mind.

The spelling of Aughnaloopy varies considerably throughout the historical documents that have been referenced in the preparation of this book. Variants include: Aghanalooby (1613), Aghanalooby (1625), Aghnatooby (1659), Aghnaluby (1661), Aughneluby (1688), Aughnaloopy (1810, 1830, 1832), Achadh na luipe (1834) and Analoopy (gravestone inscription). Except when referencing or including original documents the spelling Aughnaloopy had been used for consistency throughout this work.

While everyone involved in this project has taken the utmost care to minimise the number of errors and inaccuracies with transcriptions, it is inevitable that in a project of this detail that some may have slipped through. Many of the original documents have faded or have been copied badly and are at times difficult to read. Errors have also inevitably been passed down through the years. Many of the documents were completed before the majority of the population could read and write and so a neighbour, relative or friend may have provided the information. I would be delighted to hear from anyone who can add information on any of the people or places that are mentioned in this book including notification of any possible errors.

A project such as this never really comes to an end. Just as the families of Aughnaloopy continue to grow and flourish and spread their influence around the globe, so too should this project continue to record their contribution. My hope is that this publication is not the end of the story of the people of Aughnaloopy but rather a beginning of something bigger.

Fiona Doyle Jones
Winter 2011
mourneminers@optonline.net

Location of Aughnaloopy

Below is an adaptation of the Griffith's Valuation map showing the location of Aughnaloopy townland.

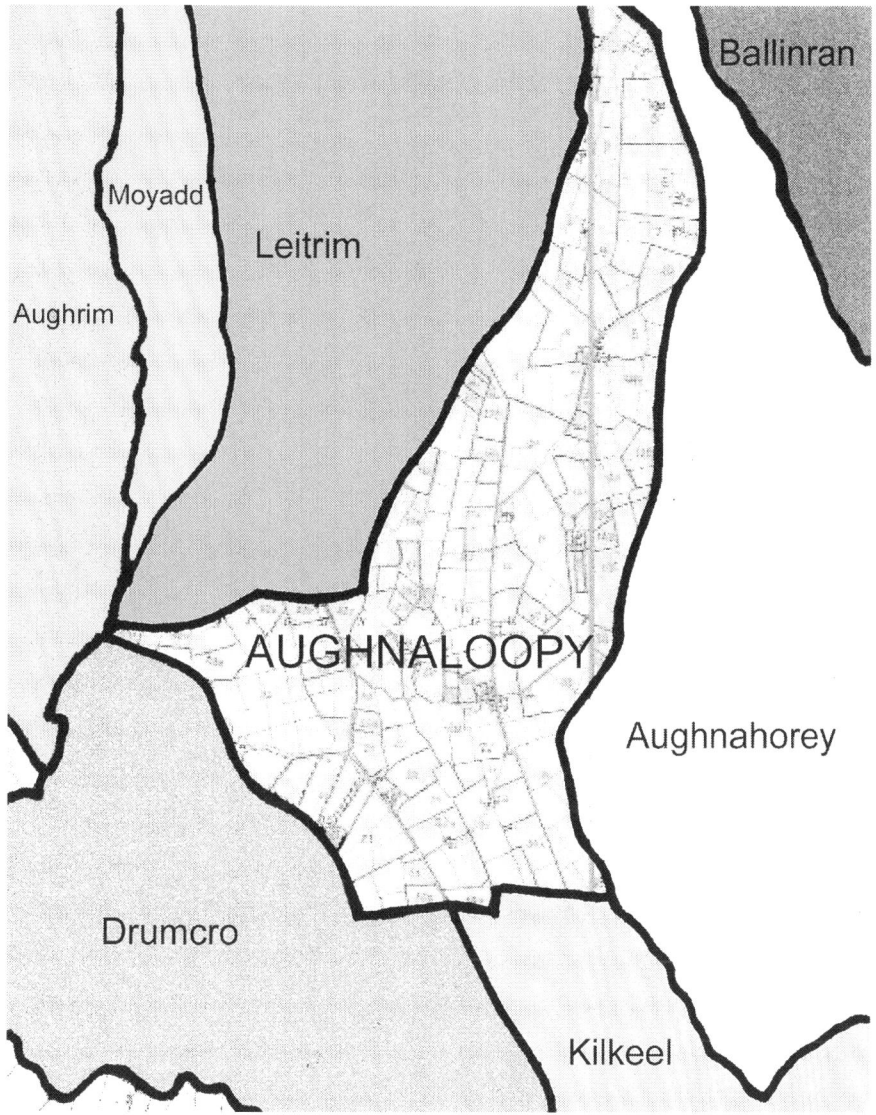

The townland consists of a little over 382 acres, in the Civil Parish and Poor Law Union of Kilkeel, in the Barony of Mourne, in the County of Down, in the Province of Ulster. It lies just to the north of Kilkeel town (Ballymageough townland). To the southwest is Drumcro townland, to the east is Aughnahorey, to the northeast is Leitrim and to the north is Ballinran. The far southwestern tip borders Aughrim townland and the southeastern tip borders Kilkeel townland.

Ann Quinn
(1840 - 1916)

It was researching the family of Ann Quinn, who married James Doyle in 1861, that led to the research in this book.

Contents

About the Researchers
Acknowledgements
Author's Preface
Location of Aughnaloopy

Part 1 The History of Aughnaloopy

Chapter 1	The Early Years	12
Chapter 2	The Nedham Days	16
Chapter 3	The Revolution	19
Chapter 4	Freeholders, Landowners and Catholic Emancipation	20
Chapter 5	Wheels of Change	24
Chapter 6	Surveys and Tithes	31
Chapter 7	Potato Famine and Poor Law	34
Chapter 8	Maps and Valuations	40
Chapter 9	Births and Marriages	45
Chapter 10	Vaccination Records	47
Chapter 11	Early Occupations	49
Chapter 12	Early Census Records	52
Chapter 13	1901 Census	54
Chapter 14	1911 Census	58
Chapter 15	Ulster Day	62
Chapter 16	Emigration	64
Chapter 17	Wills and Letters of Administration	69

Part 2 The People of Aughnaloopy

Chapter 18	Allen Family	84
Chapter 19	Annett Family	86
Chapter 20	Beck Family	88
Chapter 21	Bradley	91
Chapter 22	Campbell and Colgan	93
Chapter 23	Doran Family	94
Chapter 24	Edgar Family	104
Chapter 25	Fitzpatrick Family	105
Chapter 26	Flanagan Family	106
Chapter 27	Gonsalves Family	111
Chapter 28	Hagan Family	114
Chapter 29	Hamilton, Carvill and Murphy	118
Chapter 30	Hanna Family	122
Chapter 31	Johnston Family	127
Chapter 32	Keown Family	132
Chapter 33	Mills Family	135
Chapter 34	Moore Family	136
Chapter 35	Morgan Family	138
Chapter 36	Quinn Family	142
Chapter 37	Rogers Family	161
Chapter 38	Speers Family	162
Chapter 39	Trainor Family	170
Chapter 40	Wilson Family	174
Chapter 41	An Orphan's Tale	176
Chapter 42	Springfield Villa	179

The Loanin.
by: Shelley Jayne Crawford Maskery (Shelley Jayne Illustration)

Part 1

The History of Aughnaloopy

The Mournes

I shall not go to heaven when I die.
But if they let me be
I think I'll take a road I used to know
That goes by Slieve-na-garagh and the sea.
And all day breasting me the wind will blow,
And I'll hear nothing but the peewit's cry
And the sea talking in the caves below.
I think it will be winter when I die
(For no one from the North could die in spring)
And all the heather will be dead and grey,
And the bog-cotton will have blown away,
And there will be no yellow on the wind.
But I shall smell the peat,
And when it's almost dark I'll set my feet
Where a white track goes glimmering to the hills,
And see, far up, a light
-- Would you think Heaven could be so small a thing
As a lit window on the hills at night? --
And come in stumbling from the gloom,
Half-blind, into a firelit room.
Turn, and see you,
And there abide.
If it were true,
And if I thought that they would let me be,
I almost wish it were tonight I died.

by Helen Waddell

The author, Helen Waddell (1899 –1965) was born in Tokyo but spent much of her life in Belfast. She was a distinguished scholar and translator of medieval Latin and an authority on the church in the Middle Ages. In this poem she describes the region of Mourne adjacent to Bloody Bridge. Thank you to Sean McCartan for suggesting the inclusion of this poem.

Chapter 1

The Early Years

'Much of the abbey lands had become waste or lapsed into the hands of the Irish, and it was desirable to place them in better hands.'

Richard be Burgh, the 'Red Earl of Ulster'

From 1305 to 1326, Aughnaloopy was held by Richard de Burgh, the "Red Earl of Ulster". Richard was arguably one of the most powerful men in Ireland at the time and held his residence at the Green Castle (built during the 1230's by the Anglo Norman knight Hugh de Lacy). Ulster suffered badly during the 1315 invasion of Edward Bruce and by 1318 the area presented a pitiable spectacle. Churches and castles were destroyed, homes were burnt, crops were destroyed and famine was widespread across the land.

Upon Richard be Burgh's death on July 29, 1326, the Green Castle and associated estate passed to William 'the Brown Earl'. In the 1330's his property, which included Aughnaloopy, was the subject of a commission and the land was described as *'...a wasteland with very few tenants'*. The lives of any Aughnaloopy residents will have changed little over the next 200 years. In 1505, Aughnaloopy passed to Gerald Mór FitzGerald, 8th Earl of Kildare known variously as 'Garret the Great' (*Gearóid Mór*) or 'the Great Earl' (*An Iarla Mór*). A land survey conducted in 1540 reported that the land was *'.....in the hands of the rebels and wasted by reason of disobedience of the Maguinnesses, O'Neill's and Savages.'*

A photograph of the author Fiona Doyle Jones taken at the "Green Castle" in 1969 by photographer John Gunson.

Nicholas Bagenal

Early 16th century records referencing Aughnaloopy, link it to estate of Nicholas Bagenal, the son of John Bagnal (alias John Bagenhall) Mayor of Newcastle-under-Lyme, Staffordshire, England. Nicholas Bagenal arrived in Ulster in 1539 apparently having fled England after being implicated in a murder in the Staffordshire town of Leek. He was first employed as a mercenary soldier for the O'Neills and received a general pardon in March 1543.

'Nicholas Bagenal, or Bagnolde, or Bagenholde late of Wolston, Warwickshire, alias of Warwick, alias of Stafford, alias of Langfords, Derbyshire, Yeoman. General pardon of all murders and felonies by him committed.'

This pardon has led some historians to believe that Bagenal may have been acting as a double agent on behalf of the Crown. From 1544 to 1547, Nicholas received permission from the Dublin Privy Council to leave Ireland for service in the French Wars. During this time he acquired a fearsome military reputation for the wholesale slaughter of his enemy.

In 1547, Bagenal became a member of the Irish Privy Council and secured the position of Marshall General of Queen Elizabeth's army in Ireland. Bagenal eventually settled in the town of Newry having been granted the confiscated estates of the Cistercian Abbey along with land at Carlingford and Greencastle by King Edward VI. The lease was initially for twenty-one years, and then in 1552 Bagenal received a grant of practically the entire town of Newry along with the surrounding land, the fisheries, and the customs and tolls of the market. This had all previously belonged to the Abbey of Newry. Added to these properties and other rights and lands, he also gained the Lordship of Mourne, which extended '…..*for ten miles in length and two in breadth'*. The Privy Council thought that the continued residence of Nicholas in Newry would aid the *'civilitie'* of the natives and their obedience to the King.

> *'Much of the abbey lands had become waste or lapsed into the hands of the Irish, and it was desirable to place them in better hands.'*

Nicholas married Elenor Griffith on August 31, 1553. Eleanor was the third daughter and co-heiress of Sir Edward Griffith of Penrhyn, North Wales. Through this marriage Nicholas became seated at Plas Newydd, Near Bangor, and owner of considerable estates in Wales. The couple had many children including: Henry, Dudley, Ambrose, Frances, Mary, Margaret, Ann, Mabel and Isabel.

Around 1575 Sir Nicholas Bagnel built Saint Patrick's Church in Newry believed to be the first Protestant church to be built in Ireland. Nicholas died in Newry in 1590. His son and heir Henry was to perish just eight years later at the Battle of the Yellow Ford near Armagh, fighting against Hugh O'Neill, Earl of Tyrone. Percy Bagenal, a relative was to hold Newry awaiting the coming of age of Nicholas's grandson Arthur.

> *'... to Arthur Bagenal Esq., his heirs and assigns, the town of Newry, with all the demesne lands ...of the dissolved monastery, the manor, lordship, and castle of Greencastle, the lordship, country or territory of Mourne with two islands in the main sea; the manor of Carlingford with the monastery and its appurtenances, and the lands of Cooley; the ferry between Carlingford and Killowen; the customs and anchorage, and certain customs of goods and merchandise imported into or exported from Carlingford; the territory of Omeath, and all wrecks of sea happening on these properties. By virtue of his patent the proprietor is entitled to the tithes of the Lordship of Newry, and has the right of presentation to the rectory ...'*

William Brereton's Travels Through Ireland

Although no documents specifically relating to Aughnaloopy have been found, the following account of Ireland in 1635 is extracted from the *Travels in Holland, the United Provinces, England, Scotland and Ireland, 1634-1635, of Sir William Brereton.*

William was the eldest son of William Brereton of Handforth in Cheshire, he inherited substantial estates in Cheshire on the death of his parents around 1610. After attending Oxford and Gray's Inn, Brereton emerged as an energetic magistrate in Cheshire during the 1620s and '30s. He was made a baronet in 1627, and travelled extensively throughout Europe. He was commissioned by Parliament to supervise the transportation of troops and supplies from Cheshire to Ireland to suppress the Irish Uprising in 1641. The journal of his travels gives a detailed account of what life was like for Bagenal's tenants.

> *'July 7. We left Dromore and went to the Newrie, which is sixteen miles. This is a most difficult way for a stranger to find out. Herein we wandered, being lost amongst the Irish towns. The Irish houses are the poorest cabins I have seen, erected in the middle of the fields and grounds, which they farm*

and rent. This is a wild country, not inhabited, planted, nor enclosed, yet it would be good corn if it were husbanded. I gave an Irishman to bring us into the way a groat, who led us like a villain directly out of the way and so left us, so as by this deviation it was three hour before we came to the Newrie. Much land there is about this town belonging to Mr. Bagnall, nothing well planted. He hath a castle in this town, but is for most part resident at Green Castle; a great part of this town is his, and it is reported that he hath a 1,000£ or 1,500£ per annum in this country. This is but a poor town, and is much Irish, and is navigable for boats to come up unto with the tide. Here we baited at a good inn, the sign of the Prince's Arms.'

The Ulster Plantation

At the narrowest point, only 13 miles of sea separates Ulster and Scotland. In the beginning of the 17th Century the crossing by boat took under three hours and it is therefore not surprising that families migrated between Ulster, Scotland and England. Although no formal records exist, it is estimated that up to 200,000 Lowland Scots crossed the Channel to settle in Ulster during the 17th Century. The Plantation of Ulster took place in two stages. The first stage was primarily confined to the eastern counties of Antrim and Down and is believed to have been an initiative undertaken by individual families who saw Ulster as an attractive business opportunity. Although not a formalised plantation, it was certainly encouraged by the British Crown. The second stage of settlement was far broader in scope; conceived, planned and supervised by the British Government. The plantations included settlers from England and Scotland, although Scots outnumbered those from England by a ratio of 20 to 1. The primary purpose of the scheme was to populate the northern counties of Ireland with loyal British subjects, to counterbalance the native Irish. Scotland was only too willing to participate. It was seen as a way to eradicate Scotland of the hordes of Lowland and Border Scots, many of whom were in desperate poverty. Many were subsistence farmers barely able to support their families and thus in the early years of the Plantation, the majority of the settlers were Lowland and Border Scots seeking a better life. It is likely that some of these Scots made their way to Aughnaloopy and although it is not possible to definitively identify the origin of each family. From the extensive research of Maynard Hanna of Kilkeel, it is known that the Hanna family originated from Sorbie in Dumfriesshire and settled in Ulster in the mid to late 17th Century. Whether they arrived as a consequence of the anti-Presbyterian pogram visited upon the Lowland Scots or whether they came in the Military entourage of King William III is unknown. The name Houston also makes an appearance in the area around this time and is believed to be of Ulster-Scot origins.

The Bloodiest Century in Irish History

The 17th century was perhaps the bloodiest in Ireland's history. Two periods of civil war (1641-53 and 1689-91) caused huge loss of life and resulted in the final dispossession of the Irish Catholic landowning class and their subordination under Penal Law. In the middle of the century, Ireland was convulsed by eleven years of warfare, beginning with the Rebellion of 1641, when Irish Catholics rebelled against English and Protestant domination, in the process massacring thousands of Protestant settlers. The Catholic gentry briefly ruled the country as Confederate Ireland (1642-1649) until Oliver Cromwell re-conquered Ireland in 1649-1653 on behalf of the English Commonwealth. By it's close, up to a third of Ireland's pre-war population was dead or in exile. As punishment for the 1641 rebellion, almost all lands owned by Irish Catholics were confiscated and given to British settlers. Several hundred remaining native landowners were transplanted to Connacht.

Sir William Petty's 1659 Census

It was against this violent and unsettled backdrop that Sir William Petty conducted the so-called *1659 Census*. The document is not in reality a full enumeration of the population but rather a record of the number of adults paying tax. The document is arranged by divisions of counties, baronies, parishes and townlands, and where applicable, by cities, parishes and streets. The most influential people in society were identified as *Tituladoes*, a term coined by Petty himself to describe those individuals who are returned as paying the highest taxes. Petty wanted to ascertain the ethnic divisions living within Ireland at the time and he included a section at the end of each barony on the numbers of Irish, Scots and English living within each barony. In addition, a numerical list was made of the 'Principal Irish Names'.

Aughnaloopy is recorded in Petty's work and it is documented that eight Irish adults were living in the townland and paying tax, no English or Scots were documented. (Across Upper and Lower Mourne there were 79 English and 330 Irish taxpayers documented.

This compares with the '*Barony of ye Newry*, where there were 166 English and Scots and 765 Irish taxpayers. Patrick Modder O'Howen (O'Hoyne) Esq. was recorded as holding the lease for Aughnaloopy as well as land in the townlands of Lisnacree, Aghyoghill, Drumcro, and Greencastle. No further information is known about the origins of Patrick Modder O'Howen but evidence suggests that he may have been resident in Lisnacree.

Petty lists the principal Irish names across the Barony of Newry as O'Doran (20); O'Feggan (8); Garvy (7); McIlroy (8); O'Quinne (10); Slowan (8) and White (8).

PRONI Reference for Petty's work T371

Although Aughnaloopy remained part of the Bagenal Estate for almost two hundred years, other than receiving rent, it is unlikely that any of the Bagenals would have had reason to be involved in the life of the Aughnaloopy residents.

1663 Subsidy Roll for the Lordship of Newry and Mourne

The 1663 Subsidy Roll for the Lordship of Newry and Mourne provides the names of the major property owners who were liable to pay direct taxation to the Crown. Aughnaloopy does not warrant an individual listing but some familiar names are included. Nicholas Bagnal Esq. is recorded as being liable for £20. Patrick Modder O'Hoyne from Lisnacree is recorded as being liable for £5, Richard Houston from Cranfield paid £4 10s and Collin Wachope Esq. of Kilkeel, who was charged £3 10s.

1688 Rent Rolls for the Lordship of Mourne

The 1688 Rent Rolls for the Lordship of Mourne have survived and are archived at PRONI. Land at Aughnaloopy is listed as being let to Art mc Heroo, Thomas ma Guier (may later have been Maguire) and the rest, for the yearly rent of 6 pounds 10 shilling and 'duties' of 2 mutton. An annotation in the left column reads '*more raised Pck Mr White receives 3£.*' None of these names have survived in Aughnaloopy and their origins are unknown.

Throughout the latter part of the 17th century, the Bagenals had a policy of introducing foreign tenants to the area and it is during this time that the names Houston and Moore frequently appear in documents. One theory is that William Moore originated from the Isle of Man and he sublet land from Richard Houston. The name Modder O'Hoyne appears to die out in the area. For the next three centuries, descendants of the Moore family remain settled in Aughnaloopy and their lives were to have a major impact of the residents of the townland.

Chapter 2

The Nedham Days

'The Bagenal Mourne Rentals of 1715 documents that James Eager Senior and James Eager Junior and D A Eager paid 6 pounds and 10 shillings for use of the land at Aughnaloopy.'

Partition of the Estate

When Arthur Bagenal died his land including Aughnaloopy townland, passed to Nicholas Bagenal Jn. who died in 1712 without male issue. Nicholas's Will (dated November 13, 1708) was probated in 1713, passing the family estates to his relatives Edward Bayley (Baily) and Robert Nedham. The men were all related, Edward Bayly and Robert Nedham being descendants from other children of Sir Henry Bagenal, in the female line. The Bagenal Estate was partitioned with Bayley taking the lands in County Louth and the eastern portion of the Lordship of Newry and Nedham receiving the western portion of the Lordship of Newry and the Barony of Mourne. Whereas the ownership of Aughnaloopy had passed from the Bagenals to the Nedhams there is no evidence to suggest that much would have changed for the families living and working in Aughnaloopy. The tenant farmers may well have experienced a period of uncertainly over their tenancy and fears of rent increases.

The Arrival of the Wachop Family

The Nedhams continued with the Bagenal policy of encouraging foreign tenants to their Mourne estates. It is during this period that we begin to see the frequent occurrence of the name Wachop (with a variety of spelling variants including Wauchope, Wahap and Wahup). There are several theories on the origin and date of arrival of this family in Mourne with evidence linking the name to Germany and to Scotland. There is also evidence that at least one branch of the Wachop family were in Ulster as early as 1616. The social status of the Moore, Wachop and Houston families and the close community in which they lived will have necessitated frequent business and social interactions. It is therefore not surprising that several marriages occurred between these families.

William Wachop was the Revenue Officer for South Down and lived in Greencastle. He was married to Margaret Reman and the couple had at least seven children including: James (1697-1719), Joshua (c.1698), John (1699-1718), Hugh (1701-1722), Ann (1703-1724), Mary (1717-1724), and Thomas (c.1710). William died c.1733 and is buried in the Old Kilkeel Graveyard.

The Eagar Family of Aughnaloopy

Another now familiar Aughnaloopy name makes an appearance in the surviving archives of the townland. The Bagenal Mourne Rentals of 1715 documents that James Eager Senior and James Eager Junior and D A Eager paid 6 pounds and 10 shillings for use of land at Aughnaloopy. The lease value of the land was stated at 10 pounds. One might assume that James Eager Senior and Junior were father and son but the relationship, if any, to D A Eager is unknown. There are later references to a Doughtry Eager a landlord in the Mourne area and it is possible that D A Eager refers to Doughty. This ancient and distinguished surname is of Anglo-Saxon origin, and is derived from the Olde English pre-7th Century male personal name 'Eadgar', composed of the elements *'ead'*, prosperity, fortune, with *'gar'*, spear. In Aughnaloopy, the name appears to have become Edgar over time.

A later Rent Roll thought to be from sometime between 1716 to 1720, provides further insight into the farmers that actually worked the land at Aughnaloopy. *James Eager and partners* are noted as still renting land at Aughnaloopy. Although the name of the partners is unknown, James is most likely the James Eager Junior from the previous Rent Roll and it might be assumed that his father James Eager Senior has died during the intervening period. The agent has written *'In the chief tenants and partners hand, only one 6th part left for – '*. This presumably means that the Eagers primarily farmed the land themselves and sublet a sixth of the land for 3 pounds. Further information on the Eager (Edgar) family is given in Chapter 24.

The Moore and Wauchope Lease

On January 20, 1732, Robert Nedham Srn. granted a lease of his lands including Aughnaloopy (which was noted as comprising two-hundred and thirteen acres) to William Moore, James Moore, Charles Moore and Joshua Wauchope.

William, James and Charles Moore were all brothers from Ballynahatten; their father was William Moore and their mother was a member of the Wachop family. Joshua Wachop was born c.1698, the son of William Wachop and Margaret Redmond of Cranfield. He worked at H.M. Customs at Skerries, being described as a 'Tyde Surveyor'.

Joshua Wachop and his wife Elizabeth had two children, James and Margaret. Margaret Wachop married Joshua Moore in 1750. James died unmarried in 1756, and administration of his goods was granted to *'Margaret Moore otherwise Wahab (wife of Joshua Moore of Moran) his natural and lawful sister and next of kin'*. The grant was signed by Joshua Moore, George Wahab, and James Seed on March 19, 1756.

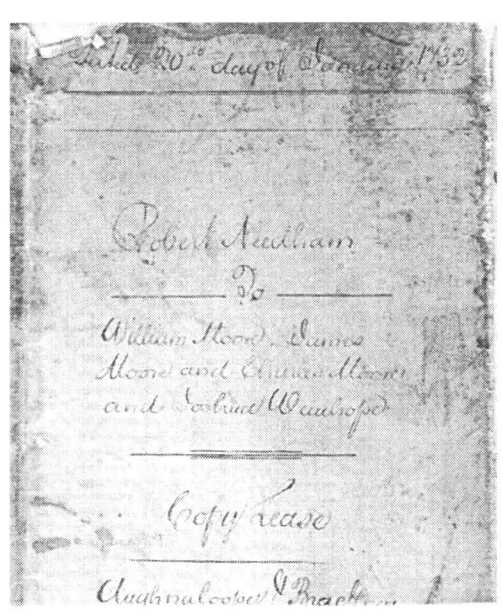

Lease from Robert Nedham, Newry to Wm. Jas. and Chas. Moore, Ballynahatten, Co. Down and Joshua Wauchop, Skerries, Co. Dublin, Aughnaloopy and Brackney PRONI Reference T618/2

Joshua's clear and concise Will states:

> *In the name of God, amen, I Joshua Wahab now of the town of Galloway, gentleman, being weak in body but of sound disposing mind and memory, do make this my last Will and Testament in manner and form following:*
> *I bequeath my soul into the hands of him that gave it, hoping for salvation thro' the merits of my Blessed Redeemer, my body to be buried in such order and such depency as John Disney, Esq., Collector of Galloway shall think fit, and as to such worldly substance either real or personal as I am possessed of or entitled unto, I leave and bequeath unto my well beloved wife Elizabeth Wahab, and my two children, James and Margaret, to be equally divided between them, share and share alike, and the distribution to be made by my Executors to my said children, at such seasonable times as my Executors shall think proper, first paying all my legal and just debts.*
> *My will is that in case any of my said children or wife should dye before such distribution be made, then shall the portion of such of them so dying devolve to ye Survivor or Survivors of my said children, share and share alike.*
> *I appoint Henry Cottingham Esq., and Ambrose Wheeler, Harmer, Executors to this my last will and Testament.*
> *Witness my hand and seal this 12th day of October, 1737*
> *Robert Westicoat Napper Gifford JOSHUA WAHAB. Robert McMullen*
> *Notary Public.*

The Will was proved on November 3, 1738.

Both James and Margaret are mentioned in a deed dated 1756 concerning the transference of the Aughnaloopy and Brackenagh property held by the late Joshua Wahab to Joshua Moore, his son-in-law.

Estate Agent

According to information from PRONI, John Bayly appears to have been the primary estate agent from 1721, after Sir Edward Bayly's dismissal of Nicholas Bagenal's agent, Hans Hamilton Esq. No mention is made of another estate agent between 1740 and 1765, and it is difficult to say whether there was any intervening person between John Bayly and John Hutcheon, who first appears in 1765. It is suspected that John Bayly was related to the landowning Bayly family.

1715 Lease - PRONI

Chapter 3

The Revolution

*'Soldier, soldier, will you marry me,
With your musket, fife and drum?
Oh, how can I marry such a pretty girl as you,
When I have no coat to put on?'*

Men of Mourne Volunteer Corps

Although isolated geographically from the centres of political development, Aughnaloopy failed to remain unscathed by the turmoil of the late 18th Century. When France allied with the American colonies in their revolt against British rule, troops were removed from Ireland to assist the British monarchy in its attempt to crush the revolution. This left only 9000 or so members of the Irish military establishment to defend the country against the genuine possibility of a French invasion. In response, landowners and other prominent citizens took it upon themselves to form volunteer military companies. By 1779, twenty-one corps had been formed across County Down including the Men of Mourne Volunteer Corps, embodied on December 13, 1778. The Men of Mourne Volunteer Corps was under the leadership of British army officer Major General Robert Ross of Bladensburg from Rostrevor. The Minute Book of the corps has survived and is archived at PRONI. It opens with the lines:

> *'The present perilous situation of this Kingdom which is Really Defenceless for want of A sufficient Force to Repel the Depredations of Pirates or Invasions of the Common Enemy having inspired the Publick spirited throughout the Kingdom to Associate for its Internal Defence. These therefore of this Parish who would be Desirous of Forming themselves into a Volunteer Company to Act in Case of necessity, in Conduction with the Friends of Ireland, may enter their Names at Stuart Moore's of Kilkeel where a book for that purpose is opened.'*

In one document dated December 13, 1778, a list of the Committee of the Men of Mourne is published and includes John Moore from Aughnaloopy. Three other members of the Moore family are noted, John from Ballymagart, Stuart and Francis, but the relationship to John from Aughnaloopy is unknown. Other members of the committee were John Atkinson, John Thomson, George Lewis, George Atkinson, John Halyday, Joseph Jefferson, Robert Carr, Samuel Walmsley, William McComb, Joseph Nichol and William Irvine.

The name John Moore is noted again in a document dated May 24, 1780 where he is recorded as holding the post of Chair. At that meeting, a resolution was passed to form a music band and a uniform of *'White Shag Coat faced with Blue, White Waistcoat, and Breeches'* was to be made available with *'great expedition'* for the Fife and Drum band volunteers. By 1782, the volunteer forces had adopted a more overtly political role and forced the British Government to concede the independence of the Irish Parliament. The question of Catholic emancipation caused divisions within the organisation and by 1784, they started to loose any national influence.

Chapter 4

Freeholders, Landowners and Catholic Emancipation

'Gentlemen, you may soon have the alternative to live as slaves or die as free men'
Daniel O'Connell

Political Change

The late 18th Century saw the introduction of great political changes that were to have an enduring impact on the lives of the families living in Aughnaloopy and indeed those of their descendants. Progress was finally underway in the development of Catholic Emancipation across Great Britain and Ireland. This process involved reducing and removing many of the existing restrictions on Roman Catholics that had been introduced by the Act of Uniformity, the Test Acts and the Penal Laws. These changes eventually gave way to Roman Catholics having the right to vote and own land.

From 1727 to 1793 only Protestants with a freehold worth at least 40 shillings a year had been legally permitted to vote. A freeholder was a man who owned his land outright (in fee) or who held it by lease that could be for one or more lives (for example, his own life or for the lives of other people named in the lease). As detailed in Chapter 2, Robert Nedham Srn. granted a lease of two hundred and thirteen acres of his land at Aughnaloopy to William Moore, James Moore, Charles Moore and Joshua Wauchope in 1732. This act was to have a lasting impact on the lives of Aughnaloopy residents for the next three hundred years.

The first Catholic Relief Act was eventually passed in 1778; subject to an oath against Stuart claims to the throne and the civil jurisdiction of the Pope. The passing of this Act, allowed Roman Catholics in Great Britain to own property, inherit land, and join the army. Further relief was given in 1791. The Irish Parliament passed similar acts between 1778 and 1793.

Forty-Shilling Freeholders

The 1793 Act created a class of tenants, Catholics and Protestants, known as 'Forty Shilling Freeholders' who had the right to vote in parliamentary elections. The Nedham family had political ambitions and were keen to create voters and thus they began a process of granting of leases to some eligible tenants. In return for a lease, the tenants were expected to vote for the Nedham interest. This vote was guaranteed, since before the 1872 Ballot Act that introduced the secret ballot, voters were required to stand up and declare publicly their electoral allegiance. The fear of going against the landlords' wishes resulted in a substantial number of candidates returned being either landlords or their relations. In 1829, the voting franchise level was increased to 10 pounds, so the 40-shilling freeholders were no longer allowed to vote. This measure increased the influence of the landlord class by effectively confining membership of Parliament to the propertied or monied ranks.

Several Freeholder Lists have survived that document individuals living in Aughnaloopy. A list, dated 1786, archived at PRONI includes several members of the Moore family: John (Kilkeel), Charles (Cranfield), Hugh, and Nicholas. At this time, the freehold was registered at Kilkeel Court House. The names John and Charles were common in the Moore family throughout the years and the Charles of Ballynahatten and Charles of Cranfield are grandsons of the original William Moore who was granted the 1732 lease.

On October 14, 1805 Nicholas Moore is again listed as a Freeholder at Aughnaloopy. A document listing the 40-shilling freeholders for the Barony of Mourne, commencing January 1813 to January 1821 has survived and is held at PRONI. Although Aughnaloopy is not specifically mentioned, the list of names includes William Moore from Ballynahatten. William was another member of the Moore family that held the Aughnaloopy lease from 1732.

In 1824, two names are given for Aughnaloopy: William Davidson, Kilkeel, Aughnaloopy and Magheramurphy and John Moore, Aughnaloopy. So it seems that despite the political advances that were being made, very little change had come to Aughnaloopy, with land ownership and voting rights still being held within a few established families. In addition to the advancement being made in land ownership and voting privileges, Catholics also had the legal right to enter professions from which they had previously been excluded. However, it would be several years before this would have a significant impact on the career choices available to Aughnaloopy residents.

1803 Agricultural Census

International affairs were also having a direct role in the life of Aughnaloopy residents during this time. In March 1802, France and Britain made peace with each other and entered into the Treaty of Amiens. Both sides remained suspicious of each other and in May 1803, Britain was once more at war with France. During 1803, many were fearful of the French invading Ireland and a census was compiled to collate information on categories of livestock and dead stock (crops), numbers of *'cars and carts'*, of people *'able to drive cattle and load carts'* and those *'willing to serve the Government gratuitously or for hire'*. This legislation coming after the 1801 Act of Union, thus applied also to Ireland. The returns for County Down were made to Robert Stewart, the 1st Marques of Londonderry. Presumably, he received returns for each parish, although it is clear from the surviving records that there was considerable variation in their content. The returns for the Agricultural Census of 1803 are included in the Londonderry Papers of the 1st Marques, and are available at PRONI (D/654/A2). For Kilkeel, the information enumerated includes: cows, young cattle, sheep and goats, pigs, riding horses, draft horse horses, cars, barrels of wheat, barrels of oats, barrels of barley, sacks of potatoes, hay and straw.

Hunting Lodge at Mourne Park

In addition to granted leases, this was also a time of family change for the Nedhams. Robert Nedham's descendant, William Nedham, died in 1806 and bequeathed his property to Robert Needham (with two e's), Viscount Kilmorey of Shavington in Shropshire. The family built a property in the townland of Ballyrogan, called Siberia (and later renamed Mourne Park). This is the only demesne completely within the Kingdom of Mourne and was situated on the slopes of Knockcree, overlooking the square tower of Greencastle and Millbay. The building served as a hunting lodge for the family who retained their seat in Shropshire, England.

Catholic Emancipation taken to the People

Initially, the campaign for Catholic Emancipation in Ireland was mainly the preserve of an intellectual minority but that changed in 1823 when it was taken to the people by Daniel O'Connell. He started a campaign for repeal of the Act of Union, and took Catholic Emancipation as his rallying call, establishing the Catholic Association. All Irish citizens were encouraged to join O'Connell's Catholic Association. They paid a *Catholic Rent* of 1d per month, collected after Mass on Sunday. This was used to finance the Association's activities and was used as an insurance fund for members who were evicted for being members of the Association. In its first year, the Association had an income of £1,000 per week (960,000 pennies a month) and at the end of the year it had £10,000 invested. The campaign was non-violent but agitation was constant and by 1825 the Association was so active that it was declared to be illegal. O'Connell simply changed its name and continued as before.

In 1828 O'Connell stood for election in County Clare, and was elected even though he could not take his seat in the House of Commons. He repeated this in 1829, and the resulting commotion led the Duke of Wellington and Sir Robert Peel, to introduce another major Catholic Relief Act in 1829, removing many of the remaining substantial restrictions on Roman Catholics in the United Kingdom. At the same time, the property franchise in Ireland was tightened, reducing the total number of voters (and especially voting Roman Catholics), although this was later loosened in successive Reform Acts. The year 1829 is therefore regarded as marking Catholic Emancipation in the United Kingdom. However, the obligation to financially support the established Anglican Church remained, resulting in the Tithe War.

US Library of Congress Public Domain

The passing of the 1829 Act was a momentous victory for O'Connell and the Catholic middle class, and he became known as 'The Liberator' and the 'Uncrowned King of Ireland'.

A succession of further reforms were introduced over time, leaving the Act of Settlement as one of the few provisions left which still discriminates against Roman Catholics, and then only those who wish to be King, Queen, or Royal Consort - probably not a major concern for most residents of Aughnaloopy!

Catholic Landowner – Mary Murphy

An alphabetical list of individuals, who owned one or more acres of land in Co. Down, was compiled in the latter part of the 1870s. There are two references to Aughnaloopy, the first is for John Moore who owned over 50 acres and the second is Mary Murphy who owned over 26 acres. The appearance of John Moore (the husband of Elizabeth Wachope) is not a surprise as John was a direct descendant of the Moore family that had been granted a lease from the Nedhams in 1732. Mary Murphy's name on the list shows how change had finally arrived in Aughnaloopy. Mary Murphy was the widow of James Murphy and was the daughter of James Hamilton of Springfield, Aughnaloopy. Despite speculation that the Hamilton family were Presbyterian, research has revealed that they were of the Roman Catholic faith. In addition to Mary Ann Hamilton marrying James Murphy in Kilkeel Roman Catholic Church, her father James's name appears in an article entitled 'Great Catholic Meeting' published in the Freeman's Journal and Daily Commercial Advertiser (Dublin, Ireland), June 14, 1853. The article states:

> 'The audacious and insulting attempt of the bigoted fanatics to obtain legislative sanction for invading the convents, the sanctified retreats of the pious ladies who have devoted their lives to religion and works of mercy, having demanded prompt and determined opposition from the Catholics of Ireland, the aggregate meeting of yesterday, was in every aspect worthy of them of the occasion.'

This was a subject very close to James Hamilton as he had a daughter Ann who had joined the Poor Clare Convent, three years previously, becoming Sister Gertrude in religion. The convent in Newry was established in 1829 and was itself a reflection that Catholic Emancipation had finally become a reality in Ireland, being the first convent to open in this part of Ireland since the Reformation.

At the request of the Bishop of Dromore the Poor Sisters of St. Clare helped established a school in the town. Within a year of laying the foundation stone for the chapel and school, about 400 children were attending the school. A local newspaper paid tribute to the Sisters for:

> '....their instruction of poor female children in the ways of virtue, and for rescuing the orphans. Older girls were taught embroidery and lace-making. And such a high standard did they reach that, in the 1850's, prizes were won at the International Industrial Exhibition in London.'

During Ann Hamilton's time at the convent she was witness to many achievements as the Catholic community prospered. Daniel O'Connell paid a visit to St Clare's School, after which he wrote:

> 'I note especially the neatness and cleanliness of the children, the superior style of their pronunciation, and thorough understanding of what they read, the proper application of emphasis and division of sentences in reading.'

For centuries, it had only been possible for Catholics to worship at Mass Rocks, so when a Crib was erected for the first time in the convent chapel in 1858, it became a place of pilgrimage. Ann Hamilton (Sister Gertrude) died in 1899 but during her life she bore witnesses to some incredible changes across Ireland.

Chapter 5

The Wheels of Change

*'Mellow the moonlight to shine is beginning,
Close by the window young Eileen is spinning.
Bent o'er the fire her blind grandmother sitting,
Is crooning and moaning and drowsily knitting.
Merrily cheerily noiselessly whirring,
Swings the wheel spins the wheel while the foot's stirring.
Sprightly and lightly and merrily ringing,
Trills the sweet voice of the young maiden singing.'*

Flax Growing

Despite the political turmoil of the day, families in Aughnaloopy will have put most of their energies into raising their families and farming their land. While most families will have grown crops such as potatoes to feed themselves and their animals, flax was the predominant cash crop throughout the 18th and 19th Centuries. Flax growing originally existed as a subsidiary industry but its importance developed over time, particularly in the late 1770s, when cotton spinning took over at the industrial centre of Belfast. Growing and processing flax was a family affair in Aughnaloopy and indeed many families will have assisted one another to plant, harvest and process the crop.

Like most farming, a successful crop was dependent on having the right amount of rain and sunshine to produce a healthy and profitable harvest. The process would start in March with the farmer broadcasting the seed thickly by hand. Once the plants reached a few inches in height, the children of the townland will have carefully weeded between the plants. About two months after planting, blue blossoms appeared on the plants. These plants were then harvested within a few days of the flowers appearing. Harvesting was done by hand so as to ensure that the full length of the fibre was preserved. This relentless process was extremely brutal on the hands and back of the workers. Depending on the success of the growing season, pulling could also be done in mid-July, after the stems began to turn yellow and the seeds began to rattle in the seedpods, although this was less common in Mourne than in other areas. These plants were then left lying in the fields to dry and let the seeds ripen. The next step was to remove the seeds from the plant. This process known as rippling involved literally combing the seeds off with a coarse comb. Alternatively, the seeds were threshed off or simply whipped off against a small barrel or cask. These seeds were then carefully stored for planting the following year. When several acres had been planted, the seed will have been taken to the local flax mill where it was pressed to make linseed oil. The next step was known as *'retting, rotting or watering'* and required the flax stems to be sunk into streams, ponds or pools or simply laid out in fields to rot by the rain and dew. Often boulders would be gathered and placed on top of the stems to hold them under water. One can only imagine the putrid smell that emanated from the decaying plant material. This retting process dissolved the pectin that glued the flax fibre to the woody, inner core of the plant. Once retting was complete, the flax was laid out thinly in a field of clean grass or newly mowed hay and the residents of Aughnaloopy will have hoped for sunshine to help quickly dry the crop. Dry handfuls of flax were then passed through a tool called a flax brake to break up the hard inner core. The resulting little pieces of hard stalk were known as the boon or the hards. The local women and children then draped the flax over a scutching board and hit it with a wooden scutching knife to scrape off the hards. Next they will have combed handfuls of fibre through one or more combs, known as hackles or heckles, to grade the fibres. The short, coarse fibres, called tow, were used for coarse linen, while the longer fibres were saved for the production of a finer-grade linen.

Images of the Linen Making Process c.1791

Print shows the farmer plowing, another man sowing flax seed, and in the background a man driving a team pulling a harrow; on the left, a woman, with several children, seated against a tree, beckons her husband to take a break for lunch.

This view represents taking the flax out of the bog when it has lain a sufficient time to separate the rind (which is the flax) from the stem and strengthen it, spreading it to dry, stoving, beetling, and breaking it.

The bleach mill consisting of the wash mill, rubbing boards moved by a crank, and beetling engine for glazing the cloth, with a view of the boiling house.

The lapping room, with the measuring, crisping or folding the cloth in lengths, picking the laps or lengths, tying in the clips, acting by the mechanic power of the laver to press the cloth round & firm,

Spinning, reeling with the clock reel, and boiling the yarn.

The tow was bundled together and carded before spinning. The long fibres were made up into twists, ready for spinning. The flax was now ready to be spun into thread and woven into linen cloth. The weaving of linen fabric on handlooms was often performed by the menfolk and was complementary to their farming activities. During busy times of the farming year, the loom could lie abandoned ready to be utilised again during slacker times on the farm. Up until the latter half of the 1700s (when sulphuric acid, potash and lime came into usage), cow manure and buttermilk were used across Mourne to bleach the linen cloth white.

Old Wives' Tales

Farmers' wives will often have saved some seeds and flax seed oil to use medicinally in the home. Many believed that flax was good for preventing baldness, lessening inflammation, treating skin complaints, and that it increased the ability to focus and help calm you down. Several of these old wives' tales such as it being good for you heart and as a treatment for psoriasis have turn out to have scientific support being linked to the omega 3 content of the oil.

1796 Flax Growers List

In 1796, the Irish Linen Board published a list of nearly 60,000 individuals in the Spinning-Wheel Premium Entitlement List, more commonly known as the Flax Growers Bounty List, or simply the Flax Growers List. This list contained the names of farmers (usually the landowner) who had received awards for planting a specified acreage of flax. Farmers who planted one acre of flax were awarded four spinning wheels, and those growing five acres were awarded a loom.

> *'To the person who should sow between the 10th day of March and the 1st day of June 1796 with a sufficient quantity of good sound flax-seed, any quantity of land, well prepared and fit for the purpose not less than 1 Acre - 4 Spinning Wheels, 3 Roods - 3 ditto, 2 Roods -2 ditto and 1 Rood - 1 ditto. And to the person who should sow in like manner any quantity of like land, not less than 5 Acres, a loom or wheels, reels or hatchels to the value of 50 shillings, and for every 5 Acres over and above the first 5, a like premium.'*

As a result of this bonus, thousands of Irish farmers grew the crop for their livelihood. Unfortunately, the Flax Growers Lists do not name the townland but just indicated the parish, in the case of Aughnaloopy, Kilkeel. There are names appearing on the list that undoubtedly have an Aughnaloopy connection including Annett, Beck, Edgar and Flanagan. Nine members of the Moore family are on the List including Nicholas Moore who although he lived in Newry had a £50 freehold registered on October 14,1805 for Aughnaloopy.

Introduction of Flax Power Spinning

In his 1811 survey, Rev. John Dubourdieu calculated that in the Belfast area, there were 150,000 power-driven spindles making over 70 million hanks of cotton yarn. He concluded *'that not less than 30,000 individuals derive a good support from the muslin and calico branches of this trade, taking in all the different departments.'* Linen could not be produced in this way due to the nature of the flax fibres. Then in 1825 James Kay of Preston discovered that soaking flax in cold water made it slippery enough to be drawn by power-spinning machines into fine yarn. James and William Murland of Annsborough House, Castlewellan began the power-spinning of flax in 1828. In the same year Mulholland's York Street Mill, the largest cotton mill in Belfast, burned down. The proprietors decided to rebuild but not as a cotton spinning operation but rather as a facility to spin flax using the new automated spinning process. Messrs Hind and others followed in Belfast and by 1850 there were 325,000 spindles producing linen yarn across Ireland. Thread making began to develop in the Banbridge area. The first spinning mill was built on the River Bann at Hazelbank, about 1834, by Samuel Law. Four years later Hugh Dunbar, from Huntly and William Stewart of Edenderry formed a partnership to build a spinning mill at Gilford.

Collapse of the Industry

The industrialisation of flax spinning led to the collapse of the cottage linen industry in the early 1830s. Several generations of families at Aughnaloopy will have supplemented their incomes by working spinning wheels and looms from home. The mechanised factory looms could do the work of 100 hand weavers. The result was tens of thousands of people across rural Ulster lost a valuable source of income. Any weavers that lived on uneconomical farms of 12 acres, or less, suffered most. This change also provided an incentive for the young to move away from the rural areas into the new industrialised centres in search of employment.

The Reed Hanna

The influence of the linen industry in Aughnaloopy is illustrated by the designation of James Hanna as 'The Reed' Hanna. Research conducted by Maynard Hanna, from Kilkeel revealed that James Hanna moved to the townland in the early 1800's from either the Rathfriland or Dromore areas of County Down. The designation of 'The Reed' was from his occupation as a reedmaker in the linen industry. The importance of this occupation warranted an annotation on the 1865 Griffith's Valuation. In addition to his home in Aughnaloopy, 'The Reed' also had a house, office and 15 acres of land at nearby Ballinran and some mountain pastureland in Ballinran Upper. His son John also ran his property as a reed farm.

An Irish Spinning Wheel

The photograph on the left was donated by Nancy McCormack Schaalje, from Lethbridge, Alberta, Canada.

The spinning wheel belonged to her step grandmother Agnes Elizabeth McCormack nee Campbell and was in her home in Toronto for many years. Agnes moved from Belfast to Canada with her husband in 1920.

The name plate on the table of the wheel says McCreery, Belfast. James McCreery had a spinning wheel works on the Albertbridge Road in Belfast.

A Peep at the Linen Trade

The following article was published in the Traralgon Record, Victoria, Australia on September 24, 1895, and gives an interesting description of the linen industry.

What an important part is played in the world by the pretty, modest, blue-eyed flax plant! Hidden in the stalk lies that stringy, white fibre, which has to go through so many processes before it develops into snowy linen - linen which covers us in the cradle, shrouds us for the grave, and has its place at our banquets and bridals. The cultivation of flax goes back to the very earliest times. Egypt was the great flax-growing centre. The mummies found in ancient Egyptian tombs are invariably wrapped in linen. Joseph, when he went out from Pharaoh, was arrayed in a vesture of fine linen; and Solomon brought linen yarn out of Egypt. The sacred garments of the priests were invariably of linen.

Samuel ministered before the Lord, girded in a linen ephod. David was clothed with a linen ephod when be brought up the ark and danced before the Lord. Mordecai went out from the presence of Ahaserus in a garment of fine linen and purple. The dress of Dives and the clothing of the Lamb's wife - the Church - are of fine linen, which in the latter case is specially noted as being clean and white, 'for the fine linen is the righteousness of the Saints' (Rev. six. 8). The peculiar purity attached to linen comes from the fact that it is the natural product of a plant, and is not like wool, taken from animals. How linen is manufactured is very interesting to tell. Some of us can hardly realise how much care, and watching, and labour it gives to the hundreds of hands that have to gather and prepare it and make it ready for use.

It was on a fine July afternoon, as I was walking along a beautiful mountain road in the County Down, in the north of Ireland, that I first saw a field of flax, waving in the sunshine. 'What pretty blue flower is that?' asked my small nephew. He gathered a handful, and as I looked at the long stalks and delicate blossoms, I said, 'Why, this is flax!' And so it was. About three weeks afterwards, we were driving along just above the seacoast near Kilkeel, which looks out on the beautiful Bay of Carlingford, when a most peculiar, almost sickening odour came borne upon the summer air. We soon found out that it was the flax, which is pulled in bundles, then gathered up, and left to steep in tanks of water for nine days. After this, it is taken out of the water and thrown on the fields to dry. It is during the process of drying that this sickly, overpowering odour rises on the air. The stalks turn a dull yellowish-brown color, and the pretty blue flowers all wither and dry up. Women and children and a few men are employed turning them and watching them, and when they are dry enough, they are carted off to the spinning mills.

There are very large linen mills at Bessbrook, near Newry, a town which has the proud distinction of not containing a single public house. There are also numbers of mills at Portadown, Lurgan, Lisburn, and especially at Belfast, which is sometimes called Linenopolis, in distinction to Dublin, which is popularly known as Whiskyopolis. Certainly, Linenopolis has the best of it, for there are few idlers and no beggars. Huge whirling engines are going all day, giving employment to an army of skilled workers at the 850,003 spindles and 28,000 power looms that are used in the linen trade.

A capital of £70,000,000 is invested in the business. The Belfast manufacturers can not get enough Irish flax to keep their mills going and are obliged to import a great part of their supply from Russia, Holland and Belgium. One of the largest spinning mills is the York Street mill in Belfast, at which considerably over a thousand people work regularly.

As to the process of linen making, the flax stems, when dried, undergo "breaking " to prepare them for the scutching process. While passing between the rolling machine, the brittle woody parts of the stems are broken, and the better the breaking is performed, the less will be the amount of scutching required. In the mills, which are usually driven by water-power the scutching is done by a series of vertical wheels. Then comes the process of heckling, which is to separate the flax into two portions - the 'line' which is the long and best portion, and the 'two', which is the short and ravelled portion.

After the heckling the flax line is sorted and spun into yarn, which comes out an ugly greyish colour. A peculiarity in flax spinning is that for all die yarns the fibre is span wet. Dry spinning is, however, adopted for coarse and heavy yarns.

Then comes the weaving of the yarn, which is done by power looms. Warping is bringing together and arranging the threads, which are required for the web to be formed. Some of the remaining processes comprise sizing, beaming, nealding, and sleying of the yarn.

I saw a small factory at Portadown for fine handkerchiefs, where the yarn was reeled off wooden reels. Nearly all the workers – about 500 - are women and girls. Their wages average from five to eight shillings a week. Some are able to earn ten shillings, but these are exceptions. Many of them are daughters of small farmers living in the country, who help with harvest work in summer but work at the mill during the winter and spring. They begin at half past eight a.m. and work till half-past six, with an interval of an hour for dinner. In April, the fresh flax comes in, so that is the busiest time. We saw some women standing at the machines, which wind the yarn on the reels. The machines have to be very closely watched. If there is a break the ends hare to be knotted together with a weaver's knot. It was the business of one small girl to pick up the little broken bits that fall, and join them together, so that nothing should be lost. The work is exhausting, as it is all done standing, no one sitting down for a minute. The yarn has then to be woven, when it comes out in-lone breadths, unsightly in colour, and of a very unfinished appearance. It is unbleached, and the process of bleaching takes time and trouble. There are some bleaching works near Rostrevor, and there I saw piles and piles of unbleached material as it arrives. First, it has to steep in water with bleaching powder and lime, then the long breadths are wrong oat and stretched on the fields to dry. It wan such a beautiful nook in the mountains where the linen lay whitening in the sun Above was the purple heather-covered height of Lockanmore, long reaches of woods were on the other side, and beneath lay the silvery Lough of Carlingford, dotted by a white sail here and there.

In these green fields the linen soon begins to get beautifully white, and then the long rolls are pressed under a heavy pounding machine, which pounds and stamps them till they get smooth and glossy.

In the month of September, the fields in the north of Ireland, all about Lisburn, Portadown, etc., are literally white with linen. The bleaching is a most important feature in the preparation of linen and it a so employs hundreds of hands. So far, I have only spoken of plain linen, such as is used for sheets and underclothing; tablecloths, dinner napkins etc., require special care and a separate process. At Robinson and Cleaver's I saw a man at a hand-loom, working a beautiful piece of damask. The pattern was marked out with little dots on a piece of card-board, and it required great care to watch that it was reproduced accurately. At the same factory at Portadown where the reeling was done there was a room devoted to hemstitching of pocket-handkerchiefs. Most of the girls here were between 16 and 18 years; some looked almost like children their hair hanging down their backs, others were older, but all were too busy even to look up. A great engine was going, which set the sewing machines in motion, and made such a noise that it was impossible to hear any one speak. Some of the girls were busy folding down the handkerchiefs with a measuring line, so that the borders should be exactly even. When these are folded, they are taken up and put under a machine, which does the hemstitching in a few minutes; but, of course, the girls have to watch and turn the handkerchiefs at the corners.

There is a great demand for black linen for aprons, linings, etc. At Rostrevor there are dyeing works where this is done. A pretty little gurgling stream that runs through a woody glen is quite black from the dyeing stuffs, which have to be used. One great end is effected by these small industrial works-they give employment during the long winter, and many of the girls and women, who would be sitting by the fire doing nothing, are enabled to earn something for themselves. The spirit of independence and the love of work is very visible amongst all classes in the north of Ireland, and this is largely due to the famous linen trade.

(C.J.H.)

These images were first published c.1890 to c.1900 by the Detroit Publishing Company. They are entitled 1. Irish Peasant Farmer, 2. Irish Spinning Wheel and 3. & 4. Irish Colleen.

Chapter 6

Surveys and Tithes

'...there was no opposition to the resident Clergyman receiving his rights.'

Dubourdieu's Statistical Survey

In an 1802 statistical survey performed by the Rev. John Dubourdieu (Rector of Annahilt), the Lordship of Mourne with the town of Kilkeel was measured at 30,000 acres and the Lordship of Newry with Newry town at 9,500 acres. Rent was estimated at 20 shillings per Irish acre for cultivatable land. Dubourdieu gives a detailed and fascinating description of the houses that were common throughout the countryside at the time.

> *'...they consist for the most part of a low cottage, the dwelling house, which contains a kitchen, and two or three rooms on the ground floor opening into each other, without any apartments over head and seldom containing any other fire place than that of the kitchen; those in the other rooms having been shut up on the alteration in the hearth-money tax. Had parliament at that period made every house with two fire-places pay for one, at the usual rate, little loss would have accrued to the revenue, as very few would in that cafe have built up the second; but the additional two and eight-pence-halfpenny, on one side, paid for two hearths, and the temptation of not paying any thing by having but one, has operated both against the revenue and the comfort of the people, who for forfeiting a consideration have deprived themselves of the satisfaction of a second fire, and consequently no longer profits the advantage of ventilation, which from an open chimney they formerly obtained in their bed rooms, in which a circulation of air is not at present known, the vent which produced it, in concert with the casual opening of the door, being now closed; besides, the windows are seldom made to open, and where they have been made with that intention, they are for often out of order, or have for many things laid upon the inner sash, that being a work of time to accomplish it, it is seldom attempted. It must in a great measure be owing to the closeness of these apartments, to the total exclusion of fresh air, that fevers, when once got into a family, seldom leave it, until they have attacked every individual.'*

The hearth-money tax referenced, refers to a 1664 tax was levied on the basis of the number of hearths in each house; these rolls listed the householders' names, as well as this number. Unfortunately, no known source of documentation for County Down still exists. On the issue of tithes, Dubourdieu comments:

> *'....are very moderately set in the county of Down, Incumbency bargains are very common; the rate from 1s to 1s 6d per acre on the whole farm; one or more substantial men binding themselves in each townland, for the payment of the whole tithes of it. Potatoes do not pay tithe; in some parishes there is a modus for flax, in others none. Upon the whole, the people are at least as leniently dealt with by the clergy, as they are by those proprietors, in whole hands the tithes of their representatives are vested; and the interference of a tithe farmer being in general dispensed with, and as well as annual setting, the whole business is generally settled in an amicable manner, so highly creditable to the clergy, and so comfortable for the people.'*

1830 Tithe Applotment Book

Tithes (from Old English *teogoþa* meaning 'tenth') were the taxes due by landholders in rural areas to support the Church of Ireland (the established church until 1869). The Tithe Applotment Books archived at PRONI record the results of a unique land survey taken to determine the amount of tax payable. They are known as the Tithe Applotment Books because the results of this land survey were originally compiled in nearly 2,000 hand-written books. For historians and genealogists, this data set represents a virtual census for pre-famine Ireland.

Each landholder was recorded along with details such as townland name, the size of holding, land quality and the types of crops grown. The amount of tithe payable by each landholder was based on all of these factors and calculated by a formula using the average price of wheat and oats from 1816-23. Kilkeel parish had a tithe survey conducted in 1830, and 42 names are listed in the Applotment Books for Aughnaloopy. This is the earliest remaining record that gives details on the families living in Aughnaloopy townland and enables us to make determinations about family structures as several members of the same family are often listed.

Aughnaloopy Residents in 1830

Moore
In Aughnaloopy, there are three members of the Moore family listed in the Applotment book; John, Hugh who had over 7 acres of land together as well as as the Widow Mary Moore who had just over an acre of land.

Beck
Two members of the Beck family are also listed as landholders, Hugh Beck with over 7 acres and Thomas with over 8 acres. This is the only mention of Hugh Beck in surviving documentation. Hugh was born in 1766. He died on April 4, 1847 and is buried in Mourne Presbyterian Graveyard with his wife Jane who died on August 12, 1852. Nothing more is known about Thomas.

Quinn
By 1830, the Quinn family (Edward and William) have become major landholders in the townland paying tithes on almost 14 acres of land. Edward's land eventually passed to his son John. William Quinn is believed to be the father of Thomas Quinn who married Margaret Donaldson (of the Kilkeel bakery family). In addition to farming William was involved on the linen trade.

Rogers
There are three members of the Rogers family listed (Francis, James and Patrick) who held almost 14 acres of land between them. Francis was the father of James. Their relationship to Patrick is unknown. Francis died in 1889 at age 70.

Edgar
The Edgar family is well established in the townland (John Jnr., Snr, and William) paying tithes on over 21 acres of land.

Fitzpatrick
Patrick Fitzpatrick had a sizeable piece of land (over 12 acres), as did the Flanagan family who had over 14 acres divided between Edmund, Felix, Henry, John and Margaret. Henry's property passed to his son Henry and is currently the home of his Great Great Grandson Peter.

Bradley
The Bradley family is established in Aughnaloopy in the 1830s with Felix holding 5 acres and James a little over 2 acres.

Annett
There are three members of the Annett family (Charles, James and John) listed with over 7 acres of land between them. The relationship between the men is unknown. By 1864, Alexander Annett was listed as farming 12 acres of land in the townland but he did not live there.

Doran
In 1830, the Doran family held over 8 acres (Bernard, Francis and John). Bernard held two sites totalling a little over 6 acres and Francis and John held an acre each. The nature of the relationship, if any, between Bernard, Francis and John is unknown.

Keown
Robert and Charles Keown have over 7 acres of land in 1830.

Speers
Samuel Spiers (Speers) had two pieces of land totalling over 16 acres and Alexander Wilson also had two plots totalling over 11 acres.

The remainder of the 217 acres is divided between Stephen Byrne, Henry Campbell, John Donnelly, William Hagan, Richard Johnson, Michael Kelly, Patrick McParlin, James McVeagh and John Small, Widow Jane Mills and Widow Nancy McAvoy.

The residents of Aughnaloopy were responsible for a total amount of £14 1s 56d being paid to the Church of Ireland. The tithes system caused a great deal of unrest among Roman Catholics and Presbyterians, however a newspaper article from January 1831, reported that in Kilkeel parish:

'.....here was no opposition to the resident Clergyman receiving his rights.'

Photograph taken by Ciera E. Jones in July 2011, showing a view of the Mournes from Aughnaloopy.

Chapter 7

Potato Famine and Poor Law

The Miseries and Beauties of Ireland

Jonathan Binns was born in 1785 in Hanover Street in Liverpool, England. In 1837, he travelled around Ireland in his capacity as Assistant Agricultural Commissioner of the Irish Poor Inquiry and recorded his observations on the lives of Irish tenants. His publication 'The Miseries and Beauties of Ireland' paints a vivid picture of housing conditions in the Mournes in the mid 19th century:

> 'The cabins are in general from fifteen to eighteen feet long, and from ten to twelve feet wide, are composed of stones and mud rudely put together. In many cases they consist of but one room but in some a small portion is screened off for a sleeping apartment. In such cases, the kitchen or room in which the inmates live during the day, is about two thirds of the entire cabin. The cabins never possess a second story – the thatch being the only shelter from the weather. In general it is tolerably good, but in some cabins we found it full of holes; in wet weather the inhabitants are obliged to remove the bed from one part of the hut to the other. In all cabins the floors are formed of clay; in some cases nothing whatever being done to the ground, which is left in exactly the same state as it was before the house was built. The floors for the most part are uneven and full of holes, containing dirty water, through which the pigs and ducks trample; and in many cases they are lower than the ground outside and admit the rain in wet weather. Most of the cabins have low chimneys, composed of mud and sticks; in some instances an old firkin is made to answer the purpose. Grates not being required for turf are never used. The usual size of the windows is one foot square, though many are not larger than the crown of a hat : some are glazed others filled with old rags. The cost of erecting a cabin is from five to six pounds.'

The photograph on the left, taken by Ciera E. Jones in July 2011, shows Sams Cottage. The cottage has been restored and updated and is available as a holiday rental property.

However, Binns also notes:

> 'On my return from Kilkeel, I walked alone, late in the evening, over the summits of some of the mountains, as far as Hilltown, a distance of several miles. And although the country was then in a disturbed state, met with every civility. I felt confident indeed that I could have gone anywhere in the neighbourhood, day or night, without interruption, and with even less risk, then would be incurred, at the same time, in most parts of England.'

Lewis Topographical Dictionary of Ireland

In the same year that Jonathan Binns travelled through Ireland, Samuel Lewis published a topological dictionary of Ireland and a corresponding atlas. The entry for the parish of Kilkeel, which includes Aughnaloopy, is listed below. In addition to giving a description of pre-famine Ireland, it provides interesting details such as the dates that Aughnaloopy residents will have travelled in to Kilkeel town to attend the local fair. It also gives one of the earliest summaries of the establishment of schools across the parish. Across Kilkeel, 450 children were attending private schools and 770 were educated in public schools.

KILKEEL

A post-town and parish, in the barony of MOURNE, county of DOWN, and province of ULSTER, 15 miles (S. E.) from Newry, and 65 ¾ (N. N. E.) from Dublin; containing 14,806 inhabitants, of which number, 1039 are in the town. According to the Ordnance survey it comprises 47,882 ¾ statute acres, of which about 11,000 are arable and 12,000 pasture; the remainder consists of the Mourne mountains. The only creek in the twelve miles of coast that bounds the parish is Annalong, where a small dock for fishing-vessels has been excavated out of a rock.

There are coastguard stations at Annalong, Cranfield, and the Lee Stone, all in the district of Newcastle; also a constabulary police station. Fairs are held on Feb. 8th, May 3rd, Aug. 2nd, and Dec. 8th; and a manorial court is held in the sessions-house at Kilkeel, once in three weeks, for the manor of Greencastle and Mourne, by a seneschal appointed by the Earl of Kilmorey; its jurisdiction extends over the whole of the barony of Mourne, which is included in this parish, and is the property of his lordship, and pleas to the amount of £10. are determined either by attachment or civil bill.

The principal seats are Mourne Park, the splendid residence of the Earl of Kilmorey; Shannon Grove, of J. S. Moore, Esq.; and the glebe-house, of the Rev. J. Forbes Close. The living is a rectory, in the diocese of Down, united, in 1809, by charter of James I., to the rectories of Kilcoo and Kilmegan and the chapelry of Tamlaght (a small townland in Kilkeel), which together form the union of Kilkeel and the corps of the treasurership of the cathedral of Down, in the alternate patronage of the Marquess of Anglesey, and the Earl of Kilmorey. The tithes amount to £800, and of the entire benefice to £1600. The church was rebuilt in 1818, for which the late Board of First Fruits granted a loan of £2160. The glebe-house is situated on a glebe of 30 acres, valued at £37. 10. per annum, but subject to a rent of £19. 7. 9., payable to the Earl of Kilmorey.

In the R. C. divisions the parish forms two districts, called Upper and Lower Mourne, the former containing a chapel at Ballymaguagh; the latter, one at Glassdrummond and one at Ballymartin. There are a Presbyterian meeting-house in connection with the Synod of Ulster, and one of the third class in connection with the Seceding Synod, also meeting-houses for Wesleyan Methodists, Baptists, and Moravians. About 770 children are educated in eight public schools, to one of which the Earl of Kilmorey contributes £31, and to another, Mrs. Keown £10. annually. Needham Thompson, Esq., built and principally supports the school at Mullartown; and that for girls, at Ballinahatton, was built by the Rev. J. F. Close, who clothes and educates 65 children there. About 450 children are taught in 10 private schools; and there are six Sunday schools and a dispensary.

English Poor Law System

In 1838, one year after Binns made his observations, the English Poor Law system was introduced to Ireland, to try and address some of the difficulties resulting from poverty. The system was a replica of that devised by Edwin Chadwick in England, which was designed to cope with the problem of an urban, industrial proletariat. Chadwick's system required the entire country to be divided into Unions, with a workhouse at the centre of each union. The workhouse was to provide relief to the destitute but the able-bodied were to be kept out so that they would be compelled to enter the labour market. This notion may have had some validity in industrial England but was totally impractical in rural Ireland. Kilkeel Poor Law Union was formally declared on July 29, 1839, it covered an area of 127 square miles and included Aughnaloopy townland. The Poor Law system was overseen by an elected Board of Guardians. The population falling within the Union at the time of the 1831 census was 26,833 with the population of Kilkeel at 3,544. Construction of the Kilkeel Union Workhouse began in 1840 on a 7.5-acre site at the north side of Newry Street. Designed by the Poor Law Commissioners' architect George Wilkinson, the building was based on one of his standard plans to accommodate 300 inmates. The construction costs were £4,050 plus £767 for fittings. The workhouse was declared fit for the reception of paupers on August 16, 1841 and admitted its first inmates on September 1, 1841. It served a Poor Union comprising 81,785 acres divided into ten divisions: Rostrevor, Killowen, Greencastle, Mourne Park, Kilkeel, Ballykeel, Mullartown, Maghera, Bryansford, and Fofanny. Charles Moore and his brother John Moore are both members of the Board of Trustees for the workhouse. During the mid-1840s, a 40-bed fever hospital was erected at the east of the site and a dispensary was located on the roadside to the east of the workhouse.

The Great Famine

The Great Famine began in 1845 and was caused by a blight that attacked and destroyed the potato crop, the main staple of Ireland's peasantry. The potatoes rotted in the fields, leaving millions with nothing to eat and unable to pay their yearly rents to the landlords. Relief measures were introduced but when the crop failed the following year the crisis became a catastrophe. Government initiated schemes to distribute food and provide work for men and at the local level relief committees were set up through which better off people did what they could to help their neighbours. While there is little documentation on individual families or townlands, it is known that between 1845-1850 the population of Ireland fell from around eight million to about five million. As many as one million died from hunger and disease (mainly typhus, cholera, dysentery, small pox and relapsing fever) and another two million tried to escape the same fate by emigrating on crowded coffin ships.

Unlike many counties in Ireland, Down's population was not decimated by the famine, but still there was widespread suffering and hardship on an enormous scale across the county. In a newspaper article dated October 8, 1845, James Kennedy Thompson who was the last Seneschal of Mourne wrote:

> *'I have not heard of any remedy being tried to prevent this rot in the ground, nor do I think that any effectual means can be applied this year. If they could be disposed of or consumed profitably, the best way to do, would be to raise the croup out of the fields where the disease has appeared and get rid of it as soon as possible.'*

On November 7, 1845 The Sun (Baltimore, USA), reported:

> *'That most dreadful of all calamities to Ireland, as well as to England's career of conquest, a failure of the Irish potato crop, is now too painfully certain. From the counties of Dublin, the two Meaths, Cork, Tyrone, Kilkenny, Carlow, Down, Roscommon, Waterford, Armagh and Kerry, embracing portions of the four Provinces, we hear of the ravages of rot, the plague, the murrain, or, as the Irish people designate it "the cholera" in the potatoes. The great "staff of life" to eight or nine millions of people is turned into a poison, while those articles of food that other countries could rely upon for a mitigation of the calamity, are being exported to England to meet the exorbitant rent extracted from Irish farmers by a foreign aristocracy.'*

Kilkeel native Anne Maddocks conducted a detailed study of the effects of the famine in Kilkeel. Her work entitled 'Poverty or Prosperity? An examination of the Mourne Community's Response to the Great Famine of 1845-49' was conducted for her 2006 B.A. Dissertation (University of Ulster). It was excerpted recently in the Journal of the Mourne Local Studies Group publication, 12 Miles of Mourne. Maddocks concluded that the Kilkeel Board of Guardians took their duties to the poor seriously, giving outdoor relief at a time when it was forbidden.

Starving families without the means to emigrate were forced to abandon their homes in the countryside and seek refuge in overcrowded and disease-ridden workhouses where death awaited many. In the terrible winter of 1846 the workhouses in Downpatrick, Kilkeel, Newry and Banbridge filled up and many died of dysentery, fever and starvation. An Extraordinary Meeting of the Kilkeel Board of Guardians was held on October 28, 1846 with Edward Senior (Assistant Poor Law Commissioner) in attendance. It was decided that '...because of the total failure this year of the potato crop, their chief support...' that the Board would provide a meal in the Workhouse. The Chairman, Lord Roden, was against this decision stating in a letter '..up to last Wednesday last there was no proof given of more than ordinary distress existing within the Union'. Despite his objections, the Guardians went ahead with the proposal to provide food to the needy.

In 1847, Kilkeel Workhouse was full. Guardian Minutes show an average weekly intake of 14 paupers a week with an average death rate of seven individuals per week. Immediate outdoor relief was being giving to over 300 people daily. Temporary Fever Hospitals were set up in Mourne Park, Greencastle and Derryogue to help cope with in increase of disease in the area. Within a two-week period in November, 39 patients were admitted to the fever hospitals. It is unlikely any survived. The effect of the famine in County Down can be seen from surviving census documents. Between 1841 and 1851 the population across Down plummeted by almost 44,000. How many of the 44,000 individuals died and how many emigrated is unknown.

It was not just the poor and destitute that left Ireland during the famine years. Although the workhouses sponsored the emigration of some of its inmates, emigration was an expensive option that most were not able to finance. The following article appeared on September 22, 1849, in The Courier, a newspaper published in Hobart, Tasmania.

> *EMIGRATION BY WHOLESALE - The extent to which emigration continues, even at this advanced period of the spring, is really marvellous; mid Ulster is now affording its full quota. Three vessels, fully freighted, sailed from Belfast on Friday morning, one for Quebec, and two for the United States. It appears from the Northern Whig that, the Canadian emigrants were of the most substantial class that have left Ulster for very many years. One of the passengers carried with him £700 in gold, and generally those emigrants took out sums of money beyond their immediate necessities. Although the poor law guardians are limited in their power to promote emigration, a considerable number of paupers are about to be sent out to Canada by the Althy, Ballinglass, and other unions, in which a certain charge is to be made on the rates for outfit, and some landlords are liberally contributing. I have learned that passages have been provided in Dublin for upwards of one thousand paupers, and that many more are to he sent out before the close of the season. The adoption of Mr. Monsell's suggestions in the New Poor Law Bill could open a wide field for this species of emigration. Many of the Human Catholic clergy are preparing to emigrate with a portion of the remnant of their flocks. The Limerick and Clare Examiner mentions several new cases ; and one in particular, of a parish priest in the diocese of Limerick, whose parish has been depopulated to so great an extent that the clergyman has been altogether bereft of income. The Rev. Dr. Moriarty, vice-general of the Augustinians, is about to proceed to the United States, accompanied by some wealthy laymen, in order to found a colony. It is thus that the failure of the potato is working a revolution in our whole social system.*

It took almost ten years for the government to openly admitted that the Poor Law policy had failed and a decision was made to issue relief in future through the free distribution of soup. The cost of this was to be borne by the ratepayer. In 1851 a document was published by the Royal Commission following an investigation into whether the size and locations of the Poor Law Unions was conducive to allowing Guardians, relieving officers and applicants for relief the opportunity of easy access to the Boards. The report gives a glimpse into life in Aughnaloopy at the time. It states that in 1841 Aughnaloopy townland occupied an area of 382 acres 3 rods and 6 perch and quotes the population at 190 people. As reference, the population of Kilkeel town was given as 1146 people. The population of Kilkeel Workhouse is quoted as 185 in 1851 and 106 in 1861 (composed of 40 men and 66 women).

Description of the Workhouse System

The following article was published on November 20, 1880 the South Australian Register newspaper, Adelaide. It gives a compelling description of the workings of the Workhouses and Boards of Guardians.

The traveller through Ireland must wonder at the number of houses of the same style of architecture and the same scanty pretensions to beauty he meets with on his journey. They are none other than the Union Workhouses, the various centres of the Poor-law Boards, and places where many a tale of misery, famine, desolation, and woe could be told. In some respects they resemble the Destitute Asylum here, bat it is more in internal matters than anything else, they are under the control of the local Government Board for Ireland, and are managed direct by Boards of Guardians, which consist of the Magistrates residing in each poor-law district, together with representatives from the sub-districts into which a Union is divided, and the elections for Guardians, which are held annually, are usually of great interest. The Chairman of each Board of Guardians is generally some large landed proprietor in the immediate neighbourhood, and when that body gives expression to any matter it is understood to represent the interests of the Union at large. It will thus be seen that when some days ago telegrams were published to the effect that a number of Poor-law Guardians had waited upon the Lord Lieutenant of Ireland and threatened to abdicate their functions if means were not taken to protect them from the lawlessness which prevailed, they simply meant nothing more than allowing the internal business of the country to go adrift - a matter in itself quite important to the Government. Each Board of Guardians meets at the workhouse once a week, where its Clerk lays all business of importance before it. The Clerk of a Union attends to all matters connected with his particular district, makes out a list of all ratepayers, and, in conjunction with the Clerk of the Peace, examines the registry of voters, and erases any name from the roll that is not entitled to be there. He is also executive sanitary officer, and thereby has direct control of the sanitary affairs of the Union. Altogether a Clerk of a Union's duties are multifarious, and to his credit be it said that be carries them out satisfactorily and efficiently. Most of the Union Workhouses were built about the year 1841. At present there are 183 Unions in Ireland. For the year ending December 31, 1878, they had afforded relief to 183,679 indoor and 68,118 outdoor paupers. The outdoor paupers are those who do not reside in the Workhouse, but receive relief in the shape of a small sum of money weekly. The expenditure for the same period was £763,155, and this included the cost of maintaining the Unions, outdoor relief, salaries of officers, and all other expenses. Each workhouse is managed by a Master and Matron, who are assisted by other subordinate officials. About the year 1847 destitution prevailed to a large extent, and the population being considerably greater than it is now, the workhouses were quite full, and consequently the poor rate, or tax levied for the support of the workhouses, was very large. The poor rate is levied under the assessment of poundage rate on the net annual value of the property rateable, which annual value is declared to be the rent for which one year with another the property might be let from year to year, the probable annual avenge cost of repairs, insurance, and other necessary expenses for repairs, and all public charges, except tithes, being paid by the tenant. The property liable to poor rates is all land and buildings, mines seven years open, commerce, rights-of-way, tolls, and other rights and easements upon land. The following kinds of property are exempt:- Turf bogs for which rent is not paid, places of worship, buildings used exclusively for charitable or public purposes, and burial-grounds. The persons liable are: - the occupier of the rateable property at the time the rate is made, and, in default of his payment, the subsequent occupier; but the occupier of tenements under £8 value in certain boroughs, and at and under £4 value elsewhere, is not liable; and in such cases the immediate lessor is to be rated instead. Persons deriving any private profit or use from property exempted are rateable for rents received in respect of such exempted property to the extent of one-half the poundage rate.

Attached or in close proximity to each workhouse is a fever hospital, which is directly under the control of the Board of Guardians, and is supported by Grand Jury presentments, Parliamentary grants, and private subscriptions. Like the workhouses in 1847, they, too, were full of patients, but now it is a rare occurrence to see three or four inmates together at a time, except in cases when scarlatina or some other malignant fever breaks out. There are also Lunatic Asylums in connection with the workhouses, the inmates of which are supposed to be but slightly deranged; and if once they show symptoms of becoming dangerous they are removed to the asylum to which the particular county in which they are subscribes, one asylum answering for three or four counties. Boards of Guardians are also empowered to form Poor-law Unions into dispensary districts, and to provide dispensaries for the same. The 163 Poor-law Unions are divided into 720 dispensary districts, giving an average of nearly five divisions to each district, the average population of the districts being about 8.003.

Each district is under a separate committee, and 1 has one or more dispensaries and medical officers, whose duties are regulated by the Medical Charities' Act. For example, before any person can see a dispensary doctor, but must first obtain from a Warden or Guardian what is known as a black ticket if to go and see the doctor, but if in the case of requiring the doctor to see him a red ticket is issued, which is supposed to be attended to at once. The number of dispensaries in these districts is 1,088, the number of medical officers being 804. In some districts an apothecary is also appointed, the total number of these officers being 41. The total number of midwives employed by Boards of Guardians is 217. Another matter which Boards of Guardians have authority over is the sanitary state of the country. They act in that capacity like the Boards of Health here, and appoint Inspectors, who report each time the Guardians meet upon the sanitary condition of their districts. Previous to the passing of the Act appointing Boards of Guardians sanitary authorities it was usual to observe in the country the most disgusting filth heaped outside the door, and the pig and donkey were looked upon as rightful residents of the dwelling-house. But now all this is changed. It is compulsory to remove dung-heaps a certain distance from dwellings, and the pig must find lodgings further away than he was in the habit of doing. For the infringement of the Act the penalty is rather heavy, but people have learned by this time the necessity of removing the rubbish away from their doors, and consequently the duty of the Sanitary Inspectors is not very heavy. Although in some respects Poor-law Unions are a necessary evil they affect a considerable amount of good. They keep the country on the alert as to the number of paupers in it, and as that fact presses unduly heavily sometimes it is to every one's interest to see the poor rates diminished. Should a pauper be a long time in the workhouse it is usual for one of the Guardians to interest himself to have him charged to the Union at large instead of a particular district, and this generally has the effect of easing the rates a little. Every little relief is felt by the Irish farmer, and his principal object is to return as Poor-law Guardian some one who will oppose taxation tooth and nail. As long as the Unions steer clear of politics - and unfortunately a number of them cannot do that - they are able to devote more attention to the particular business for which they assemble together, and the keeping down of the poor rate ought to be the main object of every earnest Poor-law Guardian

The old Kilkeel Workhouse gates closed after the last meeting of the Council on August 4, 1966.

Chapter 8

Maps and Valuations

'Not slothful in business, fervent in spirit, Serving the Lord.' (Richard Griffith's Epitaph)

Richard Griffiths 1784-1878

Richard Griffiths
Richard Griffiths was born in Dublin in 1784. In 1825 he was appointed by the government to carry out a boundary survey of Ireland in preparation for the first Ordnance Survey. He was also called upon to assist in the preparation of a parliamentary Bill to provide for the general valuation of Ireland. This Act was passed in 1826, and he was appointed Commissioner of Valuation in 1827.

1834 Griffiths Townland Valuation
The Griffiths Townland Valuation of 1828-40 was primarily a land valuation but some buildings were included. Initially houses and outbuildings with an annual value of £3 or more were noted and then in 1838 the value was increased to £5. Such valuations meant that most houses in the countryside were not included.

The Townland Valuation of Aughnaloopy was conducted in 1834. In the valuation book held at PRONI three houses were noted in Aughnaloopy with the name of the head of household. Hugh Beck is the first name listed followed by Patrick Doran (who had under two Irish acres) and John Moore. All of their properties were valued initially over the £3 valuation but were then determined to be under the final £5 valuation and so an annotation has been added 'Under Value'. Patrick Doran is likely the same Patrick who is listed on the 1864 version of the Griffith Valuation listed as property number 43ABC. He was a blacksmith by trade and it is possible that his forge added to the value of his home resulting in the initial inclusion. It is quite surprising that John Moore's property was not more significant considering the social status of the Moore family in the townland.

1861 Griffith's Revaluation
In October 1861, some land revaluations were made prior to the final version of the Griffiths Valuation being issued. Notably, James Murphy, a minor at the time, took over leases previously held by James Lewis Carvill who had died on October 13, 1864. James Lewis Carvill was the son of Francis Carvill, an iron, timber and shipping merchant from Buttercrane Quay in Newry and Margaret Hamilton from Aughnaloopy. Margaret's father James Hamilton was also a successful merchant and had lived in Springfield, Aughnaloopy. It is likely, but difficult to confirm that the Thomas Quinn mentioned in 1861 as living at number 40 on the valuation was the husband of Margaret Donaldson. Thomas Quinn was originally listed as leasing the property and land from James Lewis Carvill but this land that was taken over by James Murphy who had also became the lease holder on the nearby property identified as number 41. James Murphy was the son of John Murphy and Mary Ann Hamilton. He was a first cousin of James Lewis Carvill through the marriage of his mother's sister Margaret Hamilton to Francis Carvill. It is difficult to confirm but the links between these families suggest that the mother of the previously mentioned Thomas Quinn's mother was also a member of the Hamilton family and likely a sister of Mary Ann and Margaret.

Final Valuation

The final version of the Griffith's Valuation is regarded as one of Ireland's premier genealogical resources and provides an invaluable reference for the study of the families in Aughnaloopy. It was executed under the direction of Sir Richard Griffith to determine the amount of tax each person should pay towards the support of the needy within their poor law union (which in the case of Aughnaloopy was Kilkeel). The process involved determining the value of all privately held lands and buildings to determine the rate at which each unit of property could be rented annually. The original volumes of the survey are held in the National Archives, Dublin and at PRONI, Belfast. Recently access has also been made available on the Internet at http://www.askaboutireland.ie/griffith-valuation/index.xml

Each section of land in Aughnaloopy was allocated a number (and sometimes letter) referencing the location on the relevant ordinance survey map. Next the occupier's name was listed followed by the immediate lessor. The immediate lessor was the person the occupier (usually a leaseholder) held their land from usually by payment of rent. This could be the outright owner who held the freehold, or a middleman who held an estate by some form of leasehold and sub-let the premises to the actual occupier. A description of the tenement followed along with the area of the holding. The rateable annual value of the building and the land was quoted followed by the total annual valuation of the rateable property.

Aughnaloopy Landowners

In Aughnaloopy, 45 separation holdings were listed and marked on the corresponding ordinance survey map. The landowners in the townland were: James Moore, Alexander Annett, John and Hugh Moore, Hugh Moore, William Orr and J L Carr, Thomas F Moore, James Murphy, and William Orr. James Murphy also had land identified as number 41, which was held 'in fee'. This meant that the land was under a freehold tenure, derived from a grant from the Crown. The properties in Aughnaloopy are generally numbered in order from the northern end of the townland (towards Ballinran) down to the south towards Kilkeel town.

The first ten locations are all rented from James Moore and all tenants rented a house, an office and some farmland. Henry Flanagan was noted as holding over 11 acres identified as GV1 and John Flanagan over 8 acres at GV2. It is likely, but not confirmed that the two were brothers. After the death of John Flanagan in 1875, the property identified as GV2 passed to his widow Margaret Doran and eventually to the Hanna family. The property at GV1 remains occupied by the Flanagan family today and is shown in the photograph below.

This photograph taken by Ciera E. Jones in July 2011, shows the house located at Griffiths Valuation number 1. It is currently the residence of Peter Flanagan, a descendant of the original owner.

William Speers farmed over 6 acres of land to the south of the Flanagan property marked as number 3 and Samuel Speers occupied a relatively large farm of over 10 acres identified as number 6. It is likely, but not possible to confirm that Samuel and William were brothers. Another possible brother was John Speers who had a house and land at site number 8a consisting of over 11 acres.

On John Speer's land was a small site and property that was leased to John Wilson (8b). John Wilson also farmed a 5-acre site identified by the number 9. This site was occupied by the Hanna family in 1911. A possible brother of John was Alexander Wilson who had over 12 acres of farmland at number 10 A and B.

John Skillen lived at a site of over 6 acres marked as GV7. By 1872, the house on this site was taken down and the land was taken over by Alexander Wilson for a couple of years. From then up until the time of the 1911 census, it remained as farming land only being leased by Alexander Beck of Aughnaloopy.

James Hanna, a reedmaker is identified as leasing two sites, one marked as GV4 that consisted of over 6 acres of land and the other site where his house was that occupied another 6 acres, identified as GV5. This property was still occupied by the Hanna family at the time of the 1911 census.

Margaret Doran held land that was over 11 acres that she rented from James Moore, identified as number 15. This was an increase in the amount of land held by several members of the Doran family (Bernard, Francis and John) held at the time of the 1830 Tithes.

Patrick Fitzpatrick had a sizeable area of land that was split into 6 sites identified on the Griffith's Valuation as 16 and 17ABCDE. His land was disjointed and was interspersed by land leased by Edward Quinn, identified as 18ABCD. Both the Edward Quinn and Patrick Fitzpatrick had leased this land since the time of the 1830 Tithes. It may be speculated, but is impossible to confirm that these families were related and that a common ancestor of the two men originally held the land.

Mark Quinn (who is believed to be a brother of Edward) leased a site measuring 10 acres 2 rods 10 perches, identified as GV27. Mark's property was leased from William Orr and J L Carr. His farm was located on both sides of the Moyadd Road, just opposite Springfield Villa on the one side and just below Springfield Villa on the other side.

At the time of the Griffith's Valuation, Springfield Villa was unoccupied but it was owned by James Murphy. James Campbell had a small house on the land surrounding Springfield Villa.

Behind Mark Quinn's property towards the Aughnaloopy Road was a site of over 8 acres leased by Thomas Quinn from James Murphy. Across the Aughnaloopy Road, was a 10-acre farm occupied by James Quinn. This site was leased from Thomas F Moore.

There was a Blacksmith's forge in Aughnaloopy at the time of the Griffiths Valuation. This was leased by John Flanagan from William Orr and J L Carr and is located at number 26A on the ordinance survey map. On the site, there are two houses, one occupied by John Flanagan and the other by Daniel Small. The forge was in operation until at least 1901 when it was leased by blacksmith James Norris. John Flanagan also leased an acre of land at location GV26B.

William Wheraghty leased two small sites from William Orr and J L Carr, identified as GV24 and GV25. The site where his home was located was on the east of the Moyadd Road at site GV24 and he had farming land just opposite Springfield Villa neighbouring Mark Quinn's home. When William died in 1889, his house passed to his unmarried daughter Susan Wheraghty and the lease for the land was taken over by James Morgan.

To the north of James Murphy's property at Springfield Villa bordering Drumcro townland was a large farm of over 26 acres (GV23) with buildings owned by Hugh Moore and leased to John Moore. John also had a smaller site (GV22) of an acre across the Moyadd Road.

There were three siblings of the Johnson family with land in Aughnaloopy at the time of the Griffith's Valuation: George, Richard and William. Richard Johnston lease three fields, identified as GV38, totalling 6 acres in size but he had no property on the site. William had an acre site at GV36b and GV37. George had over six acres of farmland and he had property on the site identified as GV36a. It is suspected that their father was the Richard Johnson that was listed in the 1830 Tithes Applotment Book.

David (GV13ABC) and John Beck (GV14ABC), both lease farms approximately 12 acres from James Moore. Their property was location between the Aughnaloopy Road and Aughnahorey Road. James Moore also leased a house and garden to John Mills (GV12).

Another family with a considerable holding was the Edgar family. Robert Edgar leased over 26 acres (GV19ABaC) and James had over 6 acres (GV21ABCDEF). Both men leased the land from John and Hugh Moore. The exact relationship between Robert and James is not certain but they are both descendants of the Edgar (Eager) family that were documented on the Bagenal Mourne Rentals of 1715. Francis Rogers had a small home on the Robert Edgar's site at 19B. He also leased three separate sections of land (GV42ABC) from William Orr, and 6 acres at GV20 from John and Hugh Moore.

Jane Allen leased a house and just over 6 acres of land from Thomas F Moore. The property is identified as number 39 on the Griffiths Valuation. Jane's son John married Ellen Keown from Aughnaloopy and they continued to live on the property. Jane's daughter Margaret was married to Richard Johnston and was living in the adjoining property, identified by the number 38. James Keown leased a house and over 10 acres of land, identified as GV39, from Thomas F Moore. James Keown's wife was Jane Spears whose father Samuel Spears was resident in the townland at the site identified by Griffiths as number 6.

William Wright leased over 3 acres of land, at number 29, from Thomas F Moore, but he did not have property in Aughnaloopy. By 1866, John Moore had taken over lease of the land.

Thomas Traynor leased over 10 acres of land from Thomas F Moore. There were two farmhouses on the land positioned on opposite sides of the Aughnaloopy Road identified by Griffiths by number 30a and number 30b. The one house was the home of Thomas Traynor and the other was the home of Ann Bradley. Ann Bradley (nee Quinn) was the wife of Hugh Bradley (deceased) and she also held a 3 acres site adjoining Thomas Traynor's property. Thomas Traynor was originally from Ballymageough and moved to Aughnaloopy after his marriage to Bridget 'Biddy' Cunningham.

James Bradley had two areas of land leased from Thomas F Moore in the south-eastern section of Aughnaloopy, identified GV34AB. When James Bradley died, the property passed to his daughter Bridget who was married to Aughnaloopy man John Johnston. The property eventually passed to the Quinn family.

Patrick Doran is listed on the Griffith's Valuation with land at GV43ABC, totalling over 8 acres. Patrick was a blacksmith and was married to Bridget Trainor. His land passed to their son Patrick and on his death in 1904 to Thomas Morgan.

1882 to 1896 Return of Judicial Rents

The Griffiths Valuation provides detailed list of the landlords in Aughnaloopy from 1861. Also available for study are the 1882 to 1896 Return of judicial rents fixed by sub-commissions and civil bill courts, notified to Irish Land Commission, which states the actual rents paid from tenant to landlord.

An entry is made for July and August 1893 for Miss Lucretia Davidson Moore and her tenants John Edgar and William Shields. Lucretia had inherited her Uncle John Moore's property on his death on January 16, 1880 and also that of her father Hugh Moore. The extent of the holding for John Edgar was given as 25 acres 0 rods 25 perch and for William Shields 9 acres 2 rods 5 perch. The poor law valuation of each holding was £15 11s 0d and £9 2s 5d and the former rent was £14 0s 0d and £7 0s 0d respectively. The new judicial rent was set at £11 0s 0d for John Edgar and £6 0s 0d for William Shields.

Photograph kindly donated by Thomas Fitzpatrick of Atticall of the old forge in Aughnaloopy. he believes that this was the forge once occupied by Patrick Doran the Blacksmith.

Chapter 9

Births and Marriages

Several residents of Aughnaloopy were members of the Presbyterian Church, including the Becks, the Edgars, the Hanna family, the Moores, and the Speers. The Shields were members of the Church of Ireland. The Johnson, Quinn, Rogers, Wheraghty, Flanagan, Doran, Cunningham, Fitzpatrick, and Bradley families were all Roman Catholic. There were some Keowns who were Roman Catholic, some who were Presbyterian and others who were Church of Ireland. All church records have therefore been studied to find the records of births and marriages that relate to Aughnaloopy.

Civil Registration

Civil registration for marriages began in 1845 and the civil registration of births and deaths from 1864. The civil registration of Roman Catholic marriages took place from 1864. Some churches have kept records much earlier than these dates, including those in Upper Mourne. It is not surprising that we see several inter-marriages between the families living in Aughnaloopy and even a few *mixed marriages* in the townland.

Aughnaloopy residents worshipped at the many churches around Kilkeel and birth and marriage records have been located in the Catholic churches of Upper and Lower Mourne, Mourne Presbyterian Church, Kilkeel Presbyterian Church "Meeting House", Kilkeel Church of Ireland Parish Church, Warrenpoint Presbyterian Church, and Rostrevor Presbyterian Church. Records have also been located in some churches in Belfast.

Earliest RC Baptism Record - Patrick Bradley

Often early church records did not record the townland of residence of couples getting married or having their children baptised. Fortunately, some of the Roman Catholic records for Upper Mourne are quite detailed. The earliest surviving record Roman Catholic baptism where Aughnaloopy is specifically recorded dates back to September 21, 1845 and is for Patrick Bradley, the son of Hugh Bradley and Ann Quinn. Henry Quinn and Ellen Keown were recorded as the child's godparents.

Earliest RC Marriage Record - Brigit Bradley and John Johnson

The earliest Roman Catholic Church marriage record that specifically documents Aughnaloopy as the place of residence occurs on February 6, 1853. Again it is for a member of the Bradley family. It is the record of Bridget Bradley's marriage to local man John Johnson. James Quinn and Ellen Keown are noted as witnesses to the marriage. It is likely that the Ellen Keown was the same person who was Godmother for Patrick Bradley eight years previously. She was possibly the wife of Thomas Keown from Aughnaloopy but her maiden name is unknown. Four years later, on February 15, 1857 Aughnaloopy is noted again. The occasion this time being the marriage of Ellen Keown (daughter Ellen and Thomas Keown) to John Allen, Patrick Doran and Margaret Cunningham were witnesses to the marriage. The following year on August 22, 1858, John's sister Margaret Allen celebrated her marriage to John Johnson's brother Richard. The witnesses on this occasion were John Doran and Mary Fitzpatrick.

Aughnaloopy gets its next mention in the Upper Mourne marriage records on January 1, 1862 when John Quinn marries Margaret O'Neill from Aughrim. On this occasion, Peter Quinn and Peter Cunningham were the witnesses. Later that year on June 6, Bernard Doran and Mary Ann Rogers are married with John Quinn and Mary Ann R being the recorded witnesses.

These baptism and marriage records illustrate to closeness of families living in Aughnaloopy. In addition to neighbouring families marrying into each other, neighbours were frequently chosen as witnesses and sponsors.

Earliest Mourne Presbyterian Record - George Hanna

The earliest available baptism record for Mourne Presbyterian Church is for George Hanna who was baptised on February 8, 1840. George was the son of George Hanna and Mary Wightman. The couple had at least four more children born in Aughnaloopy: Mary Jane (b. 1842), Margaret (b. 1844), Samuel (b. 1849) and Eliza (b. 1852).

Earliest Meeting House Record - Samuel Hagan

The earliest record that has been located for a baptism in the Meeting House Lane records is for Samuel Hagan, Samuel was baptised on March 20, 1843 and his parents were Nicholas Hagan and Nancy Wilson. Sadly, he must have died during childhood because another Samuel is listed in the Meeting House Lane Presbyterian Church records with a birth date of October 12, 1854 and baptism date of July 1855.

Other early baptism records that mention Aughnaloopy include Frances, son of John Hanna, baptised on August 27, 1843 followed by a daughter Sarah Jane Hanna, baptised on November 20, 1844. On December 17, 1845 a baptism record is listed for Margaret Hanna and her fathers name is given as Joseph.

Press Announcement - James H Morgan and Minnie Murphy

In addition to registration documents, a notice was sometimes placed in the newspaper announcing a birth, marriage or death. In March 1878, a marriage announcement was published for James H Morgan and Mary Ann 'Minnie' Murphy in the New York-based newspaper The Irish American. Minnie Murphy was the daughter of John Murphy and the granddaughter of James Hamilton of Springfield House. The couple, both from Aughnaloopy were married in the Catholic Church in Kilkeel, with the Rev. George Maguire PP officiating assisted by Rev. F McGuinness CC and J M'Gahan CC.

Chapter 10

Vaccination Records

Health Epidemics
During the mid-nineteenth century there were a series of devastating health epidemics, including smallpox, cholera, and pertussis. As a response, Government Acts were passed requiring the compulsory vaccination of children and requiring that official registers were kept. Infant vaccination became compulsory in 1862 and records for the Kilkeel area are available in the minute books of the Board of Guardians records archived at PRONI. The registers record: the name of the child, their age at the time of vaccination, date the vaccination certificate was issued, name and residence of the father, mother, or person in charge of the child and a signature of the registrar and date of registration.

A study of the vaccination records for the children of Aughnaloopy reveals some interesting information. For the most part, they are what we would expect – a list of children with family names (Beck, Edgar, Speers) that we recognise from earlier Aughnaloopy records including Tithes and Griffiths Valuation but there are a few surprises.

William Newell
First we have William Newell, the son of Francis Newell. William was vaccinated on June 12, 1866 at the age of 8 months. This the earliest record of the name Newell in the townland and the family have moved away from the area by the time of the 1901 census. Further research into William unearthed a birth record for September 7, 1865 and a baptismal date of December 6, 1865. The mother's name is not recorded and the place of residence is given as Aughnahorey rather than Aughnaloopy. The marriage details for Francis Newell reveals his wife name as Eliza Scott, the daughter of Robert Scott from Ballinran. Eliza also had a sister Margaret who married John Spears from Aughnaloopy.

The Children of Charles Higton and Mary Jane Keown
An unusual surname appearing on the vaccination list is Hyden. There is a William Hyden vaccinated on July 5, 1870 at age 6 months, a girl Matilda Hyden, vaccinated at age 7 months on December 14, 1872, and a Robert vaccinated when he was 3 years old on January 27, 1880. In each case the responsible person was listed as Charles Hyden. Additional research into the corresponding civil birth registrations reveals that the more likely spelling of the surname is Higton. Charles Higton was married to Mary Jane Keown from Aughnaloopy on April 13, 1869 in Kilkeel and it appears that the family were settled in the townland at the beginning of their marriage. Charles died in 1876 at 27 years of age leaving Mary Jane with at least four young children: William, Matilda, Charles Henry and Robert. The family is not listed in the later 1901 census and several of the family eventually moved to Ohio, USA.

John McCartin
Another family that are recorded as being resident in Aughnaloopy on the vaccination record is that of John McCartin. John was born on September 18, 1869 and was vaccinated in April 1870. His parents were Patrick McCartin and Mary Bradley. It is likely that Mary is one of the Aughnaloopy Bradleys, although no marriage record of Patrick to May has been located that might have confirmed this.

The Melvin Family

The name Melvin is unusual in Mourne but it appears from the vaccination records there was a Samuel Melvin living in Aughnaloopy in 1890 who had a son Henry. Also resident was a Daniel Melvin who had at least two children while resident in Aughnaloopy – John in 1892 and Selina in 1893. By 1901 Daniel, his wife Sarah and their four children (John, Selina, Daniel and James) were living in Leitrim. Daniel gives his place of birth as the Isle of Man. It is likely that he came to Kilkeel with his brother Samuel for work.

Are you the one I'm seeking?

Are you the one I'm seeking? Are you apart of me?
I search your name in census and I'm overcome with glee.
I scan through the directories in hopes I find you there.
I cherish all the tiny clues that in your life lay bare,
I read through all the history books and find you to be fair.
I know you were most honourable a fact they all declare.
And when I finally find it, the photo of my prayer,
The face that's staring back at me is the same as mine foursquare.
I'm honoured to be part of you now that I'm aware
To be endowed with such good traits and know that I'm the heir.

Brigitte Marmion, California, USA. 2008
http://www.marmionfamilytree.com/

Chapter 11

Early Occupations

Bassett's County Down Guide and Directory, 1886

For the majority of residents in Aughnaloopy, farming will have provided the major source of income. George Henry Bassett gave some detail on the nature of the industry in Bassett's County Down Guide and Directory, 1886.

Farming in the County Down, conducted in a manner highly creditable to those engaged in it. Tillage monopolizes a large part of the energies of the farmers, and has been profitable in seasons when good prices prevailed in the markets. The total extent under crops in 1884 was 279,668 statute acres, and in 1885 it was 284,070, showing an increase of 4,402 acres, the chief contributory to which was flax. In this item alone (22,284 acres) there was an increase of 3,087 acres. Down is now by far the largest flax-growing county in Ulster. When the new system of scutching has been brought into general use, the area under the crop is likely to be doubled in a few years. It is claimed for this system that through it there will be an increase of about 40 per cent, in the amount of good rough fibre taken from the straw. Under the old system a large part was turned into tow in the process of scutching, with a proportionate reduction in the farmer's profits. The new invention releases the fibre from the straw without turning any part of it into tow.

Wheat, as a crop, is decreasing in extent. Between 1884 and 1885 the decrease was 499 acres. Oats, potatoes, turnips, and carrots, are steady crops. Down is the largest potato-growing county in Ulster. In 1885 it had 48,417 acres, an increase of three acres over the previous year. The shipment of potatoes to England and Scotland has been extensively carried on for years; in fact, potatoes are the principal freight sent from the smaller ports. The total number of acres under tillage in 1885 was 215,079, an increase of 1,749 over the previous year. The number of acres under meadow and clover in 1885 was 68,991, an increase of 2,653 over the previous year. Very nearly half the total area of the county was under crops in 1885.

The keeping of livestock was on the increase. Although the actual numbers for Aughnaloopy are not known, Bassett gives the figures for the whole of County Down.

The number of horses of all ages, in 1885 was 31,301, an increase of 357 over the figures of the previous year. There was an increase of 24 in the number of mules (119) and 285 in the number of donkeys (1,483) an increase of 2,916 in the number of milk cows (54,183) and 4,666 in the total number of cattle (149,553) an increase of 7,815 in the total number of sheep (58,203), of 220 in the number of pigs (48,612) and an increase of 12,456 in the number of poultry (625,477).

Slater's Commercial Directory

Farming was not the only form of employment. Several Aughnaloopy residents had trades or services that they advertised in Slater's Commercial Directory for Kilkeel and surrounding area. In the 1881 edition, the Reverend George Nesbitt and Mrs. Mary Murphy were listed under the *Nobility, Gentry and Clergy* section with the address of Springfield given.

The Rev. George Nesbitt was the son of William Nesbitt, from Drumshannon, Newbliss, Co. Monaghan and was married to Elizabeth Wilson, daughter of William Wilson, from Blackwatertown. In addition to being minister at the local church from at least 1856, he was also the Presbyterian chaplain at Kilkeel Union Workhouse.

Mrs. Mary Murphy was the widow of James Murphy and the daughter of James Hamilton Esq. The Murphy family held the distinction of being the first Roman Catholic landowners in Aughnaloopy. Mary Murphy's daughter Mary Ann "Minnie" Murphy was married to James Morgan and James is also listed in Slater's Commercial Directory along with his brother. The Morgan boys ran a wine and spirit merchants on Bridge Street, Kilkeel, that had previously been operated by their father James Morgan. They sold seed, iron and timber and are listed as *Hardware Dealers and Peruvian Government Guano Manure Merchants*. Guano was manure that had first been imported to Liverpool in 1839 and got its name from the Peruvian word 'huana'. It was the accumulated droppings of sea birds and was popular manure. From the year 1850 to 1870, there was a huge increase in demand for guana along with substantial price hikes and it's likely that the business was very profitable for the Morgans. John Flanagan from Aughnaloopy is listed in the directory as a Blacksmith. John died in 1898, and the business passed out of the family.

Gathering Wrack

Despite its inland location, many Aughnaloopy residents will have supplemented their incomes by gathering wrack along the Mill Bay that stretches from Greencastle to Ballyedmond Point. Wrack provided farmers with a useful fertiliser due to its quantities of nitrogen, phosphate, potassium, potash and mineral salts. There is a common saying that *'It takes a sack of sea-wrack to make a sack of potatoes'* but in truth it is the quality rather than the quantity of potatoes that is improved by the addition of wrack. Wrack rights were mentioned in Co. Down land grants dating back to 1506. The 2,000-acre expanse of the Millbay was divided into plots known as 'plans' or 'cuts' marked by boulders placed to marked the site and also encourage the growth of wrack. As these wrack beds are not directly attached to farms and homes, ownership of the beds was complicated and the rights to the wrack beds were often passed down through families. If wrack beds were sold out of the family, it often occurred through public auction and in some cases was a way to raise money for passage to America. Aughnaloopy resident Henry Flanagan made reference to a wrack bed that he bequeathed to his son Peter in 1892 and the Will of Hugh Spears who died in 1914 mentioned two seaweed beds on Mill Bay valued at £40. James Hamilton Quinn's son Thomas Quinn also made reference to a Wrack Bed in his Will of 1929. Thomas Quinn had purchased the wrack rights from Patrick Cunningham.

Wrack beds provided an important adjunct to the farmer's arable land and rents were often higher per acre than for the stony fields that the wrack enriched. So valuable was the wrack that families often brought rocks from their fields to place on the sandy beaches to encourage its growth. Watchmen or bailiffs were also appointed to prevent the wrack gatherers from venturing out of their designated areas. Gathering wrack was extremely labour intensive and it is likely that residents of Aughnaloopy assisted the Flanagan and the Speers family with their harvest. After a storm, the people would swarm to the shore to gather 'in-blown wrack', that had washed ashore. In calmer weather, they would wade out into the shallow water to gather 'cut wrack', from the seabed. The crop was harvested between March and June using knives and sickles. At the same time the rocks and boulders would be lifted, turned and re-set into the sand to encourage growth. There are three distinct species of wrack in the Millbay: 'whang wrack', 'block wrack' and 'saw or lazy wrack'.

Holy Orders

Al least three Aughnaloopy natives received Holy Orders: Ann Hamilton, Mary Ann 'Minnie' Carvill and Gertrude Morgan. James Hamilton's daughter, Ann joined the Poor Clare Convent in Newry in 1850 and took her vow of Profession in 1853 being known in religion as Sister Gertrude. Ann spent time with the Sisters of St. Clare at the convent at Keady in 1877 and returned to the Newry convent in 1879. Ann's niece (Margaret Hamilton and Francis Carvill's eldest daughter) Mary Ann 'Minnie' Carvill entered the Poor Clare convent in Newry in 1859 aged 18 years. Three years later she took her vow of Profession, being known in religion as Sister Mary Clare. In 1905, three years after her father James Hamilton Morgan died his daughter Gertrude became a member of the

Faithful Companions of Jesus, taking the name Mother Eugenia in religion. Gertrude was the grandniece of Ann Hamilton.

Women's Work

Employment options were limited for women. For most, raising their often-large families and assisting with running the home farm would leave limited time for additional employment. On the 1901 census, sewing provided an additional source of income for Elizabeth Keown, Mary Catherine Morgan, Mary and Susan Quinn, Abby Bradley, Sarah Allen, Catherine Fitzpatrick, Mary Ann Shields, Mary Doran, Mary Doran, Ellen Doran, Annie, Ellen, Maggie, Elizabeth, Mary Speers, and Mary Margaret Speers. Ellen Grant, Sarah Quinn, Teresa Quinn, Sarah Conlon and Mary Cunningham were all employed as general domestic servants. Sarah Conlon from Armagh working for the Forsyth family. Lucretia Moore's occupation was given as landowner.

The Farm Gate.
by: Shelley Jayne Crawford Maskery (Shelley Jayne Illustration)

Chapter 12

Early Census Records
'...in 1813 the population was conjectured to be 5,937,856.'

Early Enumerations and Estimates
The first documented attempt to enumerate the population of Ireland was conducted in 1672 by Sir William Petty and gave a count of 1,100,000 souls. Petty estimates that prior to the civil war of 1641 the population would have been 1,466,000. In 1694, Captain South writing in the Transactions of the Royal Society of London states a population estimate of 1,034,102. Thomas Dobbs Esq. in his essay on the trade and improvement of Ireland published in 1731 gives an estimate on the number of houses in Ireland at 2,099,094 in the year 1712, increasing to 2,169,048 in 1718, and then 2,317,374 in 1725 and 2,309,106 in 1726. These calculations were based on the results of the Hearth Tax money collectors and were estimated assuming six members per household. In 1788, an inquiry was instituted by Mr. Gervais Parker Bushe, a commissioner of the revenue. In his analysis of the Hearth Tax revenue, a population of 4,040,000 was estimated. In 1805, Major Newenham gave his population account at 5,395,456 souls. In 1812, an Act was passed to take a full account of the population of Ireland. The process was to follow that of 1810 for Great Britain. After two years, it was determined that out of the forty counties, only ten gave complete returns, in four counties the Act was completely ignored, and in the remaining twenty six, the returns were considered incomplete or defective. So rather than being able to provide an accurate enumeration, in 1813 the population was conjectured to be 5,937,856.

Full Government Census
Full government censuses were taken in County Down every ten years from 1821 until 1911. Unfortunately, the results of the 1821, 1831, 1841, and 1851 census, were largely destroyed in 1922, in the fire at the Public Record Office; and those for 1861 1871 1881 and 1891 had been completely destroyed earlier, by order of the government. A variety of documentation relating to the census data does remain and some provides quite detailed information on Aughnaloopy.

In 1821, the population in the parish of Kilkeel (excluding Kilkeel town), is quoted as 2,272 individuals living in 2,258 houses. There were 75 uninhabited houses recorded across the parish. The census data states that 7,081 people were in employment with 1,963 working in agriculture and 4,836 employed in trades or manufacture. Excluding Kilkeel town, 408 children (248 males and 160 females) were attending school. A note is made that Lord Kilmorey provides a free school in Kilkeel town for children of all denominations and that 129 boys and 105 girls attended the school.

A similar analysis is available for the 1831 census. The population in the parish of Kilkeel (excluding Kilkeel town) is quoted as 13,767 individuals living in 2,531 houses. There were 155 uninhabited houses recorded across the parish. The census data states that 1,861 families were working in agriculture, with the number of families employed in trades or manufacture was 309.

A comparative study of the returns of the 1841 and 1851 census, reports that the population in Kilkeel enumeration district had fallen from 3,896 to 3,700 individuals. This population decline fits with data in Vaughn and Fitzpatrick's book, 'Irish Historical Statistics' (Royal Irish Academy). They analysed the 1841 English census, which was the first census to distinguish Irish-born from native-born English. The census revealed that in 1841 more than 419,000 Irish-born individuals were living in England. By 1851 the number had soared to over 727,000.

Allowing for deaths and emigration on to other destinations, an estimated 500,000 Irish entered England between 1841 and 1851 and stayed long enough to be counted in both census enumerations. Unfortunately, the number of individuals that came from Co. Down and specifically Aughnaloopy, is unknown but the decline in the population in Kilkeel can certainly be explained partially by immigration into England and elsewhere.

Although the detailed information on families from the 1861 census has been destroyed, some information on the townlands remains. The 1861 census of Ireland gives a general alphabetical index to townlands and towns, parishes and baronies and includes some comparisons of 1861 with 1851 and 1841. For Aughnaloopy, the area of the townland measured 382 acres 3 rods and 6 perch. The population had grown to 215 in 1851 from 190 in 1841 and in 1861 there were 217 residents. Further breakdown shows that in 1861 there were 97 males and 120 females living in the townland. In 1841, the population lived in 36 houses with an additional four homes being constructed before 1851. Interestingly by 1861, the number had dropped to 38 houses with two now listed as uninhabited. To put this in perspective, throughout the 20-year period from 1841 to 1861 there was an average of five residents per house. This appears comparable to all areas across Ireland.

Fortunately, some newspaper articles and government records have also survived that provide a glimpse into life in Ireland in the late 19th Century and offer some detail as to how the census was conducted. The 1871 census took place on the night of Sunday April 2. A printed form was left at every house in Aughnaloopy to be completed and collected the following day. The occupier was bound by law to complete all requested information with a minimum 20 shillings fine payable for non-compliance.

For the 1881 census, Ireland was divided into 207 enumeration districts each under the supervision of a sub-inspector of the Royal Irish Constabulary. Kilkeel was the enumeration district encompassing Aughnaloopy. The 1881 census forms were distributed on the night of April 2 and their collection commenced on April 4, 1881. Data on religious denomination was collected and in County Down, the following results were obtained: there were 80,673 Roman Catholics, 62,797 Protestant Episcopalians, 112,689 Presbyterians, 4,919 Methodists, 8 Jews, 1,190 people who classified their religious affiliation as other, and 143 individuals who refused to provide the information. The population of Newry town increased by 10.6% over the ten-year period from 1871 and it is extremely likely that some residents of Aughnaloopy left the countryside in search of work in the town. Certainly, the Morgan, Murphy and Hamilton families from Aughnaloopy had connections with Newry town.

The 1891 census followed a similar process to the 1881 with Kilkeel being the enumeration district encompassing Aughnaloopy. The population of Kilkeel district fell by 8.5% over the intervening ten years; population movement to larger cities and overseas being the primary factor. Some quite detailed information on Aughnaloopy is presented in the summary documents that have survived from the 1891 census. The number of houses in the townland is reported in 1891 as being 31 of which 3 were uninhabited. There was a steady decline from 40 houses in 1851, to 38 in 1861, 35 in 1871 to just 32 homes in 1881. In 1891 there were 113 outhouses and farmstead buildings in the townland reflecting the agricultural nature of living in Aughnaloopy. The population of the townland increased by 2 people to 217 in 1861 and then declined to 205 in 1871, 158 in 1881 to 129 in 1891 (composed of 65 males and 64 females).

Chapter 13

1901 Census

'On March 31, 1901, there were 31 households recorded at Aughnaloopy with a total of 250 individuals being named as residents.'

Full government censuses were taken in County Down every ten years from 1821 until 1911. Unfortunately, the results of the 1821, 1831, 1841, and 1851 census, were largely destroyed in 1922, in the fire at the Public Record Office; and those for 1861 1871 1881 and 1891 had been completely destroyed earlier, by order of the government. The 1901 census is therefore the earliest government census to remain intact and it provides a useful insight into life in Aughnaloopy at the turn of the century.

Demographics

On March 31, 1901, there were 31 households recorded at Aughnaloopy with a total of 250 individuals being named as residents. The eldest resident was 80-year old James Keown and the youngest was 1-month old Hugh Beck (son of David Beck). On the night on the 1901 census, James's wife Jane Keown nee Speers was staying at her brother Samuel's house.

There were 37 school age children living in the townland ranging in age from 3-year old Patrick Flanagan to 15-year old John Speers.

One property was listed as uninhabited in 1901.

Houses in the Townland

The census enumerator recorded details of the houses in the townland, noting the type of roof on the building, the number of windows at the front of the house and number of rooms occupied by each family. If the walls were made from stone or brick they were rated as '1', perishable materials were rated a '0'. Roofs were also rated with a '1' for slate, iron or tiled roofs and perishable materials such as thatch was given a '0'. The number of windows at the front of the house were noted as well as the number of rooms lived in by the family according to a formula where 1 room was allocated a '1', 2, 3 or 4 rooms a '2', 5 or 6 rooms a '3', and 7, 8, or 9 rooms was granted a '4'. An overall classification was then awarded to each house based on adding the numbers together. In Aughnaloopy, there were two houses that were calculated to be 1st class residences. These were occupied by James Forsyth and his family and the other by James Morgan's children. Both 1st class properties were owned by James Morgan. The house that was occupied by the Forsyth family had originally belonged to the Rogers family but by 1891 was the property of James Morgan. The residence occupied by James Morgan and his family was now formally designated as 'Springfield House' and was originally the property of the Murphy family of Aughnaloopy.

Occupations

The men of Aughnaloopy were overwhelming involved with farming whereas the women were engaged in domestic duties. Many of the women supplemented the family income by taking on work as seamstresses. The townland also had a butcher (James Allen), a carpenter (Hugh Beck), a Master Mariner (Thomas Richard Chambers), and a shop assistant (Joseph H Morgan), although they will have had to travel into Kilkeel town to work. Thomas Richard Chambers (the son of William Chambers and Elizabeth Grills) was originally from Kilkeel town and he eventually moved back to Newcastle Street with his Aughnaloopy wife Ellen Beck. Three members of the Speers family, John, James and Samuel all worked as sett makers. Setts are small brick-shaped stores that were hand cut from Mourne granite and often exported for use in road building. This was especially gruelling work and therefore it is not surprising that the Speers boy were only 21, 19 and 17-years old respectively. It is likely that the boys took their tools to be sharpened by local blacksmith James Norris. Lucretia Moore stated her occupation as Landowner. Lurganconary born Lucretia Davidson Moore was the daughter of Hugh Moore of Aughnaloopy and Lucretia Davidson. She had inherited the land at Aughnaloopy from her uncle John Moore who is designated in early documents as being 'of Aughnaloopy'. Lucretia was living in Aughnaloopy with a female servant Sarah Quinn who was originally from Dunnaval.

The Residents

Catherine Cunningham was a member of the Aughnaloopy Johnson family. Her father was George Johnson from the townland and her mother Catherine Hagan. Her husband John Cunningham was originally from Magheramurphy but in 1898 they moved to Aughnaloopy with their four boys, Thomas, Johnny, Patrick and Joseph. Thomas and Johnny, although only 17 and 15-years old respectively were both already employed as labourers.

John Allen's wife was Ellen Keown (daughter of Thomas Keown from Aughnaloopy). One of their daughter's Jane Allen had married butcher Charles McConville in 1885 and had moved to the Mountain Rd, Kilkeel where they had a daughter Mary 'Minnie' McConville. John and Ellen's son James was also a butcher. He was living at home with his wife Sarah McCartan (daughter of Richard McCartan and Ellen Cunningham) and their son John.

John Johnson's wife was also an Aughnaloopy girl, Bridget 'Biddy' Bradley, the daughter of James Bradley. She had at least two sisters, Ann and Ellen. Her daughter Rose Ann was married to Patrick Collins (the son of James Collins) from Mahereagh and was living with John and Bridget, in 1901 along with their grandchild John Collins. Another daughter Bridget was widowed at an early age and had brought her two sons, John and William to live in Aughnaloopy. Also living in the townland was Patrick Bradley and his wife Abby who was the daughter of Alexander Callaghan and Cecilia Canavan from Ballinran. It is thought that Patrick Bradley's father Hugh Bradley and Bridget Bradley's father James Bradley were brothers. Patrick's sister was listed on the census by her married name Sarah McVeigh although she was known locally until her death as Sarah Bradley.

Mary Colgan was the daughter of John Henitty from Glenloughan. She moved to Aughnaloopy after her marriage to James Colgan (son of Daniel Colgan) from Aughrim. They moved, with their children, sometime after 1885 to a property that had been vacant for over fifteen years. James Morgan was the owner of the land.

There were two Flanagan households living in Aughnaloopy in 1901. Ann McDonald Flanagan was living with her 30-year-old unmarried daughter Ellen. Ellen's first cousin Peter Flanagan (the son of Henry Flanagan and Cecilia Doran) was living nearby with his wife Margaret McKey from Tullyframe. There were also two Doran households in 1901 but it is not yet known whether Cecilia Doran was related to either of these families. Spinsters Mary and Ellen Doran were living with their 38-year old niece, also called Mary (the daughter of Denis Doran and Mary Quinn). Denis and his wife Mary were both from Aughnaloopy but they had moved away from the townland settling in Moneydarragh Beg. Forty-two year old Aughnaloopy resident Susan Quinn was also a Doran (daughter of John Doran) from Moneydarragh. Whether John and Denis were related is unknown.

Also living nearby is 50-year old Patrick Doran. He is living with his 26-year old niece Mary Catherine Morgan and grandniece, Ellen O'Neill who was just 7-months old. Mary Catherine Morgan was the daughter of Patrick's sister Ann Doran and her husband Patrick Morgan from Maghereagh. Mary Catherine had moved to Kirkdale in Liverpool when she was an infant and is on the 1881 and 1891 census with her father Patrick. Her mother appears to have died sometime between 1881 and 1891 as she is not listed on the 1891 UK census and her father Patrick is listed as a widower. Patrick had taken in a housekeeper Margaret Kelly to help look after Mary Catherine but at some point prior to 1901 he must have decided she was better off in Ireland with her uncle.

There was another Mary Catherine Morgan living in the townland. This Mary Kate (as she was known) was 18-years old and was living with her grandmother Brigit Cunningham Trainor and her maternal uncles Thomas and James Trainor. Brigit Cunningham Trainor was the widow of Thomas Trainor who was originally from Ballymageogh townland. Mary Kate's mother had died when Mary Kate was only a baby and her father Arthur Morgan remarried in 1896. In 1901 he was living in Cranfield, with his new wife Charlotte Rogers from Ballykeel and their two sons James and Hugh. The couple were to have at least five further children, James John Arthur Joseph, Hugh and Sarah.

Little is known about siblings 64-year old Catherine, 66-year old James and 68-year old Edward Fitzpatrick who were living in the townland. Their father was likely Patrick Fitzpatrick who was listed on the 1830 Tithes document and also the 1865 Griffiths Valuation.

James Hanna, his wife Sarah Ann McKnight (from Fofanny) and their five children were living on land that had previously been in possession of the Flanagan family from before 1864 to 1886. On his wedding certificate in 1890 James states that he was from Ballinran. He was the grandson of 'The Reed' Hanna who had lived in Aughnaloopy at the time of the Griffiths Valuation. James was not at home on the night the census was taken.

Despite the distance between Moneydarragh Beg and Aughnaloopy townlands, there was considerable movement of some families between the two places. In addition to the Dorans, the Aughnaloopy Quinns also had Moneydarragh Beg connections. Ann Quinn (daughter of Thomas Quinn and Margaret Donaldson) married Thomas ('Dancing Tom') McCartan in 1857 and her sister Matilda married Thomas's brother Terence in 1866. Both girls had moved to Moneydarragh Beg after their marriage.

In 1901 there were four Morgan siblings listed as living in Aughnaloopy: 21-year old Mary Jane, 19-year old Gertrude, 17-year old Joseph Hamilton and 14-year old James Francis. Although not listed as being home the night that the census was taken, the head of household was James Morgan (son of James Morgan and Mary Clarke). James had another son John Patrick Morgan who was living and working at his father's shop in Bridge Street, Kilkeel. James Hamilton Morgan quotes his occupation as 'Shop Assistant' and this is presumably with his brother in Bridge Street. Another son James Joseph died in 1879 when just 6-months old. The sibling's mother Mary Ann 'Minnie' Murphy had died in 1896 and their father James Morgan had recently remarried Belfast girl Imelda McMullen. Unfortunately, the marriage was short-lived as James died in 1902.

In 1901, Sarah Edgar (nee Bingham) was living with her son John and his wife Sarah Cousins, the daughter of Robert Cousins from Brackney. The family lived on John's father Robert Edgar's property. Also in the home were John and Sarah's children Maggie and Sarah. The Edgars were direct descendants of the original Edgar (Eagar) family that settled in Aughnaloopy.

There were two large Speers families living in Aughnaloopy. One was headed by Alexander Speers and the other by Samuel Speers. Samuel was married to Jane McClenaghan, the daughter of Robert McClenaghan and Jane Scott. Samuel and Jane had 12 children at the time of the 1901 census but had an additional two children (Hugh and Albert Joseph) over the next three years. Samuel's sister Jane was staying with the family on the night of the census and was no doubt a great help in rearing the children and helping in the home. Alexander Speers also had a large family. In addition to having nine children of whom eight survived, in 1901 two of his sisters were living in the house, 44-year old Mary and 38-year old Jane as well as their elderly mother Elizabeth and a nephew 11-year old David Beck. The women of the household all contributed by taking in sewing work.

There were two Beck households listed on the 1901 census. 37-year old David Beck was living with his wife Ann, his three children, a niece Sarah and his widowed mother Maria. Her husband Thomas Beck had died in October 1899. Maria was the daughter of Alexander Annett from Moyadd. The other Beck family was headed by Alexander Beck who was married to Sarah Ann Baird from Aughrim. Alexander was the son of James Beck and he was a first cousin of David Beck's father Hugh Beck.

William Shields and his wife Eliza Jane Parkes (daughter of John Parkes and Mary Ann Hanna from Ballinran) were settled in Aughnaloopy along with their seven children; Sarah, Mary Ann, Hugh, John, Jane, James and Samuel. They were living on land that had originally been occupied by James Edgar, who died in 1869 and then by William Edgar until 1884.

Temporary Residents

Temporary residents of Aughnaloopy were Mrs. Margaret Gonsalves and her children. Patrick Joseph, Frank, James and Margaret. Margaret husband Joseph Gonsalves was a fisherman who was not home on census night in 1901. By 1911 Mrs. Gonsalves was living and working in Kilkeel Workhouse. Her son Joseph was living in Benagh Upper with William Newell and his family and James was living in Lurganreagh with the Magee family.

Diversity in the Townland

Aughnaloopy was a *mixed* community with Roman Catholic, Church of Ireland and Presbyterian families. There was also a little diversity in the townland provided by the Forsyth family. Head of household James Forsyth, a contractor by trade, was originally from Scotland, his wife Margaret and their eldest child Alexander were born in Kilkenny, the next son Charles was born in Galway, followed James and Annie born in Mayo, Margaret in Sligo and Harriette who was born in County Down. The Forsyth's sojourn in Aughnaloopy didn't last long and by 1911, the family had moved to the Hollywood Road, Belfast. The Norris family also moved during the 1901 to 1911 period setting in nearby Aughnahorey townland. Both the Norris and the Forsyth families rented their property from James Morgan of Springfield House.

This chapter was based on a transcription on the 1901 census by Sheila Phillips. The complete census, with images, is now available online at:
http://www.census.nationalarchives.ie/pages/1901/Down/Kilkeel/Aughnaloopy/

Chapter 14

1911 Census

'…106 outbuildings were noted composed of 19 stables, 1 coach house, 1 harness room, 26 cow houses, 3 calf houses, 2 dairies, 12 piggeries, 20 fowl houses, 1 boiling house, 11 barns, 2 turf houses, 4 potato houses, 1 shed, and 3 stores.'

On Sunday April 12, 1911, the second census of the twentieth century took place. It was the duty of the head of household to complete the census documents and have them ready for collection on the morning of April 3, 1911. The distribution and collection of forms was the responsibility of the Royal Irish Constabulary.

Detailed study of the 1911 government census has been facilitated by the recent digitisation and indexing of records by the National Archives of Ireland in partnership with Library and Archives Canada. The returns for 1911 are arranged by townland and consequently it is relatively easy to analyse the Aughnaloopy returns. Information recorded includes: name, age, sex, relationship to head of the household, religion, occupation, marital status and county or country of birth. Women were also asked to record the number of years they had been married, the totally number of births and how many of their children were still living. This information has proved invaluable in identifying second marriages or in determining whether adult children had moved out of the home and possibly married. The census also asked individuals to document their ability to read or write and facility to speak the Irish language. All of this information is given on Form A of the census, which was filled in and signed by the head of each household. Where the head of the household could not write, his or her mark, usually an X, was recorded and witnessed by the enumerator.

Houses in the Townland

As with the 1901 census the enumerator also recorded details of the houses in the townland, recording the type of roof on the building, the number of windows at the front of the house and number of rooms occupied by each family. If the walls were made from stone or brick they were rated as '1', perishable materials were rated a '0'. Roofs were also rated with a '1' for slate, iron or tiled roofs and perishable materials such as thatch was given a '0'. The number of windows at the front of the house were noted as well as the number of rooms lived in by the family according to a formula where 1 room was allocated a '1'; 2, 3 or 4 rooms a '2'; 5 or 6 rooms a '3' and 7, 8, or 9 roomed houses were granted a '4'. An overall classification was then awarded to each house based on adding the numbers together. The number of out-offices and farm buildings attached to each household is also given.

There was only one house in Aughnaloopy that was graded as a 1st class house and that was the home of James Hanna and his wife Sarah Ann McKnight. Their house had stone walls, a non-perishable roof, five rooms and eight windows at the front of the structure. Thomas Quinn's property was the largest with nine rooms. It too had a stone walls and a non-perishable roof but because it only had four windows at the front of the house, it was officially classified as a 2nd class house.

Outbuildings

In addition to the information being provided on houses, information was also recorded on the outbuildings that were in the townland. For Aughnaloopy, 106 outbuildings were noted composed of 19 stables, 1 coach house, 1 harness room, 26 cow houses, 3 calf houses, 2 dairies, 12 piggeries, 20 fowl houses, 1 boiling house, 11 barns, 2 turf houses,

4 potato houses, 1 shed, and 3 stores. There was no forge in the townland. Thomas Quinn had the most outbuildings with 13 on his property. This was followed by Hugh Speers and David Beck who both had 9 outbuildings. Thomas Quinn and Hugh Speers both had a dairy on their property.

28 Households

In Aughnaloopy, 28 households are listed in the 1911 census and we see many familiar names including: Allen, Beck, Bradley, Colgan, Cunningham, Doran, Edgar, Flanagan, Shields, Speers, Trainor, Quinn and Wherity. Two properties are listed as being unoccupied. There were a total of 131 residents composed of 68 males and 63 females. There were 60 Roman Catholic residents, 57 Presbyterians and 14 members of the Church of Ireland. All forms were collected and the census considered complete on April 17, 1911. This population summary contrasts with that of 1901 when there were 31 households and 250 residents. Over the course of ten years the townland of Aughnaloopy had lost 119 residents or nearly 48% of the population.

Employment

Thomas Speers (son of Samuel), at age 17-years had established himself as a gardener but career choices were limited for the young men of Aughnaloopy. James Bradley (son of Patrick Bradley) at 15-years old was already working with his father on the family farm, as was 15-year old James Hanna (son of James Hanna and Sarah Anne McKnight) and 15-year old John Allen (son of James Allen). 15-year old James Shields (son of William Shields), 15-year old William Quinn (son of Thomas Quinn) and 16-year old Henry Flanagan (son of Peter) were still listed as scholars but it is likely that they too helped run the family farms. As in 1901, farming remained the primary occupation for the men of the townland and the women continued to supplement the family income with dressmaking and embroidering linen handkerchiefs. It is perhaps not surprising that so many residents had left the townland to seek employment elsewhere.

Oldest Residents - James Quinn, Ellen Allen and Edward Fitzpatrick

The eldest Aughnaloopy residents were James Quinn, Ellen Allen and Edward Fitzpatrick, all who were recorded as being 84-years of age. James Quinn had never married and lived alone in a one-roomed, one-windowed thatched house. He kept a stable, a cow house, a fowl house, and a piggery. James died on April 7, 1911 however, it is noted on the census form that he completed it on April 8, 1911 perhaps this is the day that the enumerator collected the forms. Ellen Allen nee Keown was living with her 73-year old husband John, their son James, her daughter-in-law Sarah McCartan and her grandson John. Edward Fitzpatrick, at age 84, was unmarried and was living with his elderly siblings; James who was 81-years old and Catherine who was 75-years old.

Youngest Residents - Annie Beck and Thomas Beck

Ellen Allen (nee Keown) was not the only resident living in a multi-generational family. Alexander Beck and his wife Sarah Ann Baird lived with their son Thomas, his wife Eva and their four children: Thomas, Ellen, Alexander and Annie. Annie Beck was the youngest resident in the townland at just three-months old. Four-month old Thomas Beck was the other infant in the townland. He was the youngest of nine children living with his parents David Beck and Ann Irvine. David also had his 77-year old mother Maria Annett living with them.

John Edgar and his wife Sarah Cousins also had a three-generation household. John's mother Sarah was living in the house along with his wife Sarah Cousins and their seven children, ranging in ages from Maggie who was 13-years old to William who was 2-years old.

Another large family living in Aughnaloopy in 1911 was that of Samuel Speers and his wife Jane McClenaghan. In addition to six of their fifteen children who were still living at home, a three-year old granddaughter Ivy Speers was living with them. Ivy's parents are as yet unknown but it is noted that she was born in Cape Colony. The enumerator has placed an additional comment stating 'British Colony'. Several of Samuel and Jane's children had emigrated with at least two daughters settling in America.

Another family that had family members whom had immigrated to America was that of 42-year old Sarah Ann Hanna (nee McKnight). Sarah Anne was living in Aughnaloopy with two of her children, 9-year old John and 7-year old Annie. Her husband James Hanna had move to Boston in 1906 where he found work in the construction industry. Their daughters Mary Ellen and Jane had moved to the United States by the time of the census. It is likely that Sarah Ann received money from her husband in America. Their home was well-maintained with a stone walls, a non-perishable roof and five rooms.

Eighty one year old John Johnson was living with his wife Bridget 'Biddy' Bradley and their unmarried daughter Mary. Their grandson William Rogers had been reared by John and Biddy and was still living with them working on the farm.

Living Alone

Several residents of Aughnaloopy were now living alone including Susan Wherrity, Mary Colgan and Sarah McVeigh.

Susan Wherrity had lived alone in Aughnaloopy for many years. In 1911, she listed her age as 79 years but on the 1901 census she is noted as being 60-years old. She was living in a small two-roomed home with one window in the front of the house. She kept a calf house and presumably a cow to provide milk. The property she lived on was registered to William Wherrity on the 1865 Griffiths valuation (leased from William Orr & J L Carr) and it's likely that William was her father. It does not appear that Susan married and there are no known siblings.

Also living alone was 69-year old Mary Colgan. Mary Colgan was the daughter of John Henitty from Glenloughan. She moved to Aughnaloopy after her marriage to James Colgan (son of Daniel Colgan) from Aughrim. Although she had had nine children of whom eight were still living they had all moved away from home. Mary leased her home from Thomas. It consisted of two rooms and had two windows in the front. She also kept a fowl house.

62-year old Sarah McVeigh also lived alone. Although married for 25 years to Thomas McVeigh, the couple didn't have any children. Sarah still took in sewing work and lived in a two-roomed home, with two windows in the front and a thatched roof that she had inherited from her mother Ann Bradley (nee Quinn). She maintained a calf house and a fowl house. She was known locally as Sarah Bradley (her maiden name).

Patrick Quinn 'Mark's Pat'

60-year old resident Patrick Quinn lived in a two-roomed house with two windows at the front and a slate roof. He had a stable and a barn on his land. Patrick was the son of Mark Quinn and Margaret Mackin and was known locally as 'Mark's Pat'. He had married Sarah Sloan the daughter of Michael Sloan from Ballymageogh and they had had two children. One son Richard had moved to Montana, USA and the other son Joseph 'Joe' stayed at home and never married. Joe unfortunately lost his leg early in life but in order to keep working he taught himself to be a carpenter. He made himself a wooden leg, and also made coffins for people in the area. Joseph was an extremely intelligent man, known in the area as to be as good as any solicitor and many people came to him with their legal problems. In 1911 Joseph was living with his cousins Thomas Quinn and Henry Quinn. Henry Quinn remained single and helped his brother Thomas on the farm. Thomas Quinn was married to Mary Fitzpatrick (the daughter of Catherine Murphy and Patrick Fitzpatrick from nearby Leitrim townland). The couple had five children who survived childhood: William 'Strawberry Willie', Ann Teresa, Catherine, Thomas, and Mary and two who died in infancy (Mary and James). They appear to have moved to this Aughnaloopy farm around 1909. The property which was known as 'Springfield House' was large, with over ten rooms, a slate roof and four windows to the front. There were also thirteen outbuildings and no doubt Thomas relied heavily on the assistance of his brother Henry and cousin Joe in running the farm. The land had originally belonged to the Murphy family.

The Killen family had moved to Aughnaloopy around 1909 into a new house that had been built on James Morgan's land in 1906. The Norris family had previously lived on the site, followed by the Gonsalves family. Lizzie Killen (nee Higgins) was now living there with her two boys 10-year old Joseph and 6-year old James. Her husband Peter Killen was not at home when the census was taken. The property was now owned by Henry Quinn who was living nearby with his brother Thomas Quinn. Lizzie kept a fowl house but she had no other outbuildings.

Thomas Morgan, his wife Rose (nee Quinn from Moyadd) and their two children Patrick and Mary Ellen were living in a property that had previously been the home of Patrick Doran before he died in 1904.

Ellen Doran and her niece Mary were living in their house that they had previously shared with Ellen's sister Mary who had died in 1908 leaving the house to Ellen. Both women worked as dressmakers. The property had two cow houses, a fowl house and a barn.

67-year old William Sloan had only recently moved to Aughnaloopy to live with his wife Sarah when the 1911 census was taken. The couple had only been married for eight years and did not have any children. William was a widower when he married Sarah who was a spinster. There was a Sarah Quinn who was listed as a servant to Lucretia Moore in 1901. When Sarah married William Sloan she gives her occupation as servant and it is therefore likely that this is the same Sarah Quinn. William and Sarah kept a cow house and a fowl house. The property had previously belonged to the Keown family.

There was a branch of the Keown family still living in Aughnaloopy. Thomas Keown and his wife Margaret 'Maggie' Denny were living in a four-roomed house with four windows at the front, with their five children (Annie, Minnie, James, David and William Thomas). At the time of the 1901 census, Thomas's father James had been living with the family. James had died in 1903 and the farm had passed to Thomas. The family kept a stable, a piggery, a fowl house, and a barn.

William Shields and his wife Eliza Jane Parkes from Ballinran were living in the townland with five of their children (John, Jane, James, Samuel and Margaret). Eliza had given birth to nine children of whom eight were still living. All the family were listed as belonging to the Church of Ireland, but William and Eliza Jane had married in Rostrevor Presbyterian Church in 1883. The property had previously belonged to the Edgar family and William Shields appears to have move here after his marriage to Eliza Jane.

Hugh Speers and his wife Charlotte were living with their son Hugh and his new bride Annie. The men both quoted their occupation as farmer and the women worked as seamstresses. Hugh died the following year on August 16, and sadly his son Hugh died just two years later at age 38 years old. The Speers property had nine outbuildings including a dairy.

Alexander Speers had a large household. As in 1901 Alexander still had two of his sisters living at home 59-year old Mary and 54-year old Jane. His mother Elizabeth had died sometime between 1901 and 1911. He had five children still living at home (John, Samuel, Annie, Maggie and Mary Jane). His nephew David Beck who had been living with him in 1901 had moved away. The women of the household all worked at home as 'flowerers', embroidering handkerchiefs and tablecloths with delicate floral pattern. This form of home employment continued throughout the Mourne area until the 1960's. The Speers family all lived in three small rooms on a site that had belonged to the Speers family since before the time of the Griffith's Valuation in the mid-nineteenth century.

Thomas Quinn and his wife Susan (Doran) were still living with Thomas's relative Mary in their small two-roomed home. Unlike many of the households in the townlands, little seems to have changed for Thomas and Susan since 1901.

Chapter 15

Ulster Day

The Covenant and Declaration

On September 28, 1912, 25 residents of Aughnaloopy travelled into Kilkeel town to sign the Ulster Covenant and corresponding Declaration. Of those signing, nine were male and sixteen were female. Several locations were set up in Kilkeel, including the Mourne Lecture Hall, Ballinran Orange Lodge and Kilkeel Parish Church. Of the Aughnaloopy contingent, brothers Thomas and Alexander Beck travelled to the Ballinran Orange Hall to sign their names, as did John Speers. Charles Hanna, Alex and Hugh Speers and John Edgar all signed at the Mourne Lecture Hall and John and James Shields signed at Kilkeel Parish Church. All of the women from Aughnaloopy signed their names at the Mourne Lecture Hall. The women who signed were: Annie Beck, Eva Ada Nicholson Beck, Sarah Ann and Sarah Ann (Baird) Beck, Bella Scott, Annie Hanna, Jane Shields, Annie, Jane, Jane, Maggie, Mary, Mary, Mary Jane and Mary M Speers.

The wording to the Ulster Covenant signed by men was:

> *'Being convinced in our consciences that Home Rule would be disastrous to the material well-being of Ulster as well as of the whole of Ireland, subversive of our civil and religious freedom, destructive of our citizenship, and perilous to the unity of the Empire, we whose names are underwritten, men of Ulster, loyal subjects of His Gracious Majesty King George V., humbly relying on the God whom our fathers in days of stress and trial confidently trusted, do hereby pledge ourselves in solemn Covenant, throughout this our time of threatened calamity, to stand by one another in defending, for ourselves and our children, our cherished position of equal citizenship in the United Kingdom, and in using all means, which may be found necessary to defeat the present conspiracy to set up a Home Rule Parliament in Ireland. And in the event of such a parliament been forced upon us, we further solemnly and mutually pledge ourselves to refuse to recognize its authority.*
> *In sure confidence that God will defend the right, we hereby subscribe our names. And further, we individually declare that we have not already signed this Covenant.'*

The Declaration signed by women read:

> *'We, whose names are underwritten, women of Ulster, and loyal subjects of our gracious King, being firmly persuaded that Home Rule would be disastrous to our Country, desire to associate ourselves with the men of Ulster in their uncompromising opposition to the Home Rule Bill now before Parliament, whereby it is proposed to drive Ulster out of her cherished place in the constitution of the United Kingdom, and to place her under he domination and control of a Parliament in Ireland.*
> *Praying that from this calamity God will save Ireland, we hereto subscribe our names.'*

The Ulster Covenant was part of a response by Ulster Unionists to the efforts of successive Westminster governments to settle the running sore of the 'Irish Question' by giving Ireland a limited measure of local autonomy known as 'Home Rule'. The first two Home Rule Bills, in 1886 and 1893, had been rejected by Parliament, following concerted pressure from Unionists in Great Britain and Ireland. The signatures therefore give us some insight into the political persuasion of the Aughnaloopy residents and it is not surprising that several members of the same family opted to sign the Covenant and Declaration.

NAME.	ADDRESS.
Thomas Beck	Aughnaloopy
Alexander Beck	Aughanloopy
Sarah Ann Beck (7#)	Aughnaloopy
Eva Ada Beck	"
Bessie Scott	"
Mary Spurs	
Mary Spurs	
Jane Spurs	"

NAME.	ADDRESS.
Annie Beck	Aughnaloopy
Sarah Ann Beck	"
Eliza Jane Austin	"

PRONI has done a wonderful job of making the entire Ulster Covenant available on their website at http://www.proni.gov.uk/ In addition to all signatures being available for viewing, a history of the situation that led to Ulster Day is included as well as a section on the aftermath.

No Catholic residents of Aughnaloopy signed the Covenant or the Declaration. The views of non-Unionists on Ulster Day were reflected by the Irish News and Belfast Morning News Friday, September 27, 1912:

> '…….Taking the day's proceedings altogether they were tame as a demonstration of enthusiasm and highly ludicrous as an indication of the 'grim and determined' spirit. The whole grotesque production has been a political failure, though a comic success, and now that it is past and gone, one wonders how many thousands the Ulster Unionists have spent on staging it……'

Chapter 16

Emigration

*'It's not for the want of employment I'm going
O'er the dreary and stormy sea
But to seek a home for my own true love
On the shores of Amerikay.'*

As in every townland across Ireland, many left Aughnaloopy in search of work and adventure overseas. Their reasons for leaving home were variable and changed considerably over the course of history but a common characteristic is the positive impact Aughnaloopy natives had on their newfound homelands. America was a popular destination for the men and women that left Aughnaloopy, but several others from the townland settled in England, Canada and others as far away as Australia and New Zealand. For some their departure was temporary, but many others settled permanently and there are many across the globe that can trace their ancestry back to the little townland of Aughnaloopy. Emigration in the mid-nineteenth century is difficult to research. Records of residents in Ireland are scarce and passenger records such as ships manifests are limited and often not very detailed. Frequently, the place of residence is simply listed as 'Ireland' or in some cases may even have been the port of embarkation, e.g. Liverpool or Newry. Other sources that provide information on the Aughnaloopy Diaspora include personal correspondence, passport applications, census records, marriage details that state a place of birth, obituaries and Wills.

Missing Friends

One of the earliest records specifically referring to an Aughnaloopy native that had immigrated to the United States was an advertisement placed in an American newspaper. From October 1831 until October 1921, the Boston Pilot newspaper printed a 'Missing Friends' column with advertisements from people looking for *lost* friends and relatives who had emigrated from Ireland to the United States. This extraordinary collection of over 31,000 records is available as a searchable online database.

On July 27, 1859, Mary Quinn placed an advertisement in the Pilot, hoping to make contact with her husband William Quinn from Aughnaloopy. She knew that William had first started work as a miner in California in 1855 with William Cunningham. Mary wanted her husband to make contact with Mr. Thomas Rice resident at 43, Ann Street in Boston, Massachusetts. It is possible that Ann was staying with the Rice family although that is not clear from the advertisement. It is not known whether Mary heard news of her husband but no follow up message was placed in the newspaper. William Cunningham was possibly from Kilkeel but no further information is currently available.

A photograph of the Jeanie Johnston which is docked at Custom House Quay in Dublin's city centre. The vessel is an accurate replica of the original ship which sailed between Tralee in Co. Kerry and North America between 1847 and 1855. The photograph was donated by Ciera E. Jones and was taken in July 2011.

Ellis Island and Castle Garden

From 1892 until 1924, it is relatively easy to track down passengers on their w~~ York. During these years, more than 22 million immigrants, passengers, members came through Ellis Island and the Port of New York but the record been indexed and made available online for free at http://www.ellisisland.org/

From 1855 until 1890 Castle Garden in the Battery (originally known as Cas~ existed as a processing station for immigrants and although these records ar~ ~~ they are not as detailed as the Ellis Island records. Records are available to search at http://www.castlegarden.org. Approximately eight million immigrants entered America through Castle Garden.

Other Ports of Entry

While most immigrants entered the United States through New York Harbour others sailed into the ports of Boston, Philadelphia, Baltimore, San Francisco, Savannah, Miami, and New Orleans. Records at these ports are generally not as detailed to include the originating townland.

A New Jersey Connection

Fortunately, some detailed records have been uncovered. When Sarah A Beck emigrated from Aughnaloopy in December 1910 she clearly stated that she was from Aughnaloopy. Sarah was 18-years old at the time and had been living with her Uncle David Beck and his family. She was travelling with newly-weds Willie and Ida Stevenson from Kilkeel and she stated that she was going to stay with her cousin Mrs. Squires in Hohokus, New Jersey. Mrs. Squires was noted as being Ida Stevenson's sister. Mrs. Ida Stevenson was born Elizabeth Ida Anderson and at 20-years of age she had married William Henry Stevenson on November 19, 1910 in Mourne Presbyterian Church. Ida (as she was known) was from Ballinran – not far from where Sarah A Beck had been living in Aughnaloopy. Her father was Joseph Anderson and her mother Elizabeth M Beck from Aughnaloopy. Elizabeth Anderson (nee Beck) had been widowed at an early age and had at least seven children to support when she was just 40-years old. It is not surprising that many of her family had to leave home to find work. Willie and Ida Stevenson settled in Hohokus, New Jersey and had two girls, Muriel and Mary. The family became naturalised citizens on the United States and obtained a United States passport. They continued to live near the Squires family and both were listed on the 1920 United States Federal Census. Belle Squires was now a widow with two children Albert and Edith and she was living next door to Willie Stevenson. Willie was working as a private chauffeur. In June 1919, Ida took the girls back to Ireland to visit family; all three are listed on the incoming passenger list for the SS Orunda part of the Cunard shipping line. The ship landed at Liverpool and Ida would then have had to travel on the Ireland. It appears that the Stevensons stayed in Ireland for almost a year returning to New York on the SS Columbia in March 1920. They boarded the Columbia in Derry and settle back in Hohokus where they are listed on the 1930 United States Federal Census. William Henry was now employed as a truckman. What happened to Sarah A Beck is as yet unknown.

Aughnaloopy to Kirkdale

People travelled between Co. Down and England frequently, for some it was a stopping off point for future travel to America but others settled there and early census records show high numbers of County Down natives living in Cumberland, Lancashire, and Northumberland etc. Their originating townland is not recorded but if a family member returns home we are sometimes able to trace back.

One such example is for Mary Catherine Morgan the daughter of Patrick Morgan (from Maghereagh) and Ann Doran (from Aughnaloopy). When Mary Catherine was born in September 1879, her place of birth was noted as Aughnaloopy, her mother also states

Aughnaloopy on her marriage certificate to Patrick Morgan in 1877. However, in 1881 the family Patrick, Ann, Mary Catherine and an older brother Patrick, were living at 51, Darwin Street, Kirkdale, Liverpool, England and Co. Down is all that is noted for the birthplace. Ann Morgan (nee Doran) died sometime between 1881 and 1891 and Mary Catherine returned to Aughnaloopy to live with her uncle Patrick Doran. There is a 30-year old William Quinn and a 26-year old John Young lodging with the Morgan family in Liverpool and although not recorded it is possible that both William and John were from Kilkeel.

Although Margaret McCartan doesn't show up on any ship manifests, or UK census data, when her Will was proved she is listed as having lived at 161, Fountain Road, Kirkdale, Liverpool. Sometime between 1901 and 1904 she had returned to Ireland and was living in Aughnaloopy when she died on March 9, 1914 age 50-years old. Margaret had a brother Arthur McCartan, who was living in Moneydarragh Beg.

Oh Canada!

Several members of the Aughnaloopy Doran family made Canada their home. John Doran and Sally Johnson's son John is documented as arriving in Halifax, Nova Scotia on April 8, 1988 at just 19-years old. His sister Annie also moved to Canada although the details have not been confirmed. Both John and Annie married in Canada and settled in Simcoe, Ontario.

At least two of William Speers and Margaret Hanna's children settled in the Lennox area of Ontario. Although no ship manifest record has been located, the family are documented on Canadian census records.

Samuel Speers and Jane McClenaghan's son William left Belfast in March 1926 on the SS Doric sailing to Halifax, Nova Scotia. The Canadian Government supplemented the cost of his passage and he gave his address as the Government Hotel, in Toronto, Ontario. William eventually settled in Minnesota.

A San Francisco Address

Another document that refers to an address outside of Aughnaloopy is that granting Power of Attorney for the estate of Mary Davis. Mary was the daughter of James Morgan and Mary Clarke. Although born in Aughnaloopy, she settled in Dunnavan after her marriage to John Davis who was a Petty Officer in the Navy. Following Mary's death on April 13, 1913, her brother Patrick made the following statement giving an address in San Francisco for himself and also stating his nephew Joseph H Morgan's address in Belfast.

> 'Now I, the said Patrick Morgan residing at 161A Henry Street, San Francisco, and being of the age of 40 years and upwards, Labourer, as such next of kin of said Mary Davis deceased, do hereby nominate, constitute and appoint Joseph H. Morgan of 34 Agincourt Avenue, Ormeau Road, Belfast, Gentleman, to be my true and lawful Attorney for me and in my name and for my use and benefit to apply for and obtain forth of any Registry of His Majesty's Kings Bench Division in Ireland, authorised by law to issue same, a Grant of Letters of Administration, Intestate, of the Goods of the said Mary Davis.'

California Calls

On the 1910, United States Federal Census there is a 48-year old Patrick Morgan living in San Francisco who gives his place of birth as Ireland and his year of immigration as 1873. It's likely that this is Patrick (son of James Morgan) from Aughnaloopy. Patrick's nephew Joseph Hamilton Morgan (the son of James H Morgan and Mary Ann 'Minnie' Murphy) had also emigrated from Aughnaloopy. At 27-years old, he departed from Liverpool with his wife Ellen Josephine 'Nellie' Mageean (from Saintfield) and their children Joseph and David. Although he only states Kilkeel as his place of residence, he lists Mary Davis as his next-of-kin thus confirming that it is indeed Joseph H Morgan from Aughnaloopy. Joseph lists his occupation as auctioneer and states that his family are going to live in Los Angeles, California. Their ship, the SS Furnessia left Londonderry on July 30, 1900 and arrived in New York harbour on August 10. They travelled in the second-class cabin. Following, his Aunt Mary Davis death and his responsibilities as her Power of Attorney, Joseph returned to Ireland. In July 1914, he sailed again from Londonderry, this time on the SS Columbia, arriving in New York on August 4, 1914 for passage on to Los Angeles. He now states his occupation as butcher and his next-of-kin as his wife Mrs. Nellie Morgan at 24, Lavinia Square, Belfast. Lavinia Square is a continuation of Agincourt Avenue – the address listed on Mary Davis power of attorney document.

New Zealand via the Australian Goldfields

Nicholas Quinn was one of the first members of the Aughnaloopy Quinns to head to New Zealand. Nicholas apparently left Ireland in 1859, with his brother James to work on the Australian goldfields at Ballarat and Bendigo. Although, there is no record of him leaving Ireland a record remains for him arriving in Victoria on the ship 'Tudor' in July 1859. On the discovery of gold in Otago, New Zealand, Nicholas travelled on to Gabriel's Gully to mine for gold in 1861 and had considerable success. With his profits, he invested in a property 'Bellevue Farm' at Makikihi, where he worked in partnership with his brother William until 1900. Nicholas's wife Mary (nee Cunnngham) and their daughter Ann moved to New Zealand in the early 1860's. Nicholas died an extremely wealthy man, with an estate valued at over £24,000 in 1903. His Will provides several references to families still living around Kilkeel. William was also extremely successful in New Zealand. In addition to farming at his property named 'Annalong', he also established a brickworks. About 1883, another brother Patrick immigrated to New Zealand with his wife Margaret (Quinn) and their large family. They settled at a property they purchased near Nicholas, named 'Beach Farm' in Makikihi. The Quinn's success in New Zealand facilitated others members of the extended family to spend time there including Ann Quinn's son Harry Joe Doyle (from Newcastle Street, Kilkeel).

South African Birth

Sometimes, no records can be found of families that moved away from their homeland and then other times a notation appears in the most surprising place. On the 1911 census for Aughnaloopy, a 3-year old girl Ivy is listed in the home of her grandparents Samuel Speers and Jane McClenaghan. Ivy's place of birth is recorded, as being the Cape Colony and it is believed that she may be the daughter of one of the Speers boys that move to South Africa in search of work. Gladys Ivy died in 1914.

Mining in Montana

Sometimes the only records that survive concerning a family member that emigrated are oral family history records. Richard Quinn born in April 1868, the son of Mark Quinn and Sarah Sloan had a brother Patrick 'Mark's Pat' who remained in Ireland. Mark's Pat was able to relate that he had a brother and that the brother immigrated to America and spent some time working in the copper mines of Montana. Whereas no formal record has been found for Richard emigrating or settling in Montana, this is not unusual. If men remained single, didn't purchase property, didn't apply for a passport, perhaps worked at several companies or had temporary or labouring positions, it is not uncommon that they do not appear in formal records. Richard Quinn had an Uncle Richard Quinn who also emigrated from Aughnaloopy and it is possible that the two worked together. Wills sometimes provide evidence of family members who emigrated overseas when no ship manifests survive. When Mark Quinn of Aughnaloopy wrote his will in May 1873, he included a provision for his son Richard:

> 'I bequeath to my daughter Ellinor all my land property and chattels where I now live in Annalupy also all my property in Newry Street Kilkeel consisting of two Houses also all the cash I have on hand but if Richard my Son comes home from America he is to get the House that James Cunningham Taylor lives in at present.'

Emigrant Letters

Despite the fragility of handwritten letters, correspondence between family members that had left home and those who remained were treasured possessions and many have survived. Sometimes a line written in a letter is the only information that remains to indicate where Aughnaloopy residents settled. In a letter, date May 3, 1923 from Ellen Doran to her nephew John Doran in Canada, she includes the line:

> *'Johnney Cunningham is dead and Kate to both the 3 oldest boys are out in Mounttana and the youngest boy is liven alone like myself.'*

Further research based on this information revealed that Kate was Catherine Johnson from Aughnaloopy who was married to John Cunningham from Magheramurphy. The couple had at least four sons who are listed on the 1901 census: Thomas, Johnny, Patrick and Joseph. Only Joseph is at home in 1911 and so the boys referred to by Ellen are likely Thomas, Johnny and Patrick. From this information, it was possible to locate John Cunningham on a ship manifest for the SS Cymric that departed from Liverpool on April 15, 1910 sailing to Boston. John states that he is travelling to his brother Patrick in Miles City, Montana. With this additional information to aid the search, a ship manifest was then located for Thomas and Patrick Cunningham travelling together on the SS Cedric, sailing from Liverpool on April 4, 1909. Both men stated that they were travelling to Miles City, Montana. They noted that they had a cousin John Quinn who was already working in Miles City. Also travelling with Thomas and Patrick was 23-year old Frank Reilly (son of John Reilly and Mary Teggarty from Moneydarragh Beg) and 24-year old Frances Young (son of Robert Young from Ballyveaghmore).

The Brain Drain

There was a new wave of mass emigration from Ireland in the 1980s. Unskilled and semi-skilled workers continued to leave in droves but also leaving the country in high numbers were university and college graduates who despite being highly educated, were unable to find employment at home. The loss of this precious asset was popularly referred to as the 'brain drain'. In 1980, around 8 percent of college graduates left to find work and further training abroad. By the end of the decade the figure had risen to almost 30 percent. Sadly no figures are available for individual townlands.

Emigration Today

Despite a temporary reversal in the 1990's, emigration has been a dominating feature of Irish life for almost four centuries, and it continues to play an important role in the present. The Economic and Social Research Institute predicts that 100,000 Irish will be emigrating in the next two years – 50,000 in 2011 and 50,000 in 2012. These figures mean that more Irish people will emigrate this year than in 1989, when emigration last peaked and 44,000 left Ireland.

Chapter 17

Wills and Letters of Administration

While the meaning of the term Will might seem self-evident, its evolution in Ireland over the last 200 years is generally less well understood. A Will is a legal document drawn up to determine the inheritance of a person's possessions after their death. If a person had no property, or the inheritance of their property was pre-determined, they were unlikely to go to the expense of hiring a lawyer to draw up a Will. A Will only takes effect after the person dies and after the document has been proved in court, i.e. a grant of probate has been issued. The grant of probate authenticates the Will and gives the executors the power to administer the estate. Probate can take a few weeks or several years. For example, when Mary Quinn Doran's brother James Quinn passed away in 1911 at age 86 years, leaving no wife or children, his estate valued at £53 16s 6d was settled within a month. However, the estate of James Murphy of Springfield House, took 18 years to settle. A person can amend their Will at any time or several times. These amendments or codicils have to be separately dated and attested in the same way as the original Will.

Until 1858, the Church of Ireland, through the Prerogative Court of the Archbishop of Armagh and the consistorial courts in each diocese, was responsible for granting probate and letters of administration. This system was abolished in 1857 by the Court of Probate and Letters of Administration Act (Ireland) when probate matters were transferred from the ecclesiastical courts to the civil courts. The Prerogative Court and the consistorial courts were replaced by the Principal Registry in Dublin and a number of District Registries of the Probate Court (pre-1877) and of the High Court (post-1877). You could apply for a grant of probate or letters of administration at the Principal Probate Registry in all cases but application could also be made at a District Registry within whose area the deceased had a fixed place of residence. The District Registry covering Aughnaloopy was Belfast.

Will Calendars

Sadly, the original Wills of the Principal Registry up to 1904, and the District Registries up to 1899, were lost in the 1922 Dublin Courthouse fire. Fortunately, copies that had been made by the District Registries survived, as they had not been transferred to Dublin. These copies of Wills were written into large volumes and are archived and available to view at PRONI. Each year an alphabetical list of the deceased, known as Will Calendars were produced, recording the address, occupation, place of death, date of death, date of the grant of probate or letters of administration, the District Registry where the Will was proved, the value of the estate, and the names of the person or persons to whom probate or administration was granted. PRONI has recently made available an online search facility of the Will Calendars and many surviving Wills are available online and at the PRONI offices in Belfast.

A comprehensive study of the surviving Wills and administration documents relating to Aughnaloopy has enabled a detailed appreciation of the family relationships in the townland. Several of the surviving Wills are extremely detailed documents identifying siblings, sons, daughters, grandchildren, nieces, nephews, tenants and even servants. A study of the witnesses and executor's names reveals some of the relationships held with local neighbours. In addition to giving some indication of the deceased relative financial wealth, often the text of the Will gives some indication of the depth of religious devotion held by the deceased.

While the text given below is the documented Will, many families made less formal arrangements concerning the distribution of property and cash. Family property may have been been passed on prior to the preparation of a Will (when a child emigrated or married) and this is not reflected in the documented Will. Of course, many Aughnaloopy natives left their homeland and established families across the globe. Some Wills relating to Aughnaloopy diaspora that have been located are also included below. The spelling of names is often inconsistent in Wills and related documents.

John Edgar (1832)
The earliest surviving record of a Will that specifically states Aughnaloopy as the place of residence is for John Edgar whose Will was probated in 1832. The record is contained within the Newry & Mourne Wills, 1727-1858 index edited by W P W Phillimore, in 1909. No further details are given and the original Will has been destroyed. John Edgar is possibly the same John Edgar listed on the Flax Growers List in 1796 and is likely related to Robert Edgar who is listed as living at property 19a on the Griffith's Valuation in 1864. He may be the father of Robert as Robert had a son John who in turn inherited the Aughnaloopy property.

James Edgar (1869)
The next Will record is also for a member of the Edgar family. Widower James Edgar died on April 7, 1869 at Aughnaloopy. Probate was granted at Belfast to George Annett of Ballykeel who is noted as a maternal uncle and guardian (during minority only) of William Edgar, James Edgar, Margaret Edgar, Mary Edgar, Eliza Anne Edgar, Catherine Edgar and John Edgar. These seven children were all minors at the time of their father's death. James's wife Elizabeth Annett from Ballykeel had predeceased her husband. James is listed as living at property 21c on the Griffith's Valuation in 1864. He may be a brother of Robert above and may also be related to John Edgar who died in 1832. Unfortunately, as this is a pre-1900 administration document no further information is available.

James Murphy (1872)
The next document listing Aughnaloopy and more specifically Springfield House is the Letters of Administration (with the Will annexed) of the personal estate of James Murphy. James is listed as a Gentleman who died on February 3, 1872. Probate was granted to his sister Mary Anne Morgan, wife of James Morgan, the Universal Legatee. James Morgan was the son of James Morgan Snr. and Mary Clarke. Springfield House is recorded as property 41a on the 1861 Griffith's Valuation. James and Mary Ann 'Minnie' Murphy were the children of John Murphy and Mary Ann Hamilton. There were two other siblings, Hamilton Murphy and John Murphy both whom had died prior to James's death. Probate of the Will was not settled until 1890.

Mark Quinn (1874)
On February 21, 1874 Aughnaloopy farmer Mark Quinn died. His Will was proved at Belfast by the oath of Patrick Mackin of Dunnavil, Kilkeel one of the Executors and possibly Mark's brother-in-law. The other executor was his neighbour James Fitzpatrick of Aughnaloopy. Witnesses present were John Cungham (sic) and James Morgan (Jnr.)

'In the Name of God Amen. The Last Will and Testament of Mark Quinn of Annaloopy being weak of body but sound of mind I assign my soul to Almighty God and my Body to the earth from whence it came.
I bequeath to my son John One pound in cash I also bequeath to my son Patrick One pound in cash I bequeath to my daughter Ellinor all my land property and chattels where I now live in Annalupy also all my property in Newry Street Kilkeel consisting of two Houses also all the cash I have on hand but if Richard my Son comes home from America he is to get the House that James Cunningham Taylor lives in at present.
I appoint as my Executors Patrick Macken of Dunnavil and James Fitzpatrick of Annaloopy (sic). Dated this 16th May 1873. Signed with "X" Mark Quinn.'

Richard never returned from America and Mark's daughter Ellen continued to live in the property at Aughnaloopy until her death in 1895. The home then passed to her nephew John Quinn.

John Flanigan (1875)

On December 27, 1875, John Flanigan died in Aughnaloopy leaving his possessions, valued under £100 to Margaret Flanigan his widow and surviving executrix. Witnesses to the Will were James Doran (his father-in-law), and neighbours John Hanna and Robert Hanna. John was a widower when he married Margaret Doran (daughter of James from Leitrim) in 1860. There is no mention of children from either marriage.

'I leave and bequeath to my dearly beloved wife Margaret Flanigan my Farm of Land and all my stock and crops together with my houses and furniture and all the chattel property I possess and I allow my beloved wife to pay all my just debts and funeral expenses and my wife shall receive all debts due and owing to me. I hereby appoint and nominate my wife Margaret Flanigan and her Father James Doran of Leitrim as executors of this my last Will and testament bearing date this ninth day of June 1874. Signed with "X" John Flanigan.'

John Moore (1880)

John Moore died on January 16, 1880 in Aughnaloopy. In his Will, he confirms he was unmarried and that his brother was Hugh, the father of Lucretia Davidson Moore. He left his niece Lucretia all of the farmland he occupied in Aughnaloopy with dwelling house and office houses together with all chattel property. Also all his interest in all the Aughnaloopy property that was held between him and his brother Hugh as termed undivided property. Lucretia was to receive all rents out of same as he had been receiving and that she was to succeed him as owner of all his lands in Aughnaloopy after the death of her father. To his faithful servant Margaret Colgan, he gave £20. John Orr of Kilkeel and his brother Hugh Moore of Ballynahatten were appointed as executors.

Robert Edgar (1886)

Robert Edgar of Aughnaloopy, husband of Sarah Bingham, died on January 1, 1886. Probate was granted at Belfast to their son John Edgar of Aughnaloopy the residuary legatee. Robert's effects were valued at £244. Probate was not granted until July 3, 1893 presumably when John reached 21-years old. Robert's Will was witnessed by James Graham and William Hanna.

'……..I will and bequeath to my son John Edgar my farm of land situate on Aughnaloopy also all my houses on same together with all my chattel property which I may die possessed of, he my said son John Edgar being bound to support my wife Sarah Edgar as long as she remains unmarried and in case she marrys again he my said son John is no longer bound to support her. He my said son John is also bound to pay all my debts and funeral expenses. I appoint Mr. John Orr of Kilkeel and Mr. John Irvine of Aughnahoory to be the Executors of this my last Will and Testament dated the 13 July 1883.'

Letters of Administration with the Will annexed of Robert Edgar deceased granted on the July 3, 1893 to John Edgar the Residuary Legatee named in said Will John Orr and John Irvine the Executors named in said Will having duly renounced their rights to Probate.

Richard Quinn (1889)

Richard Quinn of Aughnaloopy died on 12 October 1889. Probate was granted to his daughter Ann Murray (wife of Denis Murray) of Killaghy near Lurgan. His effects were valued at under £49.

Henry Flanagan (1892)

The next surviving Will is for Henry Flanagan of Aughnaloopy who died on October 12, 1892. His Will was witnessed by Daniel Hanna and Samuel Hanna Jnr. Henry's effects were valued at £46 14s and his Will was proved at Belfast by John Clarke, Grocer and Patrick Cunningham, Bootmaker, both of Kilkeel. Henry was the husband of Cecilia Doran and the couple had at least seven children: Margaret, Catherine, John, James, Selina, Sarah and Peter. James is not mentioned in his father's Will and so he may have died prior to 1892. The Flanagan family property is listed as number 1 on the Griffith's Valuation. The property eventually passed to Henry's son Peter Flanagan in 1898.

'In the year of Our Lord 1892 June 27th I Henry Flanagan being very sick and weak of body but of perfect mind and memory do make and ordain this my last Will and Testament. First of all I give my soul to God who gave it and my body I commit to the earth to be buried in decent Christian burial and as touching such worldly estate as it has pleased God to bless me. I dispose of it in the following manner and form I bequeath to my beloved son Peter the farm in Aughnaloopy with all stock and crop and all farming utensils for his use I bequeath to my beloved daughter Sarah the sum of £10 sterling and to my grandson Henry Melvin the sum of £10 sterling to be paid when he is twelve years old, my son Peter to have my Leitrim farm also and if he has no heirs it is to go to the nearest heir, he is to have the wrack bed also for his use. My son John to get 2s 6d and my daughter Catherine 2s 6d and my daughter Selina 2s 6d and to my daughter Margret 2s 6d all these legacies to be paid by my son Peter out of my holding. I also bequeath to my beloved wife the sum of 5s per week if she cannot live with my son Peter to be paid by my son Peter. I also appoint Mr. John Clarke Newry Street Kilkeel and Mr. Patrick Cunningham Greencastle Street Kilkeel my sole executors. I also disallow and disannul all former Wills made by me whereto I sign my hand this 27th day of June 1892.'

Thomas Trainor (1892)

Thomas Trainor, originally of Ballymageough was married to Bridget 'Biddy' Cunningham of Aughnaloopy. He died on December 16, 1892. His effects were valued at £170 but probate was not granted until February 6, 1911. No age was given for Thomas on the Inland Revenue Affidavit, but it is noted that he left a widow and three lawful issue. Witnesses to the Will were John Allen and John H Eardley. The Administration Bond was signed by Thomas Trainor, Patrick H Donnelly, Merchant, Kilkeel and Alexander Beck, Farmer, of Aughnaloopy, Kilkeel.

*'All that I may die possessed of I leave and bequeath to my wife Bridget Trainor for her lifetime and at her death to my son Thomas Trainor on the condition that he pays the sum of £30 to my son James Trainor and the sum of £10 to my granddaughter Catherine Morgan on the condition that she remains with my family until her 21st year also to my step-daughter Catherine Rogers the sum of 10/- and also to my step-daughter Mary McVeigh of Maghereagh the sum of 10/- and also to my daughter Annie Canavan 10/-. I appoint as my Executor John Clarke of The Square, Kilkeel.
Dated 5th November 1892.'*

His property comprised 5 Irish acres held as a yearly tenancy under Mrs. Clarke (daughter of John Moore and sister of Hunter Moore).

Oath of Administrator: '….that John Clarke is now dead and also Bridget Trainor and that I am the lawful son of the deceased'.

Thomas's granddaughter Catherine Morgan was the only child of his daughter Margaret and her husband Arthur Morgan. Her full name was Mary Catherine Morgan and she was reared by her grandparents as her mother died either during childbirth or shortly afterwards. Mary McVeigh of Maghereagh was born Mary Bradley (the daughter of Patrick Bradley from Aughnaloopy). She was married to Thomas McVeigh from Maghereagh. Although identified as *step-children*, the exact relationship between Thomas and Mary McVeigh and Catherine Rogers is unclear. It has been speculated that Bridget 'Biddy' Cunningham was married to Patrick Bradley prior to her marriage to Thomas Trainor but this has not been confirmed.

Ann Quinn Bradley (1896)

On February 22, 1896, 84-year old widow Ann Bradley (nee Quinn) died. According to the Inland Revenue Affidavit, she left no husband and three lawful children. Her married daughter Sarah McVeigh is named in her Will, her son Patrick was living in Ballinran when his mother died but he is not mentioned in her Will and the name of her third child is unknown. The land consisted of just 2 acres and she had one cow. Her effects were valued at £31. Ann had prepared her Will 6 months previously and had it witnessed by John Allen and John Quinn.

'I Ann Bradley in the townland of Aughnaloopy in the baroney (sic) of Mouren (sic) in the county of Down Kilkeel do appoint John Allen to execute this my Will. To my daughter

Sarah McVeigh I do leave all my furniture and house and land and all therein and upon and to my grand daughter Sarah Bradley to have a home in my house with said Sarah McVeigh her lifetime in sickness as in health. Should Sarah McVeigh die first my house and furniture and land goes to my grand daughter Sarah Bradley then said Sarah Bradley may do with those things as she may think fit.'

Sarah McVeigh inherited the property and she continued to live there until her death on December 7, 1915. Sarah McVeigh may have been widowed early as she was known as Sarah Bradley throughout her life. The executor of her Will was Francis O'Hagan, Spirit Merchant of Greencastle St. Kilkeel.

Ellen Quinn (1895)

Ellen Quinn married her neighbour Hugh Keown on 31 May 1876. This was just two years after she had inherited her father Mark Quinn's farm. Ellen's parents were both ill for several years before they died and it appears that Ellen put off marrying while she stayed at home to look after them, their home and the farm. Ellen Quinn and Hugh Keown were both almost 40-years old when they married and they did not have any children. Hugh Keown was a Presbyterian by birth but he converted to Catholicism in order to marry Ellen. It appears that the marriage was not a happy one and there is a note on the Inland Revenue Affidavit that reads:

'The deceased was a married woman living separate from her husband. The property she was possessed of was bequeathed to her by her father Mark Quinn who died 21 Feb 1874. Probate granted 1 June 1874 of Belfast District Registry.'

Ellen suffered from breast cancer for two years before she died at the age of 53 on the April 19, 1895 and her effects were valued at £128 16s 1d. It is not known in what year the couple separated but Ellen made a very detailed Will to ensure that the farm she had inherited from her father did not pass to the Keown family. Ellen could not read or write and so she garnered the assistance of the parish priest, Dr. Richard Marner to write and witness her Will. She also had two respected members of the community, James Morgan of Springfield and John Fitzpatrick of Leitrim to act as executors. Ellen left everything she owned to her nephew John 'Johnny' Quinn who was present when she died. Her former husband Hugh Keown continued to live in Aughnaloopy with his brother John and his sister Elizabeth.

John Flanigan (1898)

On January 20, 1898 John Flanigan (husband of Ann McDonald) wrote a detailed Will nominating his daughter Ellen Flanigan as sole executrix. He states that he has four surviving children but in addition to Ellen only two of children are named, Catherine and Ann Flanigan, both spinsters at the time. John died on March 6, 1898 just weeks after completing his Will.

'I John Flanigan of Aughnaloopy in the County of Down, Kilkeel, do appoint my daughter Ellen Flanigan to be sole Executrix of this my last Will and testament. To her I leave all my possessions house and furniture land and chattels that she shall keep and support my wife Ann Flanigan and shall pay to my 2 daughters Catherine Flanigan and Ann Flanigan £5 each at their time of leaving as marriage and I do appoint Patrick Bradley and Hugh Keown of the farming class and residing in the townland of Aughnaloopy in the Barony of Mourne in the County of Down, Kilkeel Ireland. Dated this 20th day of January 1898.'

There were various affidavits to the Will as follows:
John Allen said that it was he who wrote the Will as John Flanigan was too ill.
Patrick Bradley was noted as an attesting witness.
Anne Clarke signed to say that she was the lawful daughter therein named as Ann Flanigan.
John Clarke of Kilkeel, Auctioneer, valued the property at £160.
An Administration Bond was signed by Anne Clarke of Aughnaloopy, married woman, wife of John Clarke of Moneydarrabeg and John Clarke of Kilkeel, Auctioneer, for £350.

Oath of Administrator

'....my sister Ellen Cambley (in said Will called by her then name of Flanigan) is the sole executrix therein named and emigrated to America and she has appointed me her lawful attorney'.

Power of Attorney to Anne Clarke
Ellen Cambley, wife of Nicholas Cambley of 1808 Franklin Street, Bellingham, Washington, USA.

John's property consisted of a small farm in Aughnaloopy of about 4 acres held under Orr and others deemed of no value. He had a heifer and a bullock valued at £9 and household goods of £2.

From the paperwork associated with the Will, it appears that Ellen had no interest in remaining in Aughnaloopy and by the time her father's estate was settled in 1908, she was married to Nicholas Cambley and had moved to the United States. Ann too moved away from Aughnaloopy. She married a widower John Clarke from Moneydarragh Beg in 1907 and she moved there with her mother Ann McDonald Flanigan. In 1908, the Flanigan property that was identified as number 26 on the Griffith's Valuation passed to Henry Quinn.

Thomas Beck (1898)

Thomas Beck from Aughnaloopy, the husband of Maria Annett (from Moyadd), died on November 29, 1898. His Will was proved on October 27 of the following year by executor Alexander Gordon of Kilkeel and by his son David Beck. David had married Ann Irvine (from Ballyveaghmore) three years previously and had settled on the family homestead in Aughnaloopy. Witnesses to the Will were John Halpin, a Solicitor from Newry and Bridget Halpin. Thomas and Maria Beck had a large family of at least 9 children but only the eldest son David was named in the Will.

'This is the Last Will and Testament of me Thomas Beck of Aughnaloopy in the County of Down Farmer. Whereas I have by deed bearing equal date herewith disposed of my real estate. Now I do hereby confirm said Deed in all respects and as to and concerning all my personal estate and any other property to which I may be entitled at the time of my decease I hereby leave devise and bequeath the same to my son David Beck absolutely whom I appoint my residuary Legatee and I appoint my said son David and also Alexander Gordon of Kilkeel Merchant executors of this my Will. In witness whereof I have here unto subscribed my name this fifth day of September 1890'.

Thomas Quinn (1899)

The following year, a member of the Aughnaloopy Quinn family died. Widower Thomas Quinn of Aughnaloopy died in June 1899. Probate valued his land and effects at £112 15s which were inherited by his son Thomas. In Thomas's Will, he refers to having previously helped his other children, of which three were still living when he made his Will. The Will was witnessed by neighbours James Quinn and John Allen.

'I Thomas Quinn of Aughnaloopy in the Barony of Mourn in the County of Down Kilkeel, do appoint John Allen of Aughnaloopy to make this my Will, all my children that has left my hous (sic), I did helpe (sic) to the best of my ability. My son Thomas who has still lived with me in my old age to said Thomas Quinn my son, I do leave my hous (sic) and lands and all that is in and in upon the said lands. Dated this Tenth day of December 1893.'

James 'Hamilton' Morgan (1902)

James 'Hamilton' Morgan the son of James Morgan and Mary Clarke died on June 16, 1902. At the time of his death, he was an extremely wealthy man, having inherited from his father's estate in 1877 and from his brother John in 1887. He had also acquired property in Aughnaloopy that had originally been occupied by Francis Rogers. John Morgan had died on April 6, 1887 and his affairs were quickly settled, probate being granted within two months. His effects were valued at £103. James 'Hamilton' Morgan was married to Mary Ann 'Minnie' Murphy the daughter of a wealthy Newry merchant James Murphy and Mary Ann Hamilton.

James 'Hamilton' Morgan was a hard-working, successful man and despite this relative wealth worked his way up through the ranks of his trade. In 1871, he left Aughnaloopy and worked in Liverpool as a grocer's assistant. Having established himself, he returned to Kilkeel where he married Mary Ann 'Minnie' Murphy in 1878 and they started their life together in Aughnaloopy. The couple had a child born a year later but the boy named James Joseph Morgan died at just 6-months old. They were to have five further children together, all born in Springfield House, Aughnaloopy.

Mary Ann 'Minnie' Murphy Morgan died on October 22, 1896 at 41-years old. No Will has been located for Mary Ann. On October 25, 1900, James married Imelda McMullen from Churchfield House, Hollywood. The couple did not have any children together.

James 'Hamilton' Morgan travelled a lot with his work as a merchant and he trained his sons John Patrick, Joseph Hamilton and James Francis to work as assistants in his shops in Kilkeel. It seems that working as a shopkeeper was not for Joseph Hamilton Morgan. He married Ellen Josephine 'Nellie' Mageean from Saintfield and along with their two boys, Joseph and David emigrated to Los Angeles, USA in 1910. Joseph had a paternal Uncle Patrick who had previously moved to California and was likely instrumental in the family's move. When his father's sister Mary Morgan Davies (wife of John Davies a Petty Officer in the Navy who had died about 20 years previously) died in 1913, she didn't leave a Will. However, she owned stocks and shares in Belfast & Co. Down Railways and the District Water Commission valued at £141. She was a widow with no children or grandchildren and so her brother Patrick Morgan, in California was her lawful next of kin. Patrick gave his power of attorney of the estate over to Joseph Hamilton Morgan to sort out her estate.

'Whereas Mary Davis, late of Dunaven (sic), Kilkeel Co. Down, a widow, died on 13th April 1913, Intestate, without child or grandchild, without parent or grandparent her surviving, but leaving me Patrick Morgan her lawful Brother and Joseph H. Morgan, Mary Josephine Sloane, James Morgan and John Morgan, the children of a deceased brother, her only next of kin her surviving. Now I, the said Patrick Morgan residing at 161A Henry Street, San Francisco, and being of the age of 40 years and upwards, Labourer, as such next of kin of said Mary Davis deceased, do hereby nominate, constitute and appoint Joseph H. Morgan of 34 Agincourt Avenue, Ormeau Road, Belfast, Gentleman, to be my true and lawful Attorney for me and in my name and for my use and benefit to apply for and obtain forth of any Registry of His Majesty's Kings Bench Division in Ireland, authorised by law to issue same, a Grant of Letters of Administration, Intestate, of the Goods of the said Mary Davis.'

James Keown (1903)
On March 22, 1903 James Keown died at age 82 years, he willed his effects, valued at £36 10s to his son Thomas, husband of Margaret Denny. He was predeceased by his wife Sarah 'Sally' Fegan from Derryogue, who died in 1885. No Will has been located for Sarah 'Sally' Fegan Keown. The couple had at least 7 children and were resident at the property identified as number 33 on the Griffith's valuation. At the time of his Will, James stated that he had four lawful issue.

'This is the last Will & Testament of me James Keown of Aughnaloopy. I leave my farm and all chattels and effects I may die possessed of to my son Thomas Keown and should he predecease me to his wife and children. Subject to the payment of my just debts and funeral expenses and to the payment of Five Pounds sterling to my daughter Annie. I appoint my said son Thomas my Executor.'

The Will was dated November 27, 1901. It was signed in his own hand and the witnesses were Hunter Moore and Samuel Shannon of Maghery. On the Inland Revenue Affidavit the only valuation was of stock and household effects, there was no land or house included.

Nicholas Quinn (1903)

When Nicholas Quinn (husband of Mary Cunningham) died in June 1903 in New Zealand, the value of his estate was approximately £23,000. He left an extremely detailed Will that has helped established his family connections in New Zealand and Ireland. Money and land bequeathed by Nicholas enabled the building of the first church in Makikihi on a five-acre site. Nicholas also left specific instructions for the procurement of a peal of bells for the use of the Catholic Cathedral at Christchurch in the Provincial District of Canterbury. He also instructed that a peal of bells be procured for his local church in Waimate to be named St. Nicholas, St. Mary and St. William.

Highlights of his Will are detailed below.

'To Peter (SWINEY?) & Henry DOYLE (equal shares as tenants in common) - both of Makikihi: 1. Share # 4606 Canterbury Farmers Cooperative Association Limited. 2. Shares # 1769 & # 1770 plus accrued bonuses, Timaru Milling Company. 3. Land - Makikihi - 1 acre Certificate of Title Vol 71 Folio 247 part Rural Section 4274 (south of the road intersecting the title).

To my brothers Henry & Thomas QUINN: 1. 500 pounds and 2. Sections in Timaru, Lots 1, 2, 3, 4, 5, 6 on Deposited Plan 763 and the buildings thereon known as Collin's Auction House, Craigies and Werry's Temperance Hotel.

To Right Reverend Bishop GRIMES - Bishop of Christchurch – or successor, 700 pounds on condition that five hundred pounds of the said legacy be expended for the purpose of procuring and erecting a peal of bells for the use of the Catholic Cathedral at Christchurch in the Provincial District of Canterbury. Remainder as liked by the Bishop.
To Reverend Father TUBMAN - Parish Priest of Timaru - or successor, 600 pounds, 300 pounds of which to go to a peal of bells to be known as St. Nicholas, St. Mary & St. William.
To Reverend Father REGNAULT - Parish Priest of Waimate - or successor, 400 pounds of which to go to a peal of bells to be known as St. Nicholas, St. Mary & St. William.
To Father GINATY of Christchurch or his successor as Director or Superintendent of the Magdalen Asylum, Christchurch - for the purposes of the Asylum.
To Right Reverend Bishop GRIMES - Catholic Bishop of Christchurch, or successor, 50 pounds.
To Reverend Father TUBMAN - Parish Priest of Timaru - or successor, 50 pounds.
To Reverend Father REGNAULT - Parish Priest of Waimate - or successor, 50 pounds.
To Reverend Father REGNAULT - Parish Priest of Waimate - or successor, for the purposes of the Catholic Church being erected at Maikikihi, 12 pounds pr annum for 5 years.
To the Local Superior of the Sisters of Joseph of the Convent of Waimate 50 pounds to be spent in respect of the convent for the benefit of the sisters.
To the Local Superior of the Convent of the Sacred Heart, Barbadoes Street, Christchurch, 50 pounds for the benefit of the sisters.
To the Local Superior of the Convent of the Sacred Heart Timaru 50 pounds.
To Reverend Father CONNELLY formerly of Waimate now of Christchurch 50 pounds.

*To my sister Margaret MOYNIHAN * 100 pounds.*
To my sister, Ann DOYLE wife of James DOYLE 50 pounds.

To Mathew QUIRK 5 pounds. To Kitty HARE 5 pounds
To Annie SIMS, Makikihi - Land and buildings at Makikihi 2 roods pt Rural Section 4274 and pt of Certificate of Title Vol 71 Folio 247(the southern half of the land on the north side of the road intersecting the land).

To Patrick QUINN son of my brother Patrick QUINN - land - Makikihi - 2 roods - pt Rural Section 4274 being pt of Certificate of Title Vol 71Folio 247 (the northern half of the land on the north side of the road intersecting the land).

To my brother William QUINN for his life - vacant allotments Sections 7, 8, 8, 9, 10, 11 on Deposited Plan 763 - and after his death to my nephews James, William and John, sons of my brother William [if any of the nephews die under age 21 without issue then the share to survivors].

My farm situate at Maikikihi aforesaid and known as Bellevue together with the furniture in the dwelling house erected on the said farm to trustees in trust for grandchildren Nicholas and Mary GEANEY, son and daughter of Humphrey GEANEY of Timaru, Butcher.

The residue of real & personal properties to trustees on trust - convert to money - pay debts and funeral expenses and legacies in this will, mortgages, etc. Balance to go to Right Reverend Bishop GRIMES for Catholic Cathedral Reverend Father TUBMAN - for church Sacred Heart at Timaru Reverend Father REGNAULT - for church at Waimate.

To Annie SIMS - for her lifetime - premiums & charge on her life policy shall be paid out of the net rents & profits of my said farm as far as as the residue may be insufficient for same.

Trustees shall let farm (Bellvue) during minority of Nicholas & Mary GEANEY. Accumulate net rents & profits and invest on behalf of same in one or more of the following modes of investment: - any real securities in New Zealand, shares of stock of any incorporated banking company or Farmers Cooperative Association, - any incorporated building society. Or, trustees can run the farm.

If Nicholas or Mary die before 35 without issue reaching 21 (or daughters marrying), then the farm goes to the survivor. If no survivor then in trust for my brothers Henry QUINN & Thomas QUINN, but issue age 21 will take their parent's share.'

Solicitors to be Percy, Percy & Kinnerney. Signed 05 December 1902
Witnesses: W.G. KINNERNEY, Solicitor, Timaru, New Zealand. Charles E. HASSAL, Solicitors Clerk, Timaru.

* His sister named as Margaret 'Moynihan' in the Will was in fact the wife of Edward Murney and was living in Ballincurry, Kilbroney.

Patrick Quinn (1903)

Nicholas's brother Patrick Quinn (husband of Margaret Quinn) died just three months later in September 1903. At the time of his death his estate was valued at £2,570NZ. Like his brother, Patrick also made sizeable donations to the local church, orphanage and convent. His widow Margaret died in October 1912. Her estate was valued at under £400NZ; most of the family money and land having already passed to the couple's ten children.

Patrick Doran (1904)

Patrick Doran of Aughnaloopy (son of Patrick Doran and Bridget Trainor) lived at the property identified as number 43abc on the Griffith's Valuation. This was land that he had inherited from his father c.1885. When Patrick died on July 22, 1904, probate was a complicated and long affair but was finally granted to Hugh Trainor on June 9, of the following year. Patrick had married his wife Ellen McDermott (from Grange) just three years before he died. The couple had no children. His original Will gives interesting details of the family relationships. The nephews Thomas and Edward Morgan and the niece Mary Morgan are children of Patrick's sister Ellen Doran and her husband Thomas Morgan from Maghereagh. His niece Mary Morgan had a child Ellen O'Neill and both Mary and Ellen lived with Patrick Doran in Aughnaloopy. The Will reads as follows:

'I give devise and bequeath to my nephew Thomas Morgan all my farm and houses in Aughnaloopy on condition that he do pay the sum of £40 sterling to my niece Mary Morgan and allow her to remain in my house for 12 years from the present time. If this farm is ever sold I Will that John Doran of Leitrim get the field called The Rocks at the river at the price of £1. I give and bequeath to my nephew Edward Morgan my Drumcrow (sic) farm without present crops on condition that he do pay to my niece Mary Morgan the sum of £110. If either Thomas or Edward Morgan want to sell these farms they must sell to one another or to their sister Mary Morgan and not to a stranger. The present crop to come home to Aughnaloopy. I give and bequeath the sum of £10 to my niece Mary Morgans' child my nephew Thomas Morgan to pay £5 and Edward to pay the remaining £5. I give and bequeath all the cow, cattle and the horse in Aughnaloopy to my niece Mary Morgan on condition that she do pay all my just debts. I give and bequeath to my

wife Ellen Doran the sum of £5, my nephew Thomas to pay half and Edward the remaining half. I give and bequeath to my nephew Thomas Morgan my seaweed bed on Killowen shore. I Will and bequeath all my money in Post Office of any property not (scored out) in my possession not herein mentioned to Charles McConville, Butcher, Kilkeel. I appoint Hugh Trainor of Aughrim (name and place scored out and replaced with Mary Morgan of Aughnaloopy) and John Edgar of Aughnaloopy executors to this my last Will and testament.'

The Will was signed in his hand and witnessed by Hugh Seed and Joseph McKibbin. Although this Will was written only days before Patrick died, there was an affidavit of the witness Hugh Seed to say that the Will had been changed since he witnessed it. Another affidavit was made by John Orr stating that he made the changes at the request of the Testator and in ignorance of the law. Patrick's wife was obviously not happy about the decisions made by her husband. There was a Civil Bill Probate Process with Hugh Trainor the Plaintiff and Ellen Doran the Defendant. John Edgar renounced his right to Probate and Ellen Doran lodged a Caveat against granting Probate to Hugh Trainor. Hugh Trainor was granted Probate by order of the Court. The property was a farm in Drumcro of over 9 acres held under Lord Kilmorey and a farm in Aughnaloopy of over 7 acres held under Mr. J M Orr. There was stock of £65 and cash of £20.

John Keown (1907)
John Keown, the husband of Ann McKnight from Leitrim, died on September 15, 1907. Probate of his Will was granted on October 7, 1908 one year after his death to his brother-in-law James Allen the Butcher from Aughnaloopy. James Allen was married to Ellen Keown, John's only surviving sibling. John's effects were valued at £22 15s 0d.

Mary Doran (1908)
Administration of the estate of 59-year old Mary Doran of Aughnaloopy who died September 28, 1908 was granted at Belfast to her sister Ellen Doran, a spinster. Mary had been living with her younger sister and their niece, Mary Doran. Her effects were valued at £137 12s 6d. Mary and Ellen had a brother Denis Doran who had married Ellen Quinn from Aughnaloopy and the couple had settled in Moneydarraghmore. Denis had died prior to 1901 and it was his daughter Mary that was living with Mary and Ellen Doran.

James Quinn (1911)
Mary Quinn Doran's brother James (son of Edward) passed away in 1911 at age 86 years. He left no wife and no children. His estate was settled with a month and was valued at £53 16s 6d.

*'I James Quin residing in the townland of Aughnaloopy in the barony of Mouren (sic), Kilkeel in the County of Down, Ireland. I do appoint my nephew Patrick Quin farmer residing in Dunavan to be my Executor of this my Will. John Allen and Thomas Quinn farmers residing in Aughnaloopy to be witnesses to this my Will, to Thomas Quin for his trouble, I leave a pound. To the reverend Father McKelope, three pounds for Masses. To my niece Mary Doran residing in Lower Mouren (sic), five pounds, then the remaining part of my estate shall be divided in equal parts between my three nephews Patrick Quin, Edward Quin and James Doran Lower Mouren (sic), this to take place when they meet together amongst themselves after all my debts and funeral expenses are paid.
Dated the fifth day of April 1911'.*

James's nephew Edward was the son of John Quinn and Catherine Fearon from Moyadd. James Doran was the son of Denis Doran and Mary Quinn.

James Fitzpatrick (1912)
James Fitzpatrick died on March 22, 1912. His estate, valued at £208 4s 8d, was quickly settled passing to his brother Edward. The two brothers had remained single throughout their life and lived at the family home with a younger sister Catherine. Edward died, two years later on March 31, 1914. Again the Estate now valued at £295 19s 6d was settled quickly. A neighbour James Allen (son of James Allen and Ellen Keown) acted as executor. There is no known connection between the Allen family and the

Fitzpatrick family. It is not known when Catherine died but no Will has been found and it is unlikely that she made one.

John Johnston (1912)
Just five days after the death of James Fitzpatrick, on March 27, 1912, John Johnston the husband of Bridget Bradley died. Probate was granted to his widow who was living with their unmarried daughter Mary and her 22-year old grandson William Rogers (son of Bridget Johnston and John Rogers).

Hugh Speers (1912)
Aughnaloopy lost another resident in 1912. On August 16, 60-year old Hugh Speers died, leaving a wife Charlotte Cousins, his son Hugh and daughter-in-law Annie Orr Speers living at home. Hugh had been married twice, and his son Hugh was from his first marriage. His effects were valued at £317 11s 9d. Witnesses to the Will were John Orr and Henry Haugh. The document was dated May 8, 1912.

'I Hugh Speers of Aughnaloopy make this my last Will and Testament. I Will and bequeath to my wife Charlotte Speers my farm land and house in Aughnaloopy the farm contains about 4 Irish Acres during her natural life and at her death all to my son Hugh Speers and I appoint my son Hugh Speers sole Executor of this my last Will. Signed by Hugh Speers.'

Affidavit of Attesting Witness John Orr

'.......that the said Will is now in the same state and condition as when executed by the said Testator being written by me on a half sheet of paper and remained in my possession from the date of same until I handed same to Hugh Speers the Executor after deceased death in order that he might prove same.' Dated October 30, 1912.

'Farm of 16a 1r 3p held in fee simple subject to yearly Head Rent of £4 and rent charge of 13s 10d - Valuation £396 3s 4d. Land of approx. 4 acres value at £67. Mortgage to Patrick Bradley of £163. 11s.3d.
Debts - Amount due on a Promissory Note and interest due to Alexander Gordon and Robert Green (the Executors of Nicholas Minnis deceased).'

Hugh Speers (1914)
It appears that the son Hugh died just two years later at age 27-years old. His effects were valued at £397 10s 2d. Francis Orr, Farmer and Andrew Orr, Merchant, were the executors. Hugh left a widow (Annie Elizabeth Orr Speers), two lawful children (Hugh and Jocelyn Speers) and two more remote lawful issue (names not given). His Will was dated March 3, 1913 and signed in his hand. The witnesses were Andrew Orr and Humphrey F Fry.

'I give devise and bequeath to my wife Annie all my houses lands farming stock crop and implements of husbandry and all other goods chattels and effects during her natural life also the care of my two children. At my wifes death I give devise and bequeath to my son Jocelyn the lands known as my fathers and Patrick Bradleys with houses thereon. I also allow all stock and crop and farming utensils to be divided equally between my two sons. Should either of my sons die before attaining the age of 21 years the survivor to get his share. In the event of my wife marrying again I allow her £100 sterling and have nothing more to do with my children or lands. I nominate constitute and appoint Francis Orr of Ballykeel, Farmer, and Andrew Orr of Kilkeel, Merchant, Trustees and executors of this my Will.'

His property was a farm in townland of Aughnaloopy of 4 acres or thereabouts statute measure held in Fee Simple subject to the terminable annuity of £1 1s 4d payable to the Irish Land Commission. The value for probate was given as £67 18s 10d. The farm in Aughnaloopy was of 16a 1r 36p held in Fee with a simple value of £396 3s 4d. He held a mortgage to Patrick Bradley dated November 9, 1901 of £163 11s 3d, stock of £121 0s 0d and two seaweed beds on Millbay valued at £40. There were debts of £354 5s 5 d which included £260 owing to Charles Minnis of Brackney on a Promissory Note.

Margaret McCartan (1914)

Spinster Margaret McCartan died in Aughnaloopy on March 9, 1914 age 50-years old. She had previously lived at 161, Fountains Road Kirkdale, Liverpool but had returned to Ireland and was working as a dressmaker. Probate was granted to her brother Arthur McCartan, Farmer. Her effects were valued at £39 14s 2d. and consisted of money in a post-office account.

William Quinn (1914)

William Quinn died on July 1, 1914 at age 80-years old from heart failure at his residence 'Annalong' Makikihi, New Zealand His Estate valued at £28,500NZ, passed to his wife Catherine 'Katie' Duggan Quinn and to their sons James Patrick, John Joseph and Henry Augustus. William and Katie's eldest son William Aloysius died just a few weeks before his father on June 11, 1914, as a result of a car accident. It is likely that the stress of losing his son in the accident contributed to 80-year old William having a heart attack.

Probate of William QUINN late of Makikihi near Waimate, Brickmaker & Farmer Value of Estate 28,500 pounds.
Administration granted to his surviving sons:
James Patrick QUINN of Makikihi, farmer,
John Joseph QUINN, farmer and
Henry Augustus QUINN who stated that William died on or about 30 June 1914 having seen the body after death.

Will: To Widow - 200 pounds per annum while she or any of my family live with her in my present house at Makikihi. If she leaves the house then 250 pounds.
To Trustees - carry on estate until youngest of children reach 21 years, equal shares to children, excepting home as above while retained by wife.
I appoint any of my sons over age and as they come of age to be executors and trustees of my Will.

Signed 10 Oct 1912
Witnesses: James FLEMING(?), Christchurch, Merchant
W. A. HOUSTON, Christchurch, Clerk.

Lucretia Davidson Moore (1915)

On May 25, 1915 Lucretia Davidson Moore of Heath Hall, passed away. Lucretia was 83-years old and was a direct descendant of the Moore family that had originally settled in Aughnaloopy. She was a wealthy landowner, having inherited her uncle John and her father Hugh's estate. Her executors were Robert G Moffatt, Insurance Broker and Robert J Long, Bank Manager (Retired) and her estate was valued at £980 7s 10d. Considering the amount of money involved, probate was settled very quickly within two months of her death. Witnesses to the Will were Hugh Beck from Leitrim and Mary Fegan of Heath Hall. Heath Hall was Lucretia's home and it appears that Mary Fegan many have been working there as a servant. Lucretia's detailed Will provides a fascinating insight into the social interactions between the residents of Aughnaloopy and the surrounding townlands. The main points of the Will were as follows:

£200 to the Mourne Presbyterian Church to be invested and the interest therefrom to be distributed annually to the sick poor of the Church, the Charity to be called the Moore Memorial Fund.
The Mortgage of £300 on House property in Belfast to Mr. Robert Moffatt of Malone Park, Belfast and his wife Mrs. Bell Moffatt or the survivor
£20 to Miss Sarah Moffatt, Clough, for her kindness to me
£100 to Hunter Moore, Solicitors, Newry
£100 to Miss Lucretia Davidson McNeilly, daughter of Joseph W. McNeilly, Glassdrummand, to be paid when she attains the age of 21 years
£20 to Miss Elizabeth Henry, Mourne Abbey, in trust for the Carginagh Episcopal Church
£20 to the Mourne Presbyterian Church for repairs to the church
£50 to Reverend Robert White, Kilkeel and his wife Mrs. White or the survivor
£10 each to the following, my tenants, viz. John Edgar, Springfield, Mrs. Sarah Edgar Jnr., Springfield, Mrs. Eliza Shields, Springfield
I leave £5 to Mrs. Sarah Sloan of Aughnaloopy, £5 to Mrs. Mary Colgan, Aughnaloopy,

£10 to Mrs. William Shiels, Aughnaloopy, £5 to Mrs. Kitty Doran, Leitrim, £5 to Mrs. Martha Highton, Kilkeel, my servant, £10 to Mrs. Jane Annett, Eastwood, Kilkeel, £10 to Miss Hilda Long, Belfast and £10 to Master Herbert McKean, The Rectory, Kilkeel these last two sums to be paid to their mothers for school books etc. as I always called them my two children

£100 for the erection of a headstone at my grave, the stone to be the same colour as that of the late Mrs. McMordie, and also to provide a granite stone boundary around the Davidson burying ground at the Mourne Presbyterian Church. I direct that a low wall be built around the grave of John Moore of Springfield, adding "In Memory of the late John Moore of Springfield"

£20 to Miss Nellie Clarke at present residing with Robert Moffatt, Belfast
£50 to Professor Todd Martin, Belfast, as a Memorial to the Moore family
£50 to Mrs. Elizabeth McNeilly, Glassdrummand, and £50 to her daughter Kathleen McNeilly on attaining the age of 21 years
£20 to Mrs. Anna McNeilly, wife of the late James McNeilly, Glassdrummand
£20 to Moore Boyle in the office of Hunter Moore, Newry

'I direct my Executors to sell all my property etc. and after paying the above legacies the residue of my Estate to go to Robert Moffatt of Belfast.'

Stocks were held by Miss Moore in the Eastern Telegraph Co. and also Arthur Guiness and son. The valuation of Heath Hall (including approx. 11 acres) was £340.

Note on the Inland Revenue Affidavit under the heading Real Property:

Lands in the townland of Aughnaloopy, Parish of Kilkeel, Barony of Mourne and County of Down containing 47 Acres, 3 Roods and 5 Perches statute measure or thereabouts, held with other lands in same townland not belonging to the deceased, under Grant in Perpetuity dated 20th January 1732. Subject to £4 being a proportionate part of the yearly rent reserved and of the Tithe Rent Charge but indemnified there from by portion of lands in said Grant sold and conveyed by the deceased in 1908.
11 acres in own occupation, the remainder occupied by Judicial Tenants.
Reps. of Patrick Fitzpatrick, William Shields and John Edgar.

Susan Wherrity (1916)
The following year, Susan Wherrity died in February. Probate was settled on March 10, 1916. Her executors were John Russell, Merchant and Thomas Quinn, Farmer. In stark contrast to Lucretia Moore's estate Susan's effects were valued at just £13 14s 1d.

Peter Flanagan (1916)
Peter Flanagan died on October 8, 1916 leaving a widow (Margaret McKey originally from Tullyframe) and nine lawful children. His farm that was held under the Irish Land Commission and measured 7 Statute Acres passed to his wife and then to his son Henry. He left £20 to his son Patrick, £10 to James and £10 to his daughter Selina. The other five children (Elizabeth, Daniel, Peter, Mary, and Mark) were not named. They were under the age of 15 when their father died.

The photograph above, taken by Ciera E. Jones in July 2011, shows a summer hedgerow in Aughnaloopy townland.

Part 2

The People of Aughnaloopy

My Brickwall

My ancestors came from both Antrim and Down.
They wore neither sashes nor medals nor crown
Nor cassock nor miter nor armor nor swords
They were not clergy or barons or lords.

They sailed before passenger lists were in vogue
And they kept to the rules - not a one was a rogue.
Therefore, they never appeared 'fore the court.
They just never got in a mess of that sort.

Of their life on the Auld Sod seems nothing's been writ,
And of their travels I know not a bit.
They seem to have transplanted lock, stock, and barrel,
No one saw reason their arrival to herald.

Connolly, Clendenin, Turner, and Craig,
Where did you come from? The townland, I beg.
If I could just find one of these on a roll,
I would have to believe I had truly struck gold.

But alas and alack, they all remain hidden,
Because none was important enough and they didn't
Go down in history, recorded for all,
So collectively they all remain my brickwall!

Ruth Ann Johnson, Iowa, USA. 2008.

Chapter 18

Allen Family

Mrs. Jane Allen (GV39)

The Allen family was established in Aughnaloopy at the time of the Griffith's Valuation with Mrs. Jane Allen leasing a house and just over 6 acres of land from Thomas F Moore. The property is identified as number 39 on the Griffith's Valuation. Jane's husband is unknown but it is believed that she had at least two children, John and Margaret.

John Allen and Ellen Keown

Jane's son John married Ellen Keown, who was also from Aughnaloopy, on February 15, 1857 at Massforth RC Church in Kilkeel. Witnesses to the marriage were Patrick Doran and Margaret Cunningham. This is one of the earliest surviving marriage records that specifically documents Aughnaloopy as the place of residence for the bride and groom. Patrick Doran is likely the resident of the property listed as number 43b, on the Griffiths Valuation. John Allen and Ellen Keown had seven children including: Annie (c.1860), Thomas (b. 1861), Jane, named after her paternal grandmother, (b. 1868), James (b. 1869) and George who was born in April 1871 and died in infancy. The names of the other children are not known.

On May 31, 1881, their daughter Annie married James Rooney (son of Patrick Rooney). Witnesses to the marriage are Margaret Doran and James Fegan. An inconsistency occurs here, as Annie Allen gives her fathers occupation as dock labourer (presumably at Kilkeel harbour), other references to John Allen state that he is a butcher or farmer. It is possible that this employment reference should relate to James Rooney's father Patrick Rooney.

John and Ellen's daughter Jane married Charles McConville from the Mountain Road on November 1, 1885. Jane was 17-years old and stated that she was a dressmaker. The couple had a daughter Mary E 'Minnie' born in 1887.

At the time of the 1901 census, John and Ellen (Keown) Allen were living with their son James, their daughter-in-law Sarah (McCartan) and their grandson John. James had followed his father's occupation and was working as a butcher. His wife, Sarah McCartan was originally from Moneydarragh Beg, the daughter of Richard McCartan and Ellen Cunningham. Sarah and James had married on February 17, 1890, when they were both 20-years old. John Quinn and Jane McCartan were witnesses to the marriage that took place at Massforth RC Church.

In 1907, Ellen Keown Allen's brother John, died. Probate of the will of John Keown was granted on October 7, 1908 one year after his death to his brother-in-law James Allen the Butcher from Aughnaloopy. John's effects were valued at £22 15s 0d.

When the 1911 Census of Ireland was conducted, John and Ellen, their son James, daughter-in-law Sarah and grandson John were all still living on the property in Aughnaloopy. The census notes that the property had three rooms, with three windows to the front of the building, stone walls and a thatched roof. John and Ellen noted that they had seven children of whom five were still living.

On March 31, 1914, Edward Fitzpatrick from Aughnaloopy died and his effects, valued at £295 19s 6d, were granted to James Allen. Any relationship, if any, between the Allen family and the Fitzpatrick family is unknown. Edward Fitzpatrick was likely from the property identified as number 17 on the Griffith's Valuation. His mother's name is not known and therefore it is possible that she was a member of the Allen family.

James Allen's name is listed on the documents relating to the 1925 Northern Ireland Land Act and the Estate of Betty Clarke (spinster). In a document published in The Belfast Gazette, dated January 10, 1930, James Allen is noted as paying rent of £7 9s 0d to Betty Clarke for just over 13 acres of land.

Margaret Allen and Richard Johnson

Mrs. Jane Allen's daughter Margaret married her neighbour Richard Johnson on August 22, 1858, also at Massforth RC Church. John Doran and Mary Fitzpatrick were witnesses to the marriage. Richard Johnson held land identified as number 38 on the Griffith's Valuation. It seems that Richard and Margaret did not have any children as when Richard died his land passed to a nephew, John Allen.

Robert Allen - Sewing Agent

The name Allen is not common in Mourne. The family of John and Ellen Allen is the only one in Kilkeel at the time of the 1901 census. There is a Robert Allen noted on the Griffith's Valuation leasing a property on Market Place in Kilkeel from Edward Carvill. This Robert is listed in the Belfast and Province of Ulster Directory for Kilkeel 1863-64 edition where he is noted as a sewing agent. No Will has been found for Robert Allen that might provide evidence as to whether he is linked to John Allen from Aughnaloopy.

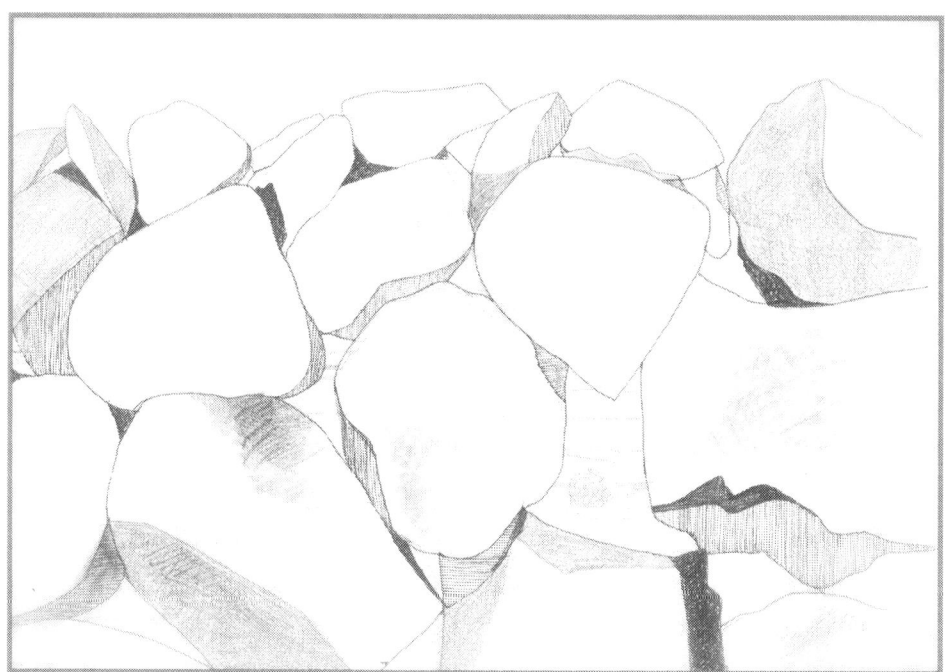

Illustration of a stone wall built by hand from Mourne granite.
by: Shelley Jayne Crawford Maskery (Shelley Jayne Illustration)

Chapter 19

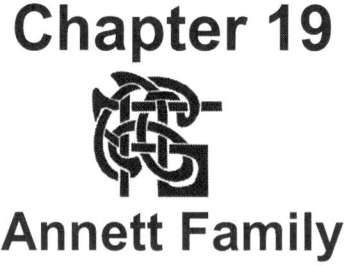

Annett Family

Charles, James and John Annett
Three members of the Annett family (Charles, James and John) are listed on the 1830 Tithes Applotment document as leasing over 7 acres of land at Aughnaloopy. Any relationship between the men is unknown.

Mary Hutchinson and Alexander Annett (GV11)
By 1864, the time of the Griffith's Valuation, there was just one member of the Annett family recorded as having land in Aughnaloopy townland. This was Alexander Annett who farmed over 12 acres of land identified as GV11 and leased from James Moore. Alexander also had a house in the townland identified as 11a, but at the time of the valuation, the house was unoccupied. Alexander also leased mountain pastureland from the Kilmorey Estate located in Mourne Mountains Upper and in Upper Moyadd townlands. He had a house and approximately 12 acres of land in Moyadd and possibly another 20 acres of land with a house in Leitrim, again leased from the Kilmorey Estate. The name of Alexander's father is unknown. There are no male members of the Annett family listed as living in Aughnaloopy at the time of the 1901 or 1911 census. Alexander and his wife Mary Hutchinson had at least three children: John (b. 1833), Maria (b. 1835) and Ellen (c.1840), and possibly another daughter Elizabeth (b. 1845). Only Maria moved to Aughnaloopy but this was to her husband Thomas Beck's property. Alexander Annett's land passed to his son John after his death around 1871. The Annett land eventually passed to the Hanna family who were related through Alexander's daughter Ellen's marriage to John Hanna in 1861. The original cottage has recently been restored and is now used as a holiday rental property. It is known as 'Sam's Cottage'.

John Annett and Mary Baird
Mary and Alexander's son John married Mary Baird from Ballinran on February 15, 1866 at Mourne Presbyterian Church in Kilkeel. Mary was the daughter of James Baird from Ballinran. The couple had at least eight children: John (b. 1869), Elizabeth (b. 1871), James (b. 1872), Mary Ann (c.1875), David (c. 1880), Samuel (c.1882), Maria (c.1884) and Adelaide (c.1886) and settled in Moyadd townland. John is noted as a widower in 1901 and is at home with his six younger children. By the time of the 1911 census only James, Adelaide and David were still at home. Also living in the house was James's wife Ellen Spears (daughter of Mary Jane and William Spears of Leitrim). James and Ellen had married on July 21, 1910 at Rostrevor Presbyterian Church.

Maria Annett and Thomas Beck
Alexander's daughter Maria married Thomas Beck on April 5, 1853 at Mourne Presbyterian Church in Kilkeel. Maria states her home as being Moyadd and Thomas documents that he is from Aughnaloopy. The couple had at least nine children and remained in Aughnaloopy on Beck land identified as number 43 on Griffiths. Their known children were Hugh (b. 1854), Alexander (b. 1856), Mary Jane (b. 1858), Elizabeth Margaret (b. 1860), David (b. 1862), Ellen (b. 1865), Lydia (b. 1867) and Maria Charlotte (b. 1869).

The children of Maria Annett and Thomas Beck

Hugh Beck and Susan Keown
Thomas and Maria's son Hugh married Susan Keown, the daughter of William Keown

and Susan Annett, and moved to Leitrim where the couple raised a family of at least nine children. The eldest was Susan (b. 1877), followed by: Alexander (b. 1879), Ellen (b. 1882), David (b. 1885), Mary Jane (b. 1892), Lydia (b. 1894), Maria (b. 1896), Ann (b. 1898) and Martha (b. 1901).

Elizabeth Margaret Beck and Joseph Anderson
Thomas's' daughter Elizabeth Margaret married Joseph Anderson on January 25, 1881 at Mourne Presbyterian Church. Joseph was the son of James Anderson from Ballinran. He died on September 20, 1893 and left a detailed Will that including the following instruction:

> *'......If what is known as the Water Scheme from Mourne to Belfast should be carried out. I am entitled to receive the sum of one hundred and fifty pounds to be divided as follows fifty pounds to my wife and an equal share to each of my children.'*

Their son Joseph eventually took over the family farm in Ballinran.

David Beck and Ann Irvine
David married Ann Irvine, daughter of Edward Irvine and Mary Hanna, on October 6, 1896 at Rostrevor Presbyterian Church. Ann was originally from Ballyveaghmore but she moved to the Beck property in Aughnaloopy after her marriage. David's father Thomas died on October 27, 1898 and David took over running the farm. His mother stayed in the home with David and his wife Ann and their nine children: David (b. 1898), Maria Charlotte (c.1899), Hugh (b. 1901), Alexander (b. 1901), Louisa (b. 1904), Edward (b. 1906), William (b. 1906), John (b. 1910) and Thomas (b. 1911). David Srn. Died in 1943 and the property passed to his son David.

Maria Charlotte Beck and Thomas Keown
On January 10, 1890, Maria Charlotte married Thomas Keown at Mourne Presbyterian Church in Kilkeel. Thomas was the son of John Keown and Mary McKee from Leitrim. Like her siblings Maria had a large family, giving birth to at least ten children: Thomas John (b. 1891), Sarah (b. 1893), David (b. 1895), Ellen (b. 1897), Robert (b. 1898), Susan (b. 1901), Mary Alice (b. 1904), Hugh (1905), William (b. 1908) and Samuel Mervin (b. 1911). The family settled on the Keown family homestead in Leitrim. Thomas died on July 4, 1941 and his property passed to his son Thomas John.

Ellen Annett and John Hanna
Mary Hutchinson and Alexander Annett's daughter Ellen was baptized in 1841 at Mourne Presbyterian Church. On May 2, 1861, she married John Hanna at the same church. John Hanna was the son of James Hanna, the reedmaker, from Ballinran. Her brother John Annett and her brother-in-law Thomas Beck were witnesses to the marriage. The couple had at least two children, John (b. 1866) and Mary Jane (b. 1873). They settled on Hanna land in Ballinran. John died prior to the 1901 census but Ellen is listed with her brother-in-law James Hanna and her son John is still at home. By 1911, James has died but Ellen and her son are still in Ballinran. John's wife Isabella is also in the home with their daughters Ellen and Mary Jane.

Chapter 20

Beck Family

Hugh and Thomas Beck

Two members of the Beck family (Hugh and Thomas) are noted on the 1830 Tithes for Aughnaloopy townland. Hugh Beck who paid tithes on over 7 acres of land and Thomas had just over 8 acres. The relationship, if any, between Hugh and Thomas is unknown.

Other than paying Tithes, nothing is known about Thomas but the name occurs frequently in later generations of the Beck family.

Hugh Beck also appears on the 1834 Townland Valuation for Aughnaloopy. His property was one of just three in the townland that was deemed to be worth £3 or more. It is thought that Hugh recorded on the Tithes document and the later Townland Valuation is buried in Mourne Presbyterian Graveyard and has the headstone inscribed:

> *Sacred to the memory of Hugh Beck, Aughnaloopy, who died 4 Apr 1847 aged 81 years. Also his wife Jane who died 12 Aug 1852 aged 79 years.*

Jane's maiden name is not known. Buried in the same plot is David Beck who died on March 28 1878, age 75-years old. This is likely a son of Hugh and Jane. Another possible son is James Beck who died on May 24, 1882, also age 75-years old.

Hugh Beck and Eliza Stevenson

In the early 19th century, there was a Hugh Beck living in Aughnaloopy townland who was married to Eliza Stevenson. It is not known if this is a son or nephew of the above-mentioned Hugh.

The Beck family were members of the Presbyterian Church and there are several occurrences of baptisms and marriages in the early Mourne Presbyterian Church records. Aughnaloopy is listed as the place of birth for Elizabeth Beck whose date of birth was December 12, 1844. She was baptised on February 9, 1845. Elizabeth was the daughter of Hugh Beck and Eliza Stevenson. The couple also had a son Thomas who was born on February 19, 1842 but his baptismal record lists his place of residence as Moyadd.

The Aughnaloopy Beck family were related to the Becks from nearly Moyadd and Leitrim and several of the families moved between the neighbouring townlands. Within the same family, baptismal records will record multiple townlands, as in the case of Hugh and Eliza's children. Their son Thomas Beck married Maria Annett from Moyadd, the daughter of Alexander, on April 5, 1853 at Mourne Presbyterian Church. The couple settled in Aughnaloopy and had at least nine children including: Hugh, Alexander, Mary Jane, Elizabeth Margaret, David, Ellen, Lydia, and Maria Charlotte. When Thomas died on November 29, 1898, the family land passed to his son David. David had recently married Ann Irvine, the daughter of Edward Irvine and Mary Hanna from Ballyveaghmore. David's older brother Hugh had by this time settled in Leitrim following his marriage to Susan Keown (daughter of William Keown and Susan Annett). His brother Alexander had settled in Aughnahorey, sister Elizabeth Margaret was married to Joseph Anderson and settled in Ballinran, Two years after her father died Maria Charlotte married Thomas Keown and move to Leitrim, close to her brother Hugh's family.

Thomas's granddaughter Maria Charlotte Beck, daughter of David Beck and Ann Irvine, sailed from Londonderry to New York on the SS Columbia arriving in America on March 8, 1920. She was 20-years old at the time and stated that she was going to stay with her cousin Ida Stevenson in Hohokus, New Jersey. Ida's full name was Elizabeth Ida Anderson and she was the wife of William Henry Stevenson from Maghereagh. Ida's mother was Elizabeth Margaret Beck a sister of Maria Charlotte's father David Beck. The Stevenson family settled in Hohokus, New Jersey where they had at least two children: Muriel (b. 1912) and Margaret (b. 1915). William Henry worked as a truckman in a granite yard and is listed on the 1930 US Federal census.

Beck on the Griffith's Valuation

At the time of the Griffith's Valuation in 1864, two members of the Beck family, David and John, both lease farms of approximately 12 acres from James Moore. Their property was located between the Aughnaloopy Road and Aughnahorey Road. David died on March 28, 1878 and was buried with Hugh and Jane in the family plot at Mourne Presbyterian Graveyard. This John Beck is believed to be the husband of Ellen Edgar. The couple had at least six children together: Jane (b. 1840), Hugh (b. 1842), Margaret (b. 1844), John (b. 1855) and James and David. Hugh married Margaret Hanna (daughter of George Hanna from Aughnaloopy) and the couple spent some time in Aughnaloopy before settling in Maghery. John Beck died on November 5, 1881. He left a Will making David his heir.

James Beck and Margaret Wilson

Although not listed on the Griffith's Valuation, there was another branch of the Beck family living in Aughnaloopy during this time period. James Beck and his wife Margaret Wilson (whose family was also from the townland) were settled in Aughnaloopy and had at least nine children: Alexander (c.1839), Thomas (b. 1841), Margaret (b. 1843), Elizabeth (b. 1845), Ann (b. 1851), Hugh (b. 1852), Jane (b. 1854), Teresa (b. 1856) and Sarah (b. 1858). The fact that James is not listed on the Griffith's Valuation would suggest that he might be a son of David, Hugh or John, but this can not be confirmed. James and Margaret's son Alexander is listed on the 1901 and 1911 census with his wife Sarah Ann Baird. Alexander and Sarah Ann married on April 22, 1864 at Mourne Presbyterian Church. Sarah Ann was the daughter of John Baird from Aughrim.

Alexander and Sarah Ann's eldest son Thomas married Eva Ada Nicholson from Derryogue, on October 26, 1904 at Kilkeel Church of Ireland Church. The couple settled in Aughnaloopy. Their daughter Ellen married Thomas Richard Chambers on February 2, 1897 at Rostrevor Presbyterian Church. Thomas Richard Chambers was from Newcastle Street, Kilkeel. He was the son of William Chambers and Elizabeth Grills. James married Margaret Orr, daughter of Samuel Orr from Ballymartin, on September 18, 1900. James stated his occupation as Provisions Merchant. Daughter Teresa married William Morris, son of William Morris and Margaret McKee, from Dunmore, on June 12, 1902. Alexander and Sarah Ann's son Hugh married Maria Grills on October 13, 1908. The couple settled on Bridge Street, Kilkeel, where they had at least two children, Alicia and Frances. Their daughter Jane married David Edward Kenmuir on November 1, 1900 and moved to Greencastle Street.

Elizabeth Margaret Beck and Joseph Anderson

As mentioned above, Thomas Beck married Maria Annett on April 5, 1853 at Mourne Presbyterian Church. Maria was the daughter of Alexander Annett and Maria Hutchinson. James McComb and James Beck were witnesses to the marriage. Thomas and Maria settled in Aughnaloopy after their marriage and they had at least nine children including: Hugh (b. 1854), Alexander (b. 1856), Mary Jane (b. 1858, Elizabeth Margaret (b.1860), David (b. 1862), Ellen (b. 1865), Lydia (b. 1867) and Maria Charlotte (b. 1869).

On January 26, 1877, their son Hugh married Susan Keown and the couple moved to Leitrim where they raised a family of nine children. Their daughter Maria Charlotte married thomas Keown on January 10, 1890 and also moved to Leitrim where they had a family of ten children.

Thomas and Maria's daughter Elizabeth Margaret Beck married Joseph Anderson from Ballinran on January 25, 1881 at Mourne Presbyterian Church. The couple had eight children together including: Margaret, Isabella, Elizabeth Ida, Rachel Amelia, Maria, Ellen and Joseph. On September 20, 1893, Joseph died leaving Maria to rear her children who ranged in ages from Margaret who was 11-years old to Joseph who was just 4-years old. Margaret Anderson had to curtail her education prematurely and started work when she was just 13-years old in order that she could assist her mother financially. Despite this apparent disadvantage, Margaret's hard work and determination enabled her to eventually be recognised as *'one of Mourne's greatest people'*.

Mourne's Florence Nightingale

Lydia Annett has published a wonderful history of Margaret Anderson in the Journal of the Mourne Local Studies Group publication '12 Miles of Mourne'. She was assisted in her research by Margaret Baird and Jean Stevenson.

Margaret Anderson started work when she was 13-years old as a receptionist for Dr. Ewing in Waringstown. Dr. Ewing encouraged Margaret to pursue a career in nursing and she eventually moved to England where she began her training in Leeds Union Infirmary. In 1916, she joined Queen Alexandra's Imperial Military Nursing Reserve and was posted for a time at Mont Dore Military Hospital in Bournemouth. In 1919, King George V awarded Nurse Anderson the Royal Red Cross for her war time service. Two years later Margaret headed to Iraq where she continued nursing until 1924. On her return to England, she was appointed Assistant Matron at the Royal Infirmary in Truro, Cornwall.

From 1926 until 1932, Margaret returned to Ireland and lived in Ballinran. She was given charge of the temporary hospital in the Silent Valley. The hospital was necessary to provide care for the two thousand strong workforce that was involved with constructing the dam. Sadly her mother Maria Beck Anderson died in 1926, shortly after Margaret had returned home, but the post at the temporary hospital gave Margaret time with her extended family in Ballinran. Margaret returned to England in 1932 and was appointed Matron of Wallingford Farm Training School near Oxford. When World War II broke out in 1939, she rejoined the nursing reserve and assisted in the evacuation of injured soldiers from Dunkirk. When the War ended in 1945, Margaret returned to the training school in Wallingford where she stayed until her retirement in 1953. She once again returned home to be with her family in Ballinran. In 1956, Margaret was honoured by Kilkeel Urban District Council. The council chairman Mr. R A Linton, said that *'Miss Anderson would go down in history as one of Mourne's greatest people'*. Sadly Nurse Anderson's retirement was a short one as she died on October 13, 1956. An obituary notice described her as 'Mourne's Florence Nightingale'.

Chapter 21

Bradley Family

The Bradley family was established in Aughnaloopy since before the 1830 Tithes document. Two names were listed, Felix with 5 acres and James with a little over 2 acres. It is possible that Felix also had land in Tullyframe townland. There was also a Hugh Bradley and a Patrick Bradley living in Aughnaloopy during this time period. Any relationship between Felix, James, Hugh and Patrick is unknown.

By the time of the Griffith's Valuation, two members of the Bradley family are noted, James and Ann. James had two areas of land leased from Thomas F Moore in the south eastern section of Aughnaloopy, identified as 34A and 34B and Ann Bradley was at number 30b.

Hugh Bradley and Ann Quinn (GV30b and GV31)

Ann Bradley (nee Quinn) who was listed on the Griffith's Valuation was the wife of Hugh Bradley (deceased). She held a 3-acre site adjoining Thomas Trainor's property and had a small farmhouse on the land, positioned on opposite sides of the Aughnaloopy Road identified by Griffiths by number 30b.

Just one Bradley family is listed on the 1901 census as living in Aughnaloopy. This was Patrick Bradley, the son of Hugh and Ann (Quinn) who had married Abigail 'Abby' Callaghan (daughter of Alexander Callaghan) from Ballinran, on June 11, 1895. James Trainor and Annie Cunningham were witnesses to the marriage that took place at Massforth RC Church in Kilkeel. Patrick and Abby had three children: James (c.1886), Annie Mary (c.1889) and Sarah (c.1892), all of whom are listed on the 1911 census. Patrick died on February 12, 1924 and his estate passed to his wife. Abigail Callaghan Bradley is listed in the paperwork relating to the 1925 Northern Ireland Land Act and the Estate of Betty Clarke (spinster). In a document published in The Belfast Gazette, dated January 10, 1930, Abigail Bradley (widow) is noted as paying rent of £6 10s 0d to Betty Clarke for just over 10 acres of land.

Hugh Bradley and his wife Ann Quinn are known to have had a daughter Sarah who married into the McVeigh family. Nothing is known about her husband and it does not appear that the couple had any children. Sarah died on December 7, 1915 and the probate of the will states her name as *'Sarah McVeigh known as Sarah Bradley'*. She left everything to her nieces Sarah Bradley, United States, America and Sarah Bradley of Aughnaloopy. Her executor was Francis O'Hagan, Spirit Merchant of Greencastle Street, Kilkeel. Her 2 acres of land were held on a yearly tenancy.

Biddy Bradley and John Johnson

On February 6, 1853, Bridget 'Biddy' Bradley married her neighbour John Johnston at Massforth RC Church in Kilkeel. James Quinn and Ellen Keown were witnesses to the marriage. Biddy's father was James Bradley who may have been a brother of Hugh who had married Ann Quinn. John and Biddy settled in Aughnaloopy and had at least seven children: William (b. 1853), James (b. 1855), Mary (b. 1858), Patrick (b. 1861), Bridget (b. 1865), John (b. 1867) and Rose (b. 1873). The family is recorded on the 1901 census. At home with their parents were John, Mary and Bridget and also their married daughter Rose Ann Collins, grandson John Collins, as well as nephews John Sloan (Mary Johnston's son) and John and William Rogers (Bridget Johnston's children). Rose Ann Johnston had married Patrick Collins from Magheragh on September 14, 1899 at Massforth RC Church in Kilkeel. Patrick was the son of James Collins and Sarah Burns.

Witnesses to the marriage were Patrick's brother Charles Collins and Ellen Flanagan. Patrick was at home with his father in Maghereagh at the time of the 1901 census, along with his brother Charles and sister Lizzie who was married to Richard McVeigh. Lizzie's children Mary, James, Richard and Sarah Elizabeth were also living in the house.

Ellen Bradley and Richard Sloan

Ellen Bradley married Richard Sloan from Tullyframe on August 17, 1869 at Massforth RC Church in Kilkeel. Richard's father was Henry and it is thought that Ellen was the daughter of James Bradley and a sister of Biddy. Ellen and Richard had four children: twins Ellen and Susan born in 1869 and then Mary (b. 1871) and Rose (b. 1873). Ellen may have died during childbirth because on May 1, 1873 Richard married Mary Bradley from Ballymageough. Any relationship between Ellen and Mary is unknown. Richard stated that he was a widower at the time of his marriage to Mary. John Bradley and Ellen Cunningham were witnesses to the wedding. The couple had a son Patrick born the following year.

Chapter 22

Campbell and Colgan

James Campbell rented a small house from James Murphy from the time of the Griffith Valuation until about 1869 when the house became vacant. The house was identified as number 41b and was on land owned by the Murphy family. It is possible that James Campbell was employed by James Murphy or he may have been a relative of the family. No documented relationship has been found between these families. There are no members of the Campbell family living in Aughnaloopy at the time of the 1901 or 1911 census and no Will has been found for James Campbell. The small home remained vacant for many years. In 1885 James Colgan and his family moved into the house. James Colgan was from Aughrim and had married Mary Hennity from Glenloughan on November 22, 1868. The couple reared at least nine children but by the time of the 1911 census, the house was solely occupied by 69-year old Mary Colgan. Details on the 1911 census return note that Thomas Quinn was now the owner of the building. An Ann Quinn was a witness at Mary Hennity's marriage to James Colgan and so perhaps some connection existed between the Quinns of Aughnaloopy and the Hennitys from Glenloughan.

On First Entering Port Philip Heads

Bright and clear the sun-beam's shine
Upon you lovely land,
Like a floating gem on an azure sea
Lies the fair Australian strand!

We have roamed a long and weary way
O'er oceans trackless path;
And felt the might of the billows foam,
And the tempest in its wrath.

And now you beauteous land appears
Before our wave worn barque;
As welcome as the white winged dove
To the dwellers of the Ark.

Wondrous tales are told to us
Of the wealth of the golden streams,
But oh! the land looks beautiful!
Be they false as fairy dreams!

Its skies to us seem sapphire blue,
Its grass as emerald green,
And radiant as the diamond flash
Its crystal waters sheen;

And tho' we have left our childhood's stars,
And the homes of those we love;
Earth's fairest forms around us smile,
And the southern cross above.

Emily E. B. Kilmore, January 1856.
Transcribed by Lyn Nunn Aug 2005 from The Examiner, 'Original and Select Poetry', January 25, 1856 n.p. Kilmore, Victoria, Australia.

Chapter 23

Doran Family

'I am very glad to hear of your grand family, the name is nearly run out in Ireland there is not one of them names in Aughnaloopy or miles round but myself.'

Early Doran Records

The earliest surviving record that references the Doran family in Aughnaloopy is the 1830 Tithes Records. The names mentioned are Bernard, Francis and John. Bernard held two sites totalling a little over 6 acres and Francis and John held an acre each. The nature of the relationship, if any, between Bernard, Francis and John is unknown.

In the Aughnaloopy Townland Valuation which was conducted in 1834, Patrick Doran is recorded as having a home valued at over £3 (this was one of only three in the townland). This Patrick Doran is likely the same Patrick who is listed on the later version of the Griffith Valuation with his property identified as 43ABC. He was a blacksmith and it is possible that his forge added to the value of his home resulting in its initial inclusion in the townland valuation.

Doran on the Griffith Valuation

At the time of the Griffith's Valuation in 1863, four members of the Doran family are documented as living in Aughnaloopy townland. These are Patrick Doran, Margaret Doran (who was married to John Flanagan), Cecelia Doran (married to Henry Flanagan), and Margaret Doran. It is unknown whether this is Margaret's married or maiden name but it is speculated that she was the wife of Francis Doran listed on the 1830 Tithes document. Patrick Doran is listed on the Griffith's Valuation leasing land in the south west of the townland identified as 43ABC. The land measures a little over 8 acres, composed of three lots. It is possible that the 6 acres site that has the house built on it (GV43B) was the land previously leased by Bernard, Francis and John in 1830. This farm borders Drumcro townland and indeed Dorans were listed in the 1803 Agricultural Census for Drumcro.

Margaret Doran was married to John Flanagan on November 9, 1860. John was the son of Henry Flanagan from Aughnaloopy and was a widower. Margaret was the daughter of James Doran from nearly Leitrim townland and his land bordered that of John Flanagan. John and Margaret leased the site in the north of the townland, identified as number 2 on the Griffith's Valuation, from James Moore. On John Flanagan's death in 1875, the property passed to his widow. There was no mention of any children in John's Will.

In the farm adjoining Margaret and John Flanagan lived Henry Flanagan and his wife Cecilia Doran. Henry and John were likely brothers and it is possible that Cecilia and Margaret were sisters. This 11-acre site was in the far north of the townland and is identified as number 1 on the Griffiths Valuation. It was also leased from James Moore.

The property identified as number 15 on the Griffith's Valuation, was leased by Margaret Doran and refers to a site of over 11 acres held by James Moore. It is not known whether Margaret was unmarried or a widow.

Although the exact family units are unknown, it is clear that from 1830 to 1864, the land held by the Doran family in Aughnaloopy increased from 6 to 19 acres, with John Flanagan and his wife Margaret Doran holding an additional 8 acres and Henry Flanagan and Cecilia Doran another 11 acres.

Francis Doran

Francis Doran was born c.1800 and is listed on the 1830 Tithes Records. He may also have held land in neighbouring Drumcro townland. No further information is known about Francis but it is possible that Francis is the unknown Doran married to Margaret listed below.

Margaret Doran (GV15)

This branch of the Doran family occupied the property identified as number 15 on the Griffith Valuation. Margaret Doran is not confirmed as being married. She may have been a sibling of the other Dorans mentioned. However as there were male offspring in the family, it would be unlikely that Margaret would be the head of household. It is speculated that Margaret, living at number 15, is the wife of Francis Doran and that there were at least four offspring: Dennis, John, Mary and Ellen.

Dennis Doran and Mary Quinn

Dennis Doran was born c.1835 and died prior to the 1901 census. He married Mary Quinn on February 19, 1860. Dennis Doran and Mary Quinn were native to Aughnaloopy. Mary was the daughter of Edward Quinn at GV18. However, after their marriage they settled in Moneydarragh Beg where they raised their family. The couple had at least five children: Mary (b. 1861), Arthur (b. 1865), John (b. 1866), Catherine (b. 1868) and James (b. 1870). When their maternal uncle James Quinn died on April 7, 1911, Mary inherited 5 pounds and James Doran a third of his uncle's estate in Aughnaloopy. No provision was made for Arthur, John or Catherine and they are not living at home at the time of the 1911 census.

John Doran and Sarah Johnson

Dennis's brother John Doran married Sarah Johnson c.1855. This was a union of two established Aughnaloopy families. As with Doran, the Johnson family is recorded in the 1830 Tithes document and both families are likely to have been in Aughnaloopy for many years prior to this. The Johnson family is listed in the Griffiths Valuation, occupying farms at GV 36, GV37 and GV38. These properties lie to the East of the Aughnaloopy Road, towards Aughnahorey townland. Unfortunately, no marriage record has been found for Sarah Johnson to John Doran but luckily, a baptism record exists for their daughter Margaret dated December 21, 1858. The couple had at least four other children: Catherine (b. 1864), Ellen (b. 1857), John Jrn. (b. 1869), and Annie (b. 1871). Their son John immigrated to Canada arriving in Halifax, Nova Scotia on April 8, 1888 at just 19-years old. His sister Annie also moved to Canada although the details have not been confirmed. John married Annie Laura Lavigne on January 17, 1905 and Annie married Ellis Lyons on November 12, 1918.

Sisters Mary and Ellen Doran

When John Doran Snr. died, his brother Dennis was living in Moneydarragh, and his son John had moved to Canada, this left sisters Mary and Ellen to run the smallholding in Aughnaloopy. When Mary died on September 28, 1908, the property passed to her sister Ellen who continued to live there with her niece Mary Doran. Mary's parents are unknown. We know she wasn't the daughter of Dennis (and Mary Quinn) as a Mary is listed with her mother on the 1911 census. It is possible that she was a daughter of John (and Sarah Johnson). Ellen and her niece Mary are the only remaining members of the Doran family living in Aughnaloopy at the time of the 1911 census.

John Doran Jrn. maintained contact with his family in Aughnaloopy. His grandson, also named John Doran has the following letter sent to Canada from Ellen Doran in 1923 that he has kindly allowed us to publish.

Ellen's reference to Johnney and Kate Cunningham further establishes Doran family

John Doran and Annie Laura Lavigne on their wedding day, January 17, 1905 in Simcoe, Ontario, Canada. John was the son of John Doran and sarah 'Sally' Johnson. He moved to Canada in 1888 when he was 19-years old.

connections in Aughnaloopy. John Cunningham married Catherine 'Kate' Johnson on February 6, 1883. The family settled at GV36 Aughnaloopy and had at least four children: Thomas, John, Patrick and Joseph. Kate Johnson's father was George Johnson and she is likely a sister or first cousin of Sarah Johnson who married John Doran. Her comment on the Bradley family in Leitrim indicates further family connections between the Dorans in Aughnaloopy and those in the neighbouring townland. The property occupied by James Bradley at the time of Ellen's letter was previously held from before the time of the Griffiths Valuation until 1895 by Daniel Doran. James Bradley also acquired neighbouring property originally held by Bernard Doran.

> May 3 1923
> Ellen Doran
> Aughnaloopy Kilkeel
> County Down, Ireland
>
> Dear Nephew
>
> *I write you these few line to let you know that I got your letter two months ago I was sorry to here of you not being well but I hope with the help of God that you are alright again you did not tell me what was the mater with you I hope you will excuse me for not written sooner but I was not well myself I had a very bad cold all winter but I am getten all right again thank God. The weather is very cold it is the coldest spring we ever mind in Ireland no farming work done yet. I am very glad to hear of your grand family, the name is nearly run out in Ireland there is not one of them names in Aughnaloopy or miles round but myself.*
>
> *Johnney Cunningham is dead and Kate to both the 3 oldest boys are out in Mounttana and the youngest boy is liven alone like myself. My old friends and neighbours are all dead but I have very kind neighbours still. The priest come often to see me and James Bradley of Leatim his yongest son is a priest he is on the Mission over years he comes very often to see me. The times is a little settled in Ireland but not quite yet. There is over 300 and 50 of the young men of these few counties in a transport ship in Belfast harbour 12 months and no word of getten out yet. Dear friend please write a few lines soon and let me know how you are and how yous are all no more at present from your Aunt Ellen Doran*
>
> *Please write soon*

Bernard Doran

Little is know about Bernard Doran who was born in 1835, but he is likely a sibling of one of the other Aughnaloopy families. His family is not listed on the 1901 or 1911 census and it is possible that they emigrated from Ireland. Bernard married Mary Ann Rogers on June 6, 1862 in Kilkeel – another union between two established Aughnaloopy families. The couple had at least one son Patrick, baptized on April 2, 1863. Nothing further is known about the family.

Patrick Doran – the Blacksmith (GV43)

This branch of the Doran family occupied the property identified as number 43ABC on the Griffith Valuation. Patrick was born c.1810 and is listed on the Griffiths Valuation at the property identified as number 43ABC. This property was originally included in the 1834 Townland Valuation as being one of three properties in Aughnaloopy valued at over £3. It was estimated at 2 Irish acres. Patrick worked as a blacksmith in the townland and was married to Bridget Trainor. Although no marriage record has been found, there is a baptism record for Ann Doran dated February 19, 1853 where the parents are listed as Patrick Doran and Bridget Trainor. Witnesses to the baptism were William Quinn and Bridget Trainor. The couple had at least seven more children: Ellen (c.1845), John (b.

1847), Mary (b. 1849), Patrick (c.1851), Michael (b. 1855) and Maria Rose (b. 1861). Nothing is known about John, Mary or Michael. In 1864, Patrick's property consisted of three sites: 43A which measured 1 acres, 43B which was 6 acres and 31 perch and 43C which was 1 acre and 3 rods. The homestead appears to be sited at 43C and it is likely that this house was the one valued at 3 pounds or over in 1834. The 43B site may have been acquired between 1843 and 1864, hence the discrepancy in the land size. His property is interspersed by that of Francis Rogers, and was situated in the southwestern section of the townland. Patrick also appears to have had land in neighbouring Drumcro townland, that was originally held by Francis Doran.

Ellen Doran and Thomas Morgan

Patrick and Bridget's daughter Ellen married Thomas Morgan (the son of Edward Morgan) from Maghereagh on January 31, 1867. The couple had at least four children: Mary (August 19, 1868), Patrick (March 17, 1870), Edward (February 27, 1875) and Thomas (July 7, 1877). Thomas Jnr. married Rose Quinn from Moyadd on November 8, 1906 and the couple had at least two children: Patrick (b. 1907) and Mary Ellen (b. 1910). Patrick moved to England where, in 1940, he married a girl named Ellen Whelan from Waterford, where they eventually went to live. Mary Ellen Morgan married Thomas Fitzpatrick (son of William Fitzpatrick and Mary Kate Redmond) from nearby Atticall. Thomas Fitzpatrick was born October 30, 1906 in Nipissing, Ontario, Canada, where his parents were living at the time. They moved back to Atticall soon afterwards. Mary Ellen and Thomas Fitzpatrick had nine children: Thomas, William, Peter, Noel, Seamus, Edward, Rosemary, Loretta and Patrick 'Paddy'. Mary Ellen passed away in January 2000 but her son Thomas still lives in Atticall with his wife and family.

Patrick Doran and Ellen McDermott (GV43)

Patrick was born c.1851 and married Ellen McDermott from Grange, on November 22, 1901 in Kilkeel. Patrick inherited the family farm listed as GV43, from his father Patrick Doran. When he died Patrick held the farm in Aughnaloopy under Mr. J.M. Orr, which measured 7 acres 3 rods 31 perch, and a farm in Drumcro of 9 acres 3 rods 3 perch held under Lord Kilmorey. This record of land in Drumcro establishes a link to Francis Doran named on the 1803 Agricultural Census. Patrick also owned a field known as 'The Rocks' at the river in Leitrim townland, and a seaweed bed on Killowen shore. Patrick and his wife Ellen did not have any children and so after his death, the property was occupied by his sister Ellen's son Thomas Morgan. Thomas and his wife Rose Quinn are listed at the property on the 1911 census with their children Mary Ellen and Patrick. In paperwork connected with Patrick's Will, several references are made to Hugh Trainor from Aughrim. This further suggests that Patrick's mother was Bridget Trainor and indicates that she may have been one of the Aughrim Trainors. Patrick Jrn. died on July 22, 1904 in Aughnaloopy.

Ann Doran and Patrick Morgan

Patrick and Bridget's daughter Anne was baptized on February 19, 1853 and married Patrick Morgan from Maghereagh on February 13, 1877. Patrick was the son of Charles Morgan, a shoemaker. After the birth of their two children, Patrick and Mary Catherine, the family moved to Liverpool in England. They are listed in the 1881 United Kingdom census living at 51 Darwin Street, Liverpool. Also in their home were boarders 30-year old William Quinn and 26-year old John Young from County Down. Ann Morgan (nee Doran) died c.1886. Mary Catherine gave birth to a little girl, named Ellen O'Neill Morgan in 1901 and moved into her Uncle Patrick Doran's house in Aughnaloopy. Patrick made several provisions for Mary Catherine in his Will.

Maria Rose Doran and John Donnelly

Maria Rose Doran was born c.1861. She is listed as a witness at her sister Anne's marriage to Patrick Morgan on February 13, 1877. On May 19, 1881 she married John Donnelly from Derryogue. John was the son of John Donnelly and Elizabeth

'Betty' Ann Quinn. Witnesses to the marriage were Richard Quinn and Ellen Doran. The couple had a large family including: Maria, Elizabeth Ann, John Patrick, Minnie, James, Daniel, Peggy, Ellen Teresa and Thomas Joseph. At least two of the boys Daniel and James Patrick and their sister Minnie (who married Patrick Rogers from Cranfield) eventually settled in Miles City, Montana. In 1936, the siblings made a trip back home to see their mother Maria and the event was reported on page 3 of the Billings Gazette, dated September 30, 1936. Daniel stated,

'.....that conditions in north Ireland are good with some good crops raised and harvested. The transportation system has been revolutionised by the buses, he said, and they are more numerous per population than in the United States.'

The Doran Girls (Cecelia and Margaret)

Cecilia Doran (c.1825) who was married to Henry Flanagan on October 23, 1843 and lived at the property identified as number 1 on the Griffith's Valuation. She was likely from Aughnaloopy or from a neighbouring townland but nothing is recorded on the marriage details. Margaret Doran who was married to John Flanagan on November 9, 1860 and lived at the property identified as number 2 on the Griffith's Valuation was the daughter of James Doran from Leitrim. She is possibly a cousin of the Aughnaloopy Dorans.

Susan Doran and Thomas Quinn

Susan Doran, the daughter of John Doran and Eliza Clarke, was born in Moneydarragh in 1856. On November 25, 1880 she married Thomas Quinn and moved to Aughnaloopy. The couple did not have any children. When Susan and Thomas Quinn died, their land passed on to Susan's nephew John Rooney. John was the son of Susan's sister Mary Ann Doran; he had spent some time working in America but returned to Mourne where he married Mary Bradley from Leitrim.

There is currently no known link between Dennis Doran (who married Mary Quinn) who moved from Aughnaloopy to Moneydarragh and Susan Doran (married to Thomas Quinn) who moved from Moneydarragh to Aughnaloopy.

Elizabeth Doran and John Spears

Another Doran living in Aughnaloopy was Elizabeth Doran who married John Spears. At the time of their marriage on June 14, 1846, both Elizabeth and John stated that they were from Leitrim and so they may have moved to Aughnaloopy after their wedding. John states that his father's name was William and Elizabeth gives her father's name as Patrick. She states that he is a farmer. Elizabeth was a widow when she married John but she does not appear to have had any children with her first husband. Elizabeth and John Spears had at least eight children: Ann (December 21, 1843), James (January 29, 1844) Margaret (May 1, 1849), John (c.1850), Alexander (c.1851), Eliza (October 1, 1854), Mary (May 14, 1851) and Jane (August 14, 1857) and the family lived at the site in Aughnaloopy identified by number 8 on the Griffith Valuation. The family is listed on the 1901 census for Aughnaloopy.

Doran's Well

To the north of Aughnaloopy townland is situated Doran's Well. It is possible that this was the well referred to in a poem written by John Doran (1869-1926). John was the son of John Doran and Sally Johnson and he emigrated to Canada when he was just 19-years old. John maintained a fondness for his homeland which is reflected in a series of poems that he wrote including the one below kindly donated by his grandson also called John Doran who lives in Ontario, Canada.

Old Kilkeel

One mile from old Kilkeel
There lies a place that I love most
It's memory clings around my heart,
It's called the Hannas Close
I often think of the happy days
I spent around its brays
With heart as light as the little birds
That hopped from spray to spray
I think I see the creeper bush
And the garden where the flowers grow
There often in the summer morn
I've heard the mistletoe
O down below the much loved spot
Beneath two little hills
And underneath a shady grove
Saw Walmsley's water mills
It's when these mills are working
It's a pleasant scene to see
The dusty scutchers lie
Upon the lovely green
But let us travel upwards
Along the river swell
And underneath a hazel bush
Here lies the boiling well
The well is situated
In a quite calm retreat
And many are the visitors
That round the waters meet
But let us travel onwards
I will not yours detain
The next place of attraction
We meet is Rogers stream
This lovely little streamlet
Flows round many a nook and crook
To join the brimming river
Just under Daniels bank
But further up where the holly grown
Across yon little hill
In midst of an expanding grove
Here stands the old Tuck mill
Remit me now to tell you
I have often heard it said
The mill is making money
When the owner is in bed
But let us now retrace our steps
Down by the river foam
Where ever my lot in life is cast
My heart still clings to home.

by: John Doran

*'...And underneath a hazel bush
Here lies the boiling well
The well is situated
In a quite calm retreat
And many are the visitors
That round the waters meet...'*

This photograph was taken in 2011 by Ciera E. Jones, while looking for Doran's Well. The well is apparently situated in the ditch on the right hand side of the image but on this day it was overgrown and impossible to locate.

Chapter 24

Edgar Family

This ancient and distinguished surname is of Anglo-Saxon origin, and is derived from the Olde English pre-7th Century male personal name 'Eadgar', composed of the elements 'ead', prosperity, fortune, with 'gar', spear. In Aughnaloopy, the name appears to have become Edgar over time.

From Eager to Edgar

The name Edgar was originally recorded as Eager in documents relating to Aughnaloopy. The family is one of the earliest documented in the townland, with the Bagenal Mourne Rentals of 1715 listing James Eager Senior, James Eager Junior and D A Eager. The family paid 6 pounds and 10 shillings for use of the land at Aughnaloopy that had a lease value of 10 pounds. There are some references to a Doughtry Eager a landlord in Mourne area in the early 19th century and it is possible that D A Eager refers to Doughtry. A later rent roll, thought to be from between 1716 to 1720, documents that James Eager and partners are still renting land at Aughnaloopy, although the name of the partners is unknown. The agent has written 'In the chief tenants and partners hand, only one 6th part lett for –.' This presumably means that the Eager family primarily farmed the land themselves and sub-leased one sixth part for 3 pounds. In 1830, the Tithes document lists John Edgar Jnr., John Edgar Snr., and William Edgar. Once again, the relationship, if any, between the three family members is unknown.

The earliest surviving record of a Will that specifically states Aughnaloopy, as the place of residence is for John Edgar whose Will was probated in 1832. The record is contained within the Newry & Mourne Wills, 1727-1858 Index, edited by W.P.W. Phillimore, 1909. No further details are given and the original Will has been destroyed. John Edgar is possibly the same John Edgar listed on the Flax Growers List in 1796.

By the time of the Griffith's Valuation in 1863, the Edgar family are leasing over 32 acres of land in Aughnaloopy, from John and Hugh Moore. It is thought that Robert and James may have been cousins.

James Edgar son of William (GV21ABCDE)

James's father was William Edgar as documented by his marriage record to Eliza Annett (from Ballykeel) on October 25, 1850. James held the land identified as 21ABCDE which amounted to just over 6 acres and the fields were interspersed through Robert's fields (GV19ABC). Robert and James's land lay to the west of the townland bordering neighbouring Leitrim. James married Elizabeth Annett a daughter of James Annett from Ballykeel on October 25, 1850. The marriage took place at Mourne Presbyterian Church in Kilkeel. The couple had at least eight children: William (b. 1851), James (b. 1853), Mary Ann (b. 1854), Margaret Ann (b. 1855), Mary 'Minnie' (b. 1857, Eliza Jane (b. 1858), Catherine 'Kate' (b. 1860) and John (b. 1863). When James Edgar died on April 7, 1869 at Aughnaloopy, probate was granted at Belfast to George Annett of Ballykeel who is noted as a maternal uncle and guardian (during minority only) of William Edgar, James Edgar, Margaret Edgar, Mary Edgar, Eliza Anne Edgar, Catherine Edgar and John Edgar. These seven children were all minors at the time of their father's death. Mary Ann is not noted so she presumably died in childhood. James's wife Elizabeth Annett from Ballykeel had predeceased her husband, dying sometime between the birth of John in 1863 and April 1869. In 1874, James's son William took over the land in Aughnaloopy, but he eventually settled in Ballinran with his wife Charlotte Maria Scott. In 1885, the land passed out of the Edgar family to William Shields and his wife Eliza Jane Parke (from Ballinran). The Shields family remained there until after the 1911 census. William and Charlotte Maria Edgar had at least six children: Margaret Elizabeth (b. 1875 in Kilkeel), James (b. 1878 in New Jersey, USA), Samuel (b. 1880 in Kilkeel), William (b. 1882 in Sturgeon Bay, Ontario, Canada), John (b. 1884 in Sturgeon Bay, Ontario, Canada) and Mary 'Minnie' (b. 1887 in Sturgeon Bay, Ontario, Canada). William died c.1890 in Canada and Charlotte returned to Ballinran where she is listed as a widow on the 1901 census. Three of her children are living back at home in Ballinran: Willie and John who are both working as stone cutters and her daughter Minnie who is still at school.

By the time of the 1911 census Willie and Minnie have left home but John's wife Elizabeth 'Lilly' Hanna has moved into the Edgar home in Ballinran. Lilly and John Edgar eventually had nine known children together: Charlotte, John, William, Jane, James, Mary 'Minnie', Robert, Margaret and William. William and Charlotte's older son William had married Susan Hanna from Ballinran on January 14, 1902. The couple eventually moved to South Africa where they remained until their death. William and Charlotte's son James settled in America and died in Silver City, New Mexico on October 26, 1953.

Robert Edgar son of John (GV19ABC)

Robert's father was John Edgar, as stated in his marriage record to Sarah Shields (from Carginagh) on November 29, 1869. At the time of their marriage both Robert and Sarah were widowed. Robert's previous wife was called Nancey and there is a headstone in Mourne Presbyterian burial ground noting Nancey's death in July 1868, aged 58.

It is believed that Sarah's first husband was William Shields and that her maiden name was Bingham. A marriage record has been located for a William Shields (son of Hugh Shields) to Sarah Bingham (daughter of John Bingham) in 1855. Sarah is thought to have been from Carginagh. Sarah had at least two sons by her first husband: Hugh (c.1855) and William (c. 1859).

Photograph of the headstone erected by Robert Edgar for his wife Nancey, taken by Sheila Phillips.

Hugh married Aughnaloopy girl Ann Keown in 1878 and William married Eliza Jane Parker from Ballinran in 1883.

Robert Edgar held land of over 26 acres identified on the Griffith's Valuation as number 19ABC. He leased a small house on his land to Francis Rogers (GV19Bb) but there is no known relationship between these families. Robert and Sarah had a son John born in Aughnaloopy in December 1871. Robert died on January 1, 1886 but his estate was not settled until July 3, 1893 when his land at Aughnaloopy passed to his son John who was now 21-years old. On October 9, 1894, John married Sarah Cousins at Mourne Presbyterian Church in Kilkeel. Sarah was the daughter of Robert Cousins and was originally from Brackenagh. The couple settled in Aughnaloopy and had at least ten children: Margaret (b. 1898), Sarah (b. 1900), Robert (b. 1902), John (b. 1903), Martha (b. 1906), Mary Elizabeth (b. 1908), William (b. 1910) and Jane, Anna and Thomas who were all born after the 1911 census.

John left Aughnaloopy when he was 21-years old. He travelled on the SS Alaunia from Belfast to New York, arriving on April 26, 1926. He was later joined by his brothers William and Thomas and the three men settled in New York City. Martha and Jane moved to Cleveland, Ohio. Jane remained in Ohio where she married Paul Junker on January 19, 1940. Martha married Edward Ferrier in Ohio on June 9, 1932 but in 1950 the couple then moved on to Marietta, Georgia

Sarah Bingham Edgar died in 1911, age 75-years old.

Jane Edgar daughter of John

It appears that Robert may have had a sister Jane Edgar who married James Edgar from Magheramurphy. The marriage took place on April 26, 1847; Jane's father was noted as John and her husband's father was James Edgar. It is not known if the couple had any children.

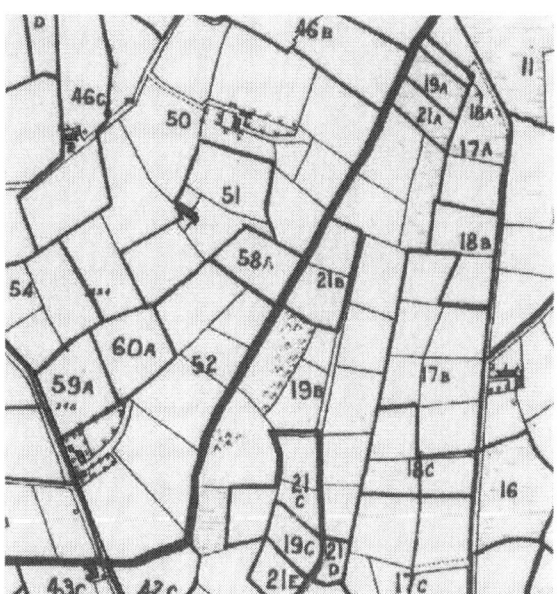

Extract from the Griffith's Valuation map of 1864 showing the location of Robert Edgar's land, marked as 19AB and C in Aughnaloopy townland. James's land is indicated by 21 ABCD and E.

Edgar Events

Considerable research has been conducted into the Edgar family. A newsletter entitled Edgar Events was started in mid-2006 to distribute to descendants of the Edgar family around the world as a way to share genealogical research. The extended family has also started a DNA Project to scientifically determine how and if branches of the family are connected. All issues of Edgar Events are available online as PDF at
http://jameswd.sasktelwebsite.net/

```
NEW SERIES LICENSE NO. A 5670    FILED AND MARRIAGE LICENSE ISSUED    July 6    1932
Name        Edward Ferrier                          Name        Martha Edgar
Age  28   Residence  555 E. 115th St.               Age  27   Residence  14736 Terrace Rd. E.C.
Place of Birth       Scotland                       Place of Birth       Ireland
Occupation           Tree Surgeon                   Occupation           Asst. Matson
Father's Name        James Ferrier                  Father's Name        John Edgar
Mother's Maiden Name Elizabeth Milne                Mother's Maiden Name Sarah Cousins
Number of times previously married    None          Number of times previously married  None
                                                    Married Name

Marriage to be solemnised by Rev. Cummins, E. 93rd St.
Consent of              Filed                 19    Consent of          Filed                19
Application taken by  Frank Zizelman   Deputy Clerk
Date of application   July 1, 1932                  License issued by  Frank Zizelman    Deputy Clerk
THE STATE OF OHIO,
  Cuyahoga County,   ss.                            RETURN
I CERTIFY, That on the 9th   day of   July          19 32 . Mr.  Edward Ferrier
and Miss   Martha Edgar                             were by me legally joined in marriage.
                                                    Rev.  John W. Cummins
```

Marriage details of Martha Edgar to Edward Ferrier

```
NEW SERIES LICENSE NO. A 67037   FILED AND MARRIAGE LICENSE ISSUED   December 28   1939
Name        Paul Junker                             Name        Jane Edgar
Age  24   Residence  7625 Lexington Ave.            Age  26   Residence  14113 ardinall ave.
Place of Birth       St. Paul, Minn                 Place of Birth       Ireland
Occupation           Ironworker                     Occupation           None
Father's Name        Harry                          Father's Name        John
Mother's Maiden Name Mamie Peters                   Mother's Maiden Name Sarah Cousins
Number of times previously married    None          Number of times previously married  None
                                                    Married Name

Marriage to be solemnized by Rev. -----
Consent of              Filed                 19    Consent of          Filed                19
Application taken by  Frank Zizelman   Deputy Clerk
Date of application   Dec. 23, 1939                 License issued by  M.L. Friebolin   Deputy Clerk
THE STATE OF OHIO,
  Cuyahoga County,   ss.                            RETURN
I CERTIFY, That on the 19th   day of   January      19 40 , Mr.  Paul Junker
and Miss   Jane Edgar                               were by me legally joined in marriage.
                                                    Rev.  N. Burnett Magruder
```

Marriage details of Jane Edgar to Paul Junker

Mrs. Ferrier

Mrs. Martha E. Ferrier, 63, of 384 Freyer Drive died Tuesday morning at Kennestone Hospital after a lengthy illness.

Services will be Thursday at 11 a.m. at First Presbyterian Church with Dr. Harry K. Holland and Rev. Wyatt Aiken Jr. officiating. Burial will be in Kennesaw Memorial Park Cemetery. Hay-Gantt Funeral Home is in charge of arrangements.

Survivors include husband, Ed Ferrier; sisters, Mrs. Jim Glenney, Mrs. James Hanna and Mrs. Anna Counsins of Kilkeel, Ireland, Mrs. Paul Junker of Cleveland, Ohio; brothers, John Edgar, William Edgar and Thomas Edgar of New York City, N. Y., Robert Edgar of Kilkeel, Ireland.

A native of Kilkeel, County of Down, Northern Ireland, Mrs. Ferrier moved to the U.S.A. in 1926. She had lived in Marietta since 1950.

Article from the Marietta Journal - March 13, 1968

Chapter 25

Fitzpatrick Family

Pat Fitzpatrick of Aughnaloopy (GV17ABCDE)

An old headstone remains at Massforth Graveyard in Kilkeel, with the inscription:

> Erected by Pat Fitzpatrick of Aughnaloopy in memory of his mother Catherine who departed this life 20th. November 1838 aged 68 years. His brother Peter is also interred here.

This suggests that the Fitzpatrick family were established in Aughnaloopy at least as far back as the mid-eighteenth century. By the time of the Griffith's Valuation, the Fitzpatrick family farmed a sizeable piece of land (over 14 acres in total) identified as GV17ABCFE, which lay to the west of the Aughnaloopy Road. Their home appears to have been located on the site identified as 17B.

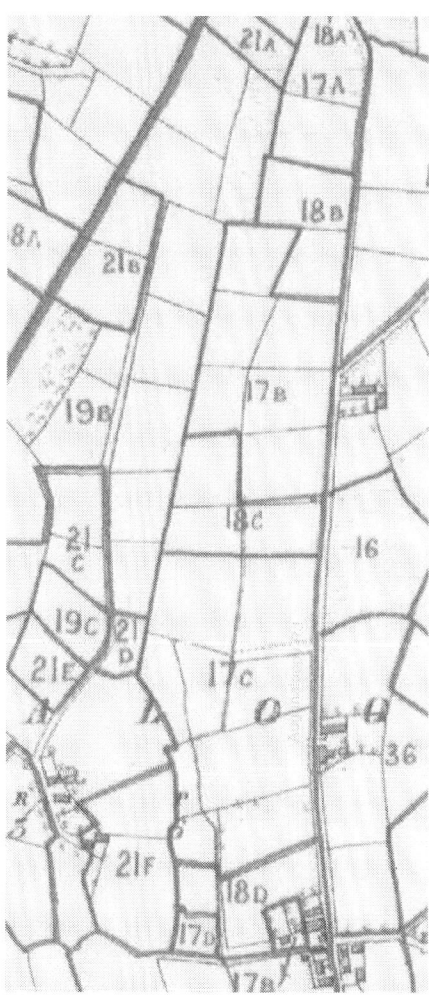

Patrick Fitzpatrick died in 1873 at age 70 but his land remained occupied by three of his children, Edward (c.1824), James (c.1828) and Catherine (c.1830), until after the 1911 census. James Fitzpatrick acted as executor for his neighbour Mark Quinn when Mark prepared his Will in 1873, indicating a trust and friendship between the two families. When James Fitzpatrick died on March 22, 1912, his estate, valued at £208 4s 8d, was quickly settled, passing to his brother Edward. Edward died just two years later, on March 31, 1914. Again the estate, now valued at £295 19s 6d, was settled quickly, passing to his sister Catherine. It is not known when Catherine died but no Will has been found and it is unlikely that she made one. It is thought that she died some time between 1917 and 1920.

An extract from the Griffith's Valuation Map of 1864 showing the Fitzpatrick land identified as 17ABCD and E. The line that runs from North to South through the centre of the townland is the Aughnaloopy Road.

Chapter 26

Flanagan Family

Many thanks to Mr. Peter Flanagan of Aughnaloopy for his kind assistance with this chapter and for providing support from the beginning of this project through to completion.

Edward, Felix, Henry, John and Margaret Flanagan

The Flanagan family is documented as living in Aughnaloopy since the early nineteenth century. Several spelling variants appear in the historical documents but Flanagan is the most frequent spelling used. There are five Flanagans mentioned in the 1830 Tithes Records: Edmund, Felix, Henry, John and Margaret. The relationship between the individuals is unknown. Edmund, Felix, and Margaret each paid tithes on 1 acre, Felix on 2 acres, John on 3 acres and Henry on 7 acres. By the time of the 1864 Griffith's Valuation, only three names are recorded: Henry, John and James. Henry is noted at the property identified as number 1 on the Griffith's Valuation. This is in the uppermost section of the townland and is still occupied by the Flanagan family today. John Flanagan occupied the adjoining property at the site identified as number 2 on the Griffith's Valuation and James leased land at GV28. Henry (Snr.) who is listed on the Tithes Document is confirmed as the father of Henry and John who are listed on the Griffith's Valuation but the relationship to James has not been determined. It is not known if Felix or Edmund married or had children.

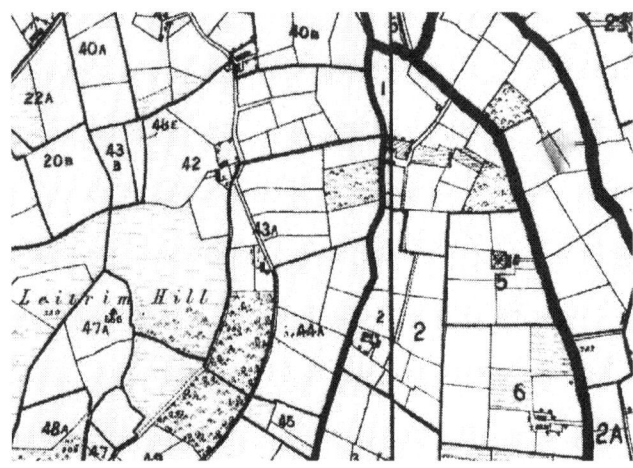

Extract from the Griffith's Valuation map of 1864 showing the location of Flanagan properties, marked as 1 and 2 in the north of Aughnaloopy townland.

Henry Flanagan (GV1)

Henry who lived at GV1 married Aughnaloopy girl Cecilia Doran on October 23, 1843 at Massforth RC Church in Kilkeel. The couple had at least seven children: Margaret (c. 1845), Catherine (b. 1848), John (b. 1850), James (b. 1852), Selina (b. 1853), Sarah (b. 1857) and Peter (b. 1860). Little is known about the older siblings.

Henry and Cecilia's daughter Sarah is known to have married Daniel Melvin from Douglas, Isle of Man on September 19, 1889 and the couple had at least five children: Henry (b. 1890), John (b. 1891), Selina (b. 1893), Daniel (b. 1895) and James (b. 1900). Sarah's sister Margaret Flanagan and Thomas Keenan were witnesses to the marriage that took place at Massforth RC Church in Kilkeel. Daniel was employed as a stonecutter in Moneydarragh at the time of their wedding. His father's name is given as John Melvin.

On October 12, 1892, Henry Flanagan passed away at age 68-years. He left a detailed Will and mentioned Catherine, Selina and Margaret. No married names were given for his daughters and it would appear that they remained single. He mentioned his daughter

Sarah and his only grandson Henry Melvin to whom he left the sum of 12 pounds to be paid when Henry reached 12-years of age. Neither John nor James was noted suggesting that they may have died previously. Daniel Hanna and Samuel Hanna Junior were witnesses to Henry's Will.

In addition to his home in Aughnaloopy, Henry Flanagan leased some bog land in Leitrim townland. In 1896, a house was erected on the site and his daughter Sarah and her family moved to Leitrim where they stayed until 1908.

The Flanagan family homestead passed to Henry's youngest son Peter. Three years later on January 3, 1895, Peter married Margaret McKey from Tullyframe (the daughter of Patrick McKey and Elizabeth Quinn) at Massforth RC Church in Kilkeel. The couple had at least nine children together: Henry (b. 1895), Patrick Joseph (b. 1898), Selina (b. 1899), James (b. 1900), Daniel (b. 1902), Elizabeth "Lizzie" (b. 1903), Daniel (b. 1904), Peter (b. 1906), Anna Mary "Annie" (b. 1907) and Mark (b. 1908).

The children of Henry Flanagan and Margaret McKey

Henry
Following the traditional family naming pattern, Henry and Margaret's eldest son was called Henry. He was born on January 7, 1895 and baptised on January 10, 1895. Sponsors at the baptism were Hugh Doran and Mary McKey. Henry died on January 10, 1979.

Patrick Joseph
Henry and Margaret's second son Patrick Joseph was born on February 11, 1898 and baptised on February 13. Sponsors to the baptism were Lizzie Quinn and Daniel McKey. Like many of his peers, Patrick Joseph left Ireland when he was 25-years old and sought work in America. For over 20 years, he farmed and worked as a shovel operator in Colstrip, which lies between Billings and Miles City in Montana. The town of Colstrip was established in 1924 by the Northern Pacific Railway as a company town tasked with providing coal for their steam locomotives. It operated open pit mining and was strategically important during World War II as it supplied coal for the Northern Pacific Railway steam locomotives hauling military equipment for the war effort. During the War, the mine was guarded from sabotage, and the employees were not allowed to quit their jobs. Patrick Joseph married Edna Ellen Sample on January 23, 1937 in Forsyth, Montana. Patrick Joseph and Edna had two daughters, Patricia and Margaret and a son Patrick. Patrick Joseph died in 1986 at Sheridan Memorial Hospital in Montana.

Selina
Henry and Margaret's eldest daughter Selina also left Aughnaloopy in search of work and adventure. A border-crossing document has been found for Selina when she crossed from Canada into Buffalo, New York on November 8, 1929. She gives her date of birth as April 18, 1899, although her actual date of birth was April 9. She stated that her mother's name was Margaret and that she had a brother Peter living in New York.

Selina made a trip back to see her family in Aughnaloopy at the end of 1930 returning to America at the beginning of 1931. She left Belfast on February 28, 1931, sailing on the SS Cedric and arrived in New York on March 10. She stated that she was 31-years old and that she was going to stay with her brother Peter. She had an immigration visa that had been issued in Washington DC on November 11, 1930. The address she gave for Peter was 526 East, 135 Street in the Bronx, New York.

Selina married at St. Luke's Church in New York on September 6, 1931 to a Norwegian man, Olaf Larson. The couple had a daughter Margaret who lives in New Jersey. Selina died on March 8, 1975 and Olaf died on June 1, 2000.

James

The couple had another son James born on June 25, 1900 and baptised four days later. Sponsors to the baptism were Henry Cunningham and Mary McKey. Like his siblings James left Aughnaloopy in search of employment in America. He travelled on the SS Regina in January 1926 stating that he was going to live in Brooklyn, New York. He noted that he had a cousin William T at 189 Cooper Street, Brooklyn.

On January 5, 1932, James returned to Aughnaloopy. He travelled from New York harbour sailing on the SS Ascania. The vessel, which was part of the Cunard White Star line, arrived in Liverpool on January 5, 1932.

James married Catherine Rooney, the daughter of Patrick Rooney from Carginagh and the couple had a son Peter and a daughter.

Peter Flanagan lives on the site that has been occupied by his family for almost 200 years.

Mr. Flanagan continues to farm the land that has been in his family since the early 19th Century.

Photograph taken by Ciera E. Jones, Summer 2011.

Elizabeth

Elizabeth 'Lizzie' Flanagan was born on May 25, 1903. Sponsors to the baptism were Patrick McConn and Mary Cunningham. Like her siblings, Lizzie left Aughnaloopy and moved to North America. She is recorded on a border crossing document travelling from Canada into Buffalo, New York, on June 27, 1937. She stated that she was 31 years old and said that she was going to see her sister Selina Larson. Lizzie died on July 27, 1992.

Daniel

Little is known about Daniel other than the date of his baptism November 17, 1904 which occurred 13 days after his birth. The baptismal sponsors were John McConn and Katie Cunningham. Daniel died c.1952.

Peter

Another son, Peter was born in Aughnaloopy on April 12, 1906 and baptised 3 days later. His baptismal sponsors were M. Cunningham and Sarah Doran.

On October 4, 1927, Peter left Ireland sailing on the SS Celtic out of Liverpool and arrived in New York on October 4, 1927. Peter named his brother James as his contact in the US and gave his address as 146 East 137 Street, Bronx. The following year on February 21, he filed his intention to become a citizen of the United States. The document filed in the US District, Southern District of New York records that Peter was living at 580 East 134 Street, Bronx. He stated that he was unmarried and that he had no children. Witnesses to the petition were Patrick J. Cunningham of 521 Union Avenue, Bronx and James Harrison of 541 East 148 Street, Bronx. From documentation completed by his sister Selina, we know that he was living at 26 East 135 Street in the Bronx, New York in 1931. On March 13, 1933 Peter swore an Oath of Allegiance to the United States and formally became a citizen of the United States. On December 10, 1934, Peter made a trip home to Aughnaloopy arriving in Belfast on the SS Transylvania. He gave his age as 28, stated his occupation as a labourer and noted that he was a US citizen. Peter died on October 23, 1958.

Anna Mary
Henry and Margaret's youngest daughter Anna Mary 'Annie' Flanagan moved to England. She married Leonard T Webber in 1941 and settled in Basingstoke.

Mark
Henry and Margaret's youngest child was born on November 25, 1911 and baptised 4 days later. Patrick McKey and Mary Killop were his godparents. Mark died October 2, 1979.

Margaret McKey Flanagan and her daughter Annie, sitting outside of the original house at GV1. Photograph kindly donated by Peter Flanagan who lives in the house today.

Bernard Flanagan (GV2)
On October 1, 1853 Bernard Flanagan from Aughnaloopy married Margaret Hanna from Ballykeel. A note was made in the records that this was a mixed marriage and that Bernard was now living in Maghereagh although his maternal home was Springfield, Aughnaloopy. Witnesses to the wedding were John Trimble and Hugh McLinden. In 1887, the land at GV2 had been purchased by brothers John and James Hanna (no known relations of Margaret). It does not appear that Margaret and Bernard had any children.

John Flanagan (GV2)
On November 9, 1860, John Flanagan married Margaret Doran, a daughter of James Doran from nearby Leitrim. John stated that he was a widower and that his father's name was Henry. His previous wife's name is not known. Alexander Beck and Bernard Boden were witnesses to the marriage. John died on December 27, 1875 and his property passed to his wife Margaret. It does not appear that the couple had any children. Witnesses to the Will were James Doran, John Hanna and Robert Hanna.

Both Bernard and John's marriages were recorded at the Kilkeel Civil Registrars Office. Although not confirmed, it would appear that they were brothers.

John Flanagan (GV26a and GV28)

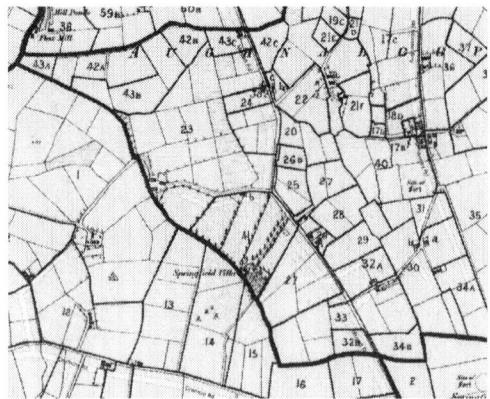

Extract from the Griffith's Valuation map showing the location of John Flanagan's farmhouse at location 26a and his adjoining land at GV28.

John Flanagan and his wife Ann McDonald lived at the property identified as number 26a on the Griffith's Valuation. Their home was located in the southern part of the townland on the Moyadd Road, opposite Springfield Villa. John Flanagan also farmed the land behind his house, noted as number 28. He also worked as a blacksmith and had a forge on the site. His home, forge and land was held by William Orr and J L Carr. No marriage record for John and Ann has been located but they are known to have had at least eight children: John (b. 1855), Margaret (b. 1857), Eliza (b. 1859), Alexander (b. 1862) who died in infancy, Alexander (b. 1864), Ann (b. 1865), Catherine (b. 1868) and Ellen (b. 1870). All the children were baptised in Massforth RC Church in Kilkeel.

A note is made on the Griffith's Revaluations that the house was extended in 1897. John died on March 6, 1898 leaving a widow and four lawful children, indicating that four of his children had predeceased him. His property noted in his Will consisted of the farm in Aughnaloopy of about 4 acres held under Orr, a heifer, a bullock and household goods.

On June 13, 1901 John's daughter Catherine Flanagan married John Cambley, a mechanic, from Brackenagh (the son of Hugh Cambley and Ann McCartan). In 1902, Catherine and John had a son Nicholas. When Nicholas was just over a year old, the family traveled out to Canada and is recorded on the border crossing documents from Canada into the United States. They arrived on August 7, 1903 aboard the SS Lake Champlain sailing from Liverpool into Quebec and then travelled on to Washington State where they settled in Bellingham. The couple had at least three more children all born in the US: Annie, Mary J and Genevieve.

John Cambley had a brother Nicholas who traveled to America aboard the SS Teutonic, arriving on November 30, 1900. He traveled with 40-year old Mary Doran, 21-year old Daniel Haughian and 21-year old James Rooney, all whom stated that they were from Kilkeel. Catherine's sister Ellen Flanagan moved out to the US in 1904, and later married Nicholas Cambley. The couple had at least two children together Hubert and Anna. Nicholas was a widower when he married Ellen, having been married previously to Sarah Burns from Brackenagh.

At the time of the 1901 census, Ann McDonald Flanagan is living in the house with her daughter Ellen.

On November 5, 1907 John and Ann's daughter Ann married John Clarke from Moneydarragh. John was a widower and had a daughter Margaret born in 1896 by his first wife. Ann moved over to Moneydarragh and is listed on the 1911 census with her mother Ann, her husband John, and his daughter Maggie.

The property at GV26a passed to Henry Quinn in 1909. The land at GV28 was taken over by James Quinn in 1897 and then passed to Henry Quinn and James Clarke in 1910 and then solely to Henry Quinn in 1911.

Chapter 27

Gonsalves Family
Special thanks to Francie and Mary Doyle, Burren, Warrenpoint

*'I must go down to the seas again, for the call of the running tide
Is a wild call and a clear call that may not be denied.'*
John Masefield.

The 1901 census documents a family with the unusual name of Gonsalves living in Aughnaloopy. There is often the assumption that families remain in an area for hundreds of years but just like today, families can move in and out of a townland and sometimes they are not listed on surviving official documents and we never know that they were there. Luckily, on this occasion, the family was documented on the 1901 census. Margaret Gonsalves was living with her four children Patrick Joseph 'Joe', Francis 'Frank', James and Margaret. Further research revealed that Margaret was also recorded on the vaccination records for Kilkeel where it was noted that she received a vaccination at three months old on July 10, 1900. The place of residence was given as Aughnaloopy and, importantly, her father was noted as Joseph Gonsalves. No marriage record could be found in Kilkeel for a Joseph Gonsalves despite trying a variety of spelling variants. Expanding the search further eventually unearthed a record for the marriage of Joseph Gonsalves to Margaret Mooney taking place in St. Vincent de Paul RC Church in Lancashire, England, on October 10, 1888. Joseph and Margaret were both living in the Toxteth Park area of Liverpool at the time of their marriage. Joseph's occupation was listed as Seaman. So it appears that some time after their marriage in 1888 and before the time of the 1901 census, the young couple returned to Kilkeel and temporarily settled in Aughnaloopy.

So why Aughnaloopy?
What would bring a young couple from Toxteth Park to move to this little townland? Further research revealed that Margaret Gonsalves nee Mooney was born on October 17, 1860 in Ballymageough, the daughter of John Mooney and Margaret Sloan. She had a brother Patrick, another brother James who married Selina Cunningham and settled in Aughrim, and a sister Mary. Therefore, the obvious answer would be that after her marriage, Margaret wished to return home to rear her family in Mourne and be closer to her parents. Joseph Gonsalves parents were originally from Portugal and as a seaman Margaret was no doubt able to convince her new husband that he would find employment working the shores around Ireland.

By the time of the 1911 census of Ireland, with Joe away at sea, Margaret had moved away from Aughnaloopy and gained employment as a ward maid in Kilkeel Workhouse on Newry Street. Their eldest son Patrick Joseph 'Joe' Gonsalves was living with William Newell and his family at Benagh and his brother James was working nearby in Lurganreagh for Ellen Magee.

On July 27, 1912 Joseph Gonsalves died at age 60 at Ballymageough, leaving his widow Margaret and their four children, Patrick Joseph 'Joe' (age 19), James (age 18), Francis (age 15) and Margaret (age 12). Joseph died in the Union Infirmary of Kilkeel from a cerebral haemorrhage, which was certified for one year. Hugh Gilleece registered the death.

Tragedy of War
With the outbreak of World War I, James left Mourne and signed up with the 19/249, 8th/9th Bn., of the Royal Irish Rifles. His brother Patrick Joseph 'Joe' worked through both

World Wars on merchantmen and had a full set of medals to prove it! Tragedy befell the Gonsalves family when on September 29, 1917 James was killed in France at age 20. He was buried in the Commonwealth War Grave in Metz-en-Couture Communal Cemetery. Joe and Margaret's son Francis was also employed as a merchant seaman throughout World War I, but he too met an untimely end, falling into a hold and was buried at sea.

A Bangor Connection

Joseph and Margaret's daughter Margaret Gonsalves married Benjamin Brierly from Bangor on November 29, 1919 and the couple had a daughter Jean born several years later. The photograph on the right, shows Margaret with her granddaughter Jean Brierly.

One advantage of tracing an unusual name is that it did not take long before contact was made with a living descendant of the Gonsalves family. The mother of Francis 'Francie' Doyle who lives in Burren near Warrenpoint was Mary Elizabeth Gonsalves. Mary Elizabeth was the eldest daughter of Patrick Joseph 'Joe' Gonsalves and his wife Mary Cunningham, who were married in Massforth Church on May 10, 1917. Francie's father was Patrick 'James' Doyle of Dunnaval, Kilkeel.

Francie Doyle remembers visiting Margaret Gonsalves and relates that she was quite a character:

> *'She lived to well over 100 and could drink Guinness with any man - and she smoked a clay pipe.'*

Joe Gonsalves sailed the Seven Seas

Patrick Joseph 'Joe' Gonsalves ID photograph

Francie was able to provide additional information including family photographs and an article on his grandfather Patrick Joseph 'Joe' Gonsalves that was printed in the Rathfriland Outlook, June 25, 1965. Joe died less than a year after the article appeared on June 6, 1966.

The article details the wonderful and varied life of Patrick Joseph 'Joe' Gonsalves as he literally sailed the seven seas. It appears that Patrick Joseph 'Joe' was in fact born in Ballymageough near what was known as Russell's School. His birth certificate states that his father Joseph was a Sea Captain and that he was born in Portugal. Patrick Joseph 'Joe' attended school with his siblings at Dunnavan, at the foot of Doran's Hill. He confesses that his biggest sin as a young boy was his love of tobacco that he smoked in clay pipes bought from Mrs. Manus's shop in Newry Street.

When he was 12-years old, Patrick Joseph 'Joe' followed his father to sea. He obtained his first employment working as a cook on the lugger "Mermaid" skippered by John Maginnis of Derryogue. After a year, he graduated to a seaman's post on the lugger, 'Ida Shannon', owned by Robert Green. Patrick Joseph 'Joe' soon moved on to working the schooners exporting granite, potatoes and scrap iron and then returning to Mourne with flour, timber and coal.

Patrick Joseph 'Joe' shared some wonderful details of his life at sea:

> 'Each Monday and Tuesday were good grub days for there was steak and this, along with potatoes and onions kept a man going. The next couple of days were alright too with broth and potatoes. At the heal of the week, it was herring and potatoes and there was always a kettle of tea on the stove.'

Crew Duff

Patrick Joseph 'Joe' also shared his fondness for crew duff – a crumbed loaf with shortening rubbed in along with brown sugar, raisins and currants, made into stiff dough and boiled for three hours.

> 'There was nothing dainty about the pudding but it was filling and sustaining in those days before such things as 'elevenses' with cream buns and tinned fruit for dessert on board our modern Mourne fishing boats.'

Patrick Joseph 'Joe' soon moved on to working the schooners; exporting granite, potatoes and scrap iron and then returning to Mourne with flour, timber and coal. This was a hard existence, controlled by the whims of the weather. A week's work often consisted of three consecutive crossings between Kilkeel and North Wales, with little time to rest. Like many an old salt Patrick Joseph 'Joe' had many tales to tell about his life at sea. He tells of one jam that he got caught up in aboard the schooner 'Catherine' when bound for Irvine in Ayrshire to pick up coal.

> 'Again, the skipper and his henchmen imbibed too freely and sold everything loose aboard, including ropes and bolts of canvas.'

Luckily for Patrick Joseph 'Joe', his friend Jimsey Maginnis was in port with his vessel 'Alpha' and was able to provide some food to the crew but as Patrick Joseph 'Joe' colourfully recalls there was not enough rope aboard *'to tether a goat'* and they had to make fast with the log line.

The Post-War Years

Following the War, some normality returned to the Gonsalves family and on May 10, 1917 Margaret's surviving son Patrick Joseph 'Joe' married Mary Cunningham from Carginagh. The marriage was blessed with three daughters, Mary Elizabeth, Ann and Eileen and three sons, James Joseph, Frank and John, ensuring that the Gonsalves name would continue for another generation in Mourne.

'Joe' on a trip to Liverpool.

After World War II, Patrick Joseph 'Joe' Gonsalves joined the Newry firm of Fishers, working the coastline of Ireland, Scotland, France and the Netherlands. He gathered several mementoes on his travels, including buffalo horns from Demerara, a model brig from Finland, and a ship carved from a Dutch clog. Joe recalled that his best mementoes were the sights he saw, such as the black pigs running wild on the coast of the Gulf of Mexico and the people he met, especially the inevitable Irishmen that turned up in the most unexpected places.

Patrick Joseph 'Joe' Gonsalves ended his working days as they had begun – working in the position as cook - in the hope that the warmth of the galley would ease the inevitable aches and pains that resulted from his hard working life on the high seas.

The 1965 Rathfriland Outlook closes by describing Patrick Joseph 'Joe' Gonsalves as *'cheerful...and the very best of company'*, traits that his grandson Francie Doyle has obviously inherited.

Chapter 28

Hagan Family

Special thanks to Andrea Picton, Durham, England and Bill Clarke, Surrey, England.

Variants of the name include Hagen, O'Hagan and O'Hagen.

William Hagan
The name Hagan first appears in the 1830 Tithes Applotment Book for Aughnaloopy with the listing of William Hagan, who is responsible for paying tithes on 3 acres of land in the townland. William's wife is not known but he had at least one daughter Margaret born c. 1830.

Margaret Hagan and John Wilson (GV8b and GV9)
William's daughter Margaret married John Wilson at the Meeting House Lane Presbyterian Church in Kilkeel on January 11, 1856. John Wilson was a neighbour from Aughnaloopy and the son of Alexander Wilson, although there is speculation that the Wilson family may have originated from Drumgath. Sarah Little was witness to the marriage. John and Margaret had at least three children: Mary Margaret baptised on December 17, 1861, Teresa born on December 26, 1865 and Ellen born on April 30, 1868. Teresa is listed on the Kilkeel Board of Guardian's Vaccination records recording her vaccination on June 5, 1866 when her age is given as 6 months. Margaret Hagan Wilson and her family settled at the property identified as number 8b and 9 on the Griffith's Valuation. By 1881, the property had passed to the Hanna family.

Nicholas Hagan and Nancy Wilson
Also living in Aughnaloopy in the mid-nineteenth century was Nicholas Hagan. He was of similar age to William and likely a brother. Nicholas had three known surviving children: Samuel, John and Ann. Although the mothers name is not recorded for any of Nicholas's children, it appears that their mother may have been Nancy Wilson (a daughter of Alexander Wilson from Aughnaloopy and a sister of John Wilson who was married to Margaret Hagan). Nicholas died prior to 1857 leaving a widow and three young children.

On June 11, 1857, Nancy, his widow, married John Skillen a bachelor of Glenloughan. Nancy and John Skillen do not appear to have had any children together. John is listed on the Griffith's Valuation holding a house, office and land at the site identified as number 7. The house was pulled down in 1872 and Alexander Wilson (likely Nancy's brother) farmed the land there until 1874 when it passed to Alexander Beck (likely Nancy's nephew – the son of James Beck and Margaret Wilson). The fact that the homestead stayed in the Wilson side of the family would indicate that this was Wilson property prior to the time of the Griffith's Valuation and that John Skillen moved into the home of Nancy Wilson Hagan after their marriage in 1857.

Samuel Hagan
Samuel was baptised on March 20, 1843. Sadly, he must have died during childhood because another Samuel is listed in the Meeting House Lane Presbyterian Church records with a birth date of October 12, 1854 and baptism date of July 1855. The mother's name appears to have been incorrectly noted as Mary Wilson. Unfortunately no further information is known about his life.

John Hagan
John was born c.1846 and worked as a labourer in Kilkeel. On May 18, 1874 he married Susan(na) Fogg who was living in Aughrim at the time. Susan Fogg was born on May

29, 1837 and baptised at St. Anthony's Church in Liverpool on August 6, 1837. Her father was James Fogg and her mother Catherine Twist. In 1851, Susanna was living on Howard Street in Liverpool with her sister Ann and her mother who kept a boarding house. The house was situated in the dockyard area of Liverpool and may have provided lodging to the many people from Kilkeel who worked in the area.

An Earlier Kilkeel Connection

Susan's connection to Kilkeel began with her earlier marriage to John Wilson from Aughrim, which took place at Mourne Presbyterian Church on February 18, 1856. John Wilson was born c.1825 and was the son of Archibald Wilson and Isabella Kernaghan. At the time of the 1861 UK census, Susan and her first husband John Wilson had returned to Liverpool and are living with their son Archibald and Susan's mother Catherine. John Wilson was employed as a dock labourer. The couple had six more children together, Isabel who died in infancy, John, Samuel, Sarah, William and Thomas. The family retained close ties with Ireland and when John took ill they returned to the Wilson family home in Kilkeel. John Wilson died in Aughrim from bronchitis on February 12, 1873 when he was just 48-years old. Susan was left with a young family and no means of support. It is not surprising that she married shortly after John's death. Her marriage to John Hagan took place at Mourne Presbyterian Church and Susan gave her place of residence as Aughrim. John Hagan was employed as a labourer and was living in Drummond at the time. Witnesses to the marriage were Samuel Wilson and May Duncan.

John Hagan and Susan Fogg had two known children, Annie and Maggie. Annie married John McMeekin in Glasgow on March 9, 1909; she remained in Scotland until her death in 1947. Their daughter Maggie is listed with her parents on the 1901 census. The family is living in Ballymageough with a cousin, 5-month old Hector Hamilton. By 1911, the family had expanded. Margaret was married to Robert Cassidy and was living with her parents and her 2-year old son John. Hector was also still with the family. Robert was working as a blacksmith and John was working as a labourer. Susan Fogg Hagan died in 1912.

Ann 'Nancy' Hagan and William Teggarty

Nicholas had a daughter Ann 'Nancy' Hagan who was baptized on February 23, 1851 at the Meeting House Lane Presbyterian Church. Nancy married William Teggarty on November 4, 1873 in Kilkeel Church of Ireland Church in Kilkeel. William was the son of Andrew Teggarty and Margaret Curren from Moneydarragh Beg and at the time of their marriage Nancy stated that she was resident in nearby Ballykeel. William and Ann 'Nancy' Teggarty had five children: William (b. 1877), David (b. 1879), Francis 'Frank' (b. 1882), Samuel James (b. 1885) and Adelaide (b. 1888). Nancy's husband William died in 1900, age 54-years old.

William and Nancy's son William married Mary Galbraith in 1904 in Warrenpoint and the couple had at least six children: Maud, Ann Elizabeth, William, John, David and Adelaide. They are listed on the 1911 census at Greencastle Street, Kilkeel, with four of their children: Ann Elizabeth, John, David and Adelaide Jane. Their children Maud and William were living nearby with their grandmother Ann Teggarty and uncles David, Frank and Samuel. The Teggarty brothers William, Frank and Samuel were all involved in the Kilkeel fishing industry.

In March 1900 William Teggarty enlisted in the Imperial Yeomanry and served in South Africa. He was invalided in December 1901 and declared medically unfit in February 1902. On his return to Ireland he was discharged from the Yeomanry. The Imperial Yeomanry was officially disbanded in 1908. William answered the call to service during World War I and travelled to Newry where he enlisted in the 13th Royal Irish Rifles. He wrote a letter to his daughter Maud in February 1916 from France after returning from home leave. Tragically, on July 1, 1916 he was killed on the battlefields of France during the Battle of the Somme. Private William Teggarty was reported missing on July 1, 1916 but was not confirmed dead until 1923 when his corpse was found. William's grandson Bill Clarke has a copy of the letter sent to his mother and has kindly agreed to share it in this publication.

William Teggarty (centre), taken in South Africa. William enlisted in the Imperial Yeomanry in 1900 and served until 1902.

Photograph reproduced with the permission of Bill Clarke.

'I received the original letter sent to my mother by her Father (William Teggarty) from France in February 1916. She would have been 11 at the time. In the letter he talks about coming home in July and taking the family to the *twelfth celebrations*. Unfortunately he was killed on the 1st July 1916. This proved quite emotional at first but very soon became just another fact from the past.'

Bill Clarke.

Catherine Hagan and John Fitzpatrick

Catherine Hagan married John Fitzpatrick on January 24, 1875 at Massforth RC Church in Kilkeel. Witnesses to the marriage were P. Fitzpatrick and Ann Rogers. Aughnaloopy is noted in the record but whether this refers to Catherine or John's place of residence is unknown. The name of the parents has not been noted. Catherine and John had moved away from Aughnaloopy prior to the 1901 census.

Catherine Hagan and George Johnson (GV36b)

Catherine married Richard Johnson's son George prior to 1846. The couple had a daughter Catherine 'Kate' who was born at number GV36b and baptised at Massforth RC Church on September 202, 1846. On February 6, 1883, Kate married John Cunningham from Magheramurphy. Bridget Johnson was a witness to the marriage. By the time of the 1901 census, John and Kate have five children living with them at the Johnson homestead in Aughnaloopy: Thomas (b. 1884), John (b. 1886), Patrick (b. 1887) and Joseph (b. 1892). From a letter written by Ellen Doran to her nephew John, living in Canada, in 1923, we learn that Thomas, John and Patrick all moved out to Montana and that Joseph remained at home unmarried.

> *May 3 1923*
>
> *Dear Nephew*
>
> *……………..Johnney Cunningham is dead and Kate to both the 3 oldest boys are out in Mounttana (sic) and the youngest boy is liven alone like myself. ………..*
> *Dear friend please write a few lines soon and let me know how you are and how yous are all no more at present from your Aunt Ellen Doran*

13/2/1910
Sunday

My Dear Maud
just the time to write till
all well and doing
all you are told Be
good to all the Rest of
your Brothers & sisters
Do what your mother
tell you I was sorry
did not Ill you that
Sunday I came away
as you went to School

But no matter I will
tell you all about the
12 of July and we
will go to the field no
no more good your
loving father

JB

Chapter 29

Hamilton, Carvill and Murphy

Special thanks to Deirdre McEvoy, Dublin, Ireland for her research into the Hamilton and Carvill families and to Bill Neal, Melbourne, Australia for his research into the Poor Clares.

James Hamilton Esq. of Springfield

James Hamilton Esq., a wealthy Catholic merchant in Kilkeel, resided in Springfield Villa, Aughnaloopy in the early 1850s. He died in Springfield Villa in Aughnaloopy on October 11, 1856 and the house was then rented to Rev. George Nesbitt (according to Slater's Directory for Kilkeel). Little is known about James Hamilton but there is reference to him in an article in the Freeman's Journal and Daily Commercial Advertiser (Dublin, Ireland), Tuesday, June 14, 1853, entitled 'Catholics of Ireland', where he attended a large gathering of the major Catholics in Ireland in protest against '...the invasion of nunneries.' He is buried in Massforth cemetery in Kilkeel along with his daughter Jane. His wife is possibly buried there too but she is not named on the headstone.

It is not known who his wife was, but James Hamilton had at least four daughters, Margaret, Jane, Ann, and Mary Ann and there is some conjecture of a daughter Rose. If he had any sons, they may have died young, as there is no mention of them in any surviving records. There is speculation that he may have had a son George who immigrated to America but this cannot be confirmed. There may also have been a son John, but again there is no evidence that he survived to adulthood.

Margaret Hamilton and Francis Carvill

James's eldest daughter Margaret Hamilton was born c.1807. In September 1829, she married Francis Carvill, a wealthy Catholic merchant (timber and iron merchant and shipbuilder) who lived in Newry but who was reputedly from Mourne. It is thought that she married in Kilkeel as her marriage is not registered in Newry. There is an application for a marriage license in their names in the Newry parish records taken out on September 19, 1829.

Margaret and Francis Carvill had at least ten children who were all baptised in Newry, however the family actually lived in Kilbroney parish, in Moygannon townland. Before her death Margaret lived at Merchants Quay in Newry but died in Killowen, Kilbroney parish. Her sons lived in Benvenue on the Hilltown Road in Rostrevor throughout the 1870s and 1880s. Margaret died in Killowen, Rostrevor on December 30, 1891.

James Lewis Carvill

Margaret's eldest son, James Lewis Carvill, was baptised in Newry on September 7, 1830. It was James who took over the family's business after his father's death in Newry in 1854. Despite taking on such responsibilities at such a young age he was extremely successful in business. In 1859 he was appointed French Vice Consul for the ports of Newry, Dundalk and Drogheda. Then in January 1862 he was appointed to the Commission of the Peace, JP for the counties of Down and Armagh.

James Lewis Carvill appears to have been a beneficiary of his grandfather James Hamilton's Will and up to his death owned Springfield Villa in Aughnaloopy along with its surrounding acres. James Lewis died suddenly, unmarried, at just 34-years old in October 1864. On his death, the house and farms were passed on to another grandchild of James Hamilton, namely James Murphy, the eldest son of Mary Ann Hamilton and John Murphy.

John, Francis and William Carvill

Margaret Hamilton and Francis Carvill had three other sons, John, Francis and William Hamilton. The first two died as infants and William Hamilton died, aged 29 in March 1865, in the family home in Rostrevor.

Patrick George Hamilton 'PGH' Carvill

Mr. P. G. Carvill.

The fifth son, Patrick George Hamilton 'PGH' Carvill was baptised on January 25, 1839. He married Frances Mary 'Fanny' Gartlan (daughter of a wealthy Catholic merchant from Monalty, near Carrickmacross) in Killanny parish on September 21, 1869. He was a JP for Counties Down and Armagh and was High Sheriff for County Armagh in 1878. PGH matriculated at the London University and was called to the English Bar in 1888. He was also involved in the family business. Following his marriage to Fanny Gartlan, he moved to Waterloo in Lancashire, England and is listed on the 1871 census as a Magistrate, Ship Owner and Timber Merchant. By the time of the 1881 census, PGH had moved to 23 Park Crescent, Marylebone, London and the couple now had four children: Francis Ignatius, Patrick George, Thomas and Christina Maria. They also employed four staff: Marie Badouard, (a nurse from St. Malo, France), Clara Futter (a cook from Norfolk), Kate Gounoude (a housemaid from Carrickmacross), Mary Grimes (a kitchenmaid also from Carrickmacross) and Patrick Kerney (a butler from Aughnacloy). PGH enjoyed travel and in 1897 took an extended tour visiting America, Australia and New Zealand. PGH became a Member of Parliament for Newry (Nationalist party but anti-Parnellite) from 1892 to 1906. He died in Roquebrune, France on January 10, 1924.

Mary Ann 'Minnie' Carvill

Margaret Hamilton and Francis Carvill's eldest daughter Mary Ann 'Minnie' Carvill, was baptised on January 28, 1841. She entered the Poor Clare convent in Newry in 1859 aged 18 years. Three years later she took her vow of Profession, being known in religion as Sister Mary Clare. She died July 26, 1878 after a long illness and is interred in the vault in the Convent Cemetery located on the High Street in Newry.

> *'She was a very prayerful Religious and a zealous teacher of the Faith.'*

Margaret Carvill

The couple's next two daughters, both called Margaret, died as infants.

Joseph Thomas Carvill

Their sixth son, Joseph Thomas Carvill, baptised on December 26, 1849, joined the family business and married Mary Margaret 'Maggie' Ryan of Mount Prospect, Newport, Tipperary in Dublin on June 19, 1870. The marriage took place at the Church of Saint Saviour, on Dominick Street and was officiated by the Rt. Rev. Dr. Leahy, Lord Bishop of Dromore, assisted by Rev. Thomas H. O'Brien. Joseph Thomas and Margaret had three children, Mary Margaret Josephine (b. 1872), Catherine Ann (b. 1873) and Francis Joseph (b. March 1875). Catherine Ann died in December 1875 when she was 2-years old. Joseph Thomas died in Corfu, Crete on May 3, 1876, at just 26-years old. His wife died soon after him in February 1879 and their two surviving children were raised by their maternal grandmother.

John Carvill

The seventh son, John Carvill, was baptised April 20, 1854, two months after the death of his father. He also joined the family firm but after the shipbuilding company collapsed in 1883, he took over the timber yards in Newry. He married Elizabeth Martin (1858-1936) on February 10, 1887. Elizabeth (b. 1858) was the seventh and youngest daughter of Robert Martin, Esq. of Kilbroney (1814-1858) and his wife Millicent Millar (1824-1858). She was the niece of 'Honest' John Martin of Rostrevor. John and Elizabeth had one daughter Ruth Martin Carvill. John was an established figure in the Newry merchant community and, like his father, before him, was involved in the Northern Ireland railroad. He was also involved in the Newry Harbour Trust, the Carlingford Lough Commissioners and the Newry Chamber of Commerce. He died on January 25, 1927 in his home on Downshire Road, Newry.

Mary Anne Hamilton and John Murphy

James Hamilton's second daughter, Mary Anne married John Murphy, an architect from Belfast (who may also have practiced in Newry), in Massforth RC Church in Kilkeel on September 5, 1841. John and Mary Ann Hamilton Murphy had three children, James, John and Mary Anne 'Minnie'. James Murphy appeared to inherit the property known as 'Springfield' and the surrounding farms from his cousin, James Lewis Carvill. James and John Murphy remained single, but their sister Minnie married James Hamilton Morgan, a merchant from Kilkeel on January 24, 1878. Mary Anne Morgan had six children: James Joseph (who died in childhood), Mary Josephine 'Geneva' (who married Edward Sloan), Gertrude (who joined the Faithful Companions of Jesus), John Patrick, Joseph Hamilton (who married Ellen Josephine 'Nellie' Mageean), and James Francis.

Ann Hamilton

James Hamilton's daughter, Ann joined the Poor Clare Convent in Newry on July 10, 1850 and received her habit January 7, 1851 being known in religion as Sister Gertrude. She took the vow of Profession on January 12, 1853. She spent time with the Sisters of St. Clare at the convent at Keady in September 1877 and returned to Newry on February 25, 1879. Sister Gertrude died August 17, 1899 '....*of decline of nature a Bronchial cold.*' and is interred in the New Cemetery.

> *'The Abbess announced to the Community that this was an exceptional case and would not be repeated in the future.'*

Jane Hamilton

James Hamilton's daughter Jane died at the young age of 21 on December 6, 1839. Her grave is located in Ballymageough cemetery, stone raised by her father, James Hamilton of Kilkeel. Next to her grave lies a stone: '*Sacred to the memory of Mary Ann Hamilton of Aughnaloopy who departed this life on 09 Mar 1859 aged 35 years.*' It is not known who this Mary Ann Hamilton is.

Rose Hamilton

It has not been confirmed but it is possible that Rose Hamilton who married James Sloan of Maghereagh was a daughter or niece of James Hamilton. The couple were married in Lower Mourne on February 4, 1842. The couple had at least ten children all baptised in Kilkeel but the family eventually moved away from the area to Belfast.

By the time of the 1901 census, the names Hamilton, Carvill and Murphy no longer exist in Aughnaloopy townland. The property 'Springfield' originally held by James Murphy had passed on to the Quinn family.

Macclesfield, in the county of Chester, Chartered Accountant, the Trustee under the liquidation, or in default thereof they will be excluded from the benefit of the Dividend proposed to be declared.—Dated this 27th day of April, 1883.
GEO. IBESON, Trustee.

The Bankruptcy Act, 1869.
In the County Court of Devonshire, holden at Exeter.
In the Matter of a Special Resolution for Liquidation by Arrangement of the affairs of Francis Edward King, of No. 22, Fore-street, Tiverton, in the county of Devon, Tobacconist.

THE creditors of the above-named Francis Edward King who have not already proved their debts, are required, on or before the 17th day of May, 1883, to send their names and addresses, and the particulars of their debts or claims, to me, the undersigned, William Webster, of Tiverton aforesaid, Accountant, the Trustee under the liquidation, or in default thereof they will be excluded from the benefit of the Dividend proposed to be declared.—Dated this 27th day of April, 1883.
WM. WEBSTER, Trustee.

The Bankruptcy Act, 1869.
In the London Bankruptcy Court.
In the Matter of a Special Resolution for Liquidation by Arrangement of the affairs of Patrick George Carvill and George McKean, carrying on business in copartnership together, and lately, but not now, with George Thomas Carvill and also with William Muirhead Simpson, as Merchants and Ship Owners, at 126, Gresham House, Old Broad-street, in the city of London, and lately at 4, Bishopsgate-street Within, in the said city of London, and at 13, Leadenhall-street, in the said city, also now or lately at 26, Chapel-street, and formerly at 3, Water-street, Liverpool, in the county of Lancashire, and at Merchants'-quay, Newry, in the county of Armagh, Ireland, under the style or firm of Francis Carvill and Son, also at St. John, New Brunswick, in the Dominion of Canada, under the style or firm of Carvill, McKean and Co., also in copartnership with Isaac Henry Mathers, at Pickford and Black's Wharf, Halifax, Nova Scotia, under the style of Isaac Henry Mathers, also in copartnership with John Mackenzie and James Gilbertson, at Post Office Box 1,863, San Francisco, under the style of Mackenzie and Gilbertson, also in copartnership with Thomas Green Barr and William Carvill, at St. Paul's-street, Montreal, in the said Dominion of Canada, under the style of Carvill, Barr, and Co., the said Patrick George Carvill also carrying on business at 22, Bridge-street, Sydney, New South Wales, in copartnership with John Carvill and John Barr Johnson, under the style of Barr, Johnson, and Co., also in copartnership with Joseph Connor, at 32, Union-street, Birmingham, in the county of Warwick, and at 155, Fenchurch-street, in the said city of London, under the style of Connor and Co., also in copartnership with Robert Nairn, at the London and North Western Bank-buildings, Castle-street, Bristol, in the county of Gloucester, under the style of R. and P. Nairn, also in copartnership with James Gilbertson, at 27, Leadenhall-street, in the said city of London, under the style of Gilbertson Brothers, also in copartnership with Joseph Crawley, at Forest Brook, Rostrevor, in the county of Down, Ireland, under the style of the Forest Brook Linen Company, also in copartnership with Archibald Lindegreen, at 154, Upper Thames-street, in the said city of London, under the style of A. Lindegreen and Co., also in copartnership with Richard Wakeham, at 42, Harrington-street, Liverpool, in the county of Lancashire, under the style of Richard Wakeham and Co., also in copartnership with William Peacop, at 19, Laurence Pountney-lane, in the said city of London, under the style of William Peacop and Co., also lately, but not now, in copartnership with John Carvill, at Newry aforesaid, under the style of Carvill Brothers, the said Patrick George Carvill now residing at 23, Park-crescent, in the county of Middlesex, and lately at Benvenue, Rostrevor, in the county of Down aforesaid, and the said George McKean at Saint John, New Brunswick aforesaid.

ALFRED GLIDDON, Cashier to the Capital and Counties Bank, of 39, Threadneedle-street, in the city of London, has been appointed trustee of the property of the debtors. All persons having in their possession any of the effects of the debtors must deliver them to the trustee, and all debts due to the debtors, must be paid to the trustee. Creditors who have not yet proved their debts, must forward their proofs of debts to the trustee.—Dated this 23rd day of April, 1883.

The Bankruptcy Act, 1869.
In the London Bankruptcy Court.
In the Matter of a Special Resolution for Liquidation by Arrangement of the affairs of Patrick George Carvill and George McKean, carrying on business in copartnership together, and lately, but not now, with George Thomas Carvill and also with William Muirhead Simpson, as Merchants and Ship Owners, at 126, Gresham House, Old Broad-street, in the city of London, and lately at 4, Bishopsgate-street Within, in the said city of London, and at 13, Leadenhall-street, in the said city, also now or lately at 26, Chapel-street, and formerly at 3, Water-street, Liverpool, in the county of Lancashire, and at Merchants'-quay, Newry, in the county of Armagh, Ireland, under the style or firm of Francis Carvill and Son, also at St. John, New Brunswick, in the Dominion of Canada, under the style or firm of Carvill, McKean, and Co., also in copartnership with Isaac Henry Mathers, at Pickford and Black's Wharf, Halifax, Nova Scotia, under the style of Isaac Henry Mathers, also in copartnership with John Mackenzie and James Gilbertson, at Post Office Box 1,863, San Francisco, under the style of Mackenzie and Gilbertson, also in copartnership with Thomas Green Barr and William Carvill, at St. Paul's-street, Montreal, in the said Dominion of Canada, under the style of Carvill, Barr, and Co., the said Patrick George Carvill also carrying on business at 22, Bridge-street, Sydney, New South Wales, in copartnership with John Carvill and John Barr Johnson, under the style of Barr, Johnson, and Co., also in copartnership with Joseph Connor, at 32, Union-street, Birmingham, in the county of Warwick, and at 155, Fenchurch-street, in the said city of London, under the style of Connor and Co., also in copartnership with Robert Nairn, at the London and North Western Bank-buildings, Castle-street, Bristol, in the county of Gloucester, under the style of R. and P. Nairn, also in copartnership with James Gilbertson, at 27, Leadenhall-street, in the said city of London, under the style of Gilbertson Brothers, also in copartnership with Joseph Crawley, at Forest Brook, Rostrevor, in the county of Down, Ireland, under the style of the Forest Brook Linen Company, also in copartnership with Archibald Lindegreen, at 154, Upper Thames-street, in the said city of London, under the style of A. Lindegreen and Co., also in copartnership with Richard Wakeham, at 42, Harrington-street, Liverpool, in the county of Lancashire, under the style of Richard Wakeham and Co., also in copartnership with William Peacop, at 19, Laurence Pountney-lane, in the said city of London, under the style of William Peacop and Co., also lately, but not now, in copartnership with John Carvill, at Newry aforesaid, under the style of Carvill Brothers, the said Patrick George Carvill now residing at 23, Park-crescent, in the county of Middlesex, and lately at Benvenue, Rostrevor, in the county of Down aforesaid, and the said George McKean at Saint John, New Brunswick aforesaid.

ALFRED GLIDDON, Cashier to the Capital and Counties Bank Limited, of 39, Threadneedle-street, in the city of London, has been appointed Trustee of the separate estate of Patrick George Carvill. All persons having in their possession any effects of the debtor must deliver them to the trustee, and all debts due to the debtor must be paid to the trustee. Creditors who have not yet proved their debts must forward their proofs of debts to the trustee.—Dated this 26th day of April, 1883.

The Bankruptcy Act, 1869.
In the London Bankruptcy Court.
In the Matter of Proceedings for Liquidation by Arrangement or Composition with Creditors, instituted by Thomas Arkell, of 42, Gilbert-street, Oxford-street, 7, Campsbourne-terrace, Hornsey, and 7, Pimlico-road, Pimlico, all in the county of Middlesex, Boot and Shoe Manufacturer, and residing at 7, Pimlico-road aforesaid.

LOUIS MICHAEL BERGTHEIL, of 3, West-street, Finsbury-circus, in the city of London, Chartered Accountant, has been appointed Trustee of the property of the debtor. All persons having in their possession any of the effects of the debtor must deliver them to the trustee, and all debts due to the debtor must be paid to the trustee. Creditors who have not yet proved their debts must forward their proofs of debts to the trustee.—Dated this 24th day of April, 1883.

The Bankruptcy Act, 1869.
In the London Bankruptcy Court.
In the Matter of Proceedings for Liquidation by Arrangement or Composition with Creditors, instituted by Charles Middlebrook, of 121, High-street, Kingsland, in the county of Middlesex, Tobacconist and Dealer in British and Foreign Cigars.

THOMAS STEPHEN EVANS, of 5 and 6, Bucklersbury, in the city of London, Chartered Accountant, has been appointed Trustee of the property of the debtor. All persons having in their possession any of the effects of the debtor must deliver them to the trustee, and all debts due to the debtor must be paid to the trustee. Creditors

This document reveals some of the business projects that were owned or managed by Patrick George Carvill. The ship building industry collapsed c.1883.

Chapter 30

Hanna Family

Special thanks to Maynard Hanna for his help researching this family.

Despite sharing Scottish origins, there is no known connection between the Hanna family of Aughnaloopy and the Hanna families in neighbouring Aughnahorey.

James Hanna 'The Reed' (GV4 & 5)

James Hanna, the reedmaker has land noted on the Griffith's Valuation at site numbers 4 and 5. The property at number 5 appears to be where the family home was situated. His land bordered Aughnahorey in the North West section of Aughnaloopy and the land that it is connected to, is held by James Hanna 'Wee'.

Despite sharing Scottish origins, there is no known connection between the Hanna family of Aughnaloopy and the Hanna families in neighbouring Aughnahorey.

Maynard Hanna, a direct descendant of James Hanna from Aughnaloopy, has researched his ancestors and discovered that his third Great Grandfather James Hanna 'The Reed' came to Mourne in the early 1800's from either the Rathfriland or Dromore areas of County Down. The designation of 'The Reed' was from his occupation as a reedmaker in the Linen Industry. This was to distinguish him from the many Hanna families already living in the area including: 'The Hannas of the Far Hill', 'Hannas of the Glen', 'The Leitrim Hannas', 'The Close Hannas' and 'The Poor Rate Hannas'. In addition to his land at Aughnaloopy, 'The Reed' also had a house, office and 15 acres of land at nearby Ballinran (identified as number 15 on the Griffith's Valuation) and some mountain pastureland in Ballinran Upper.

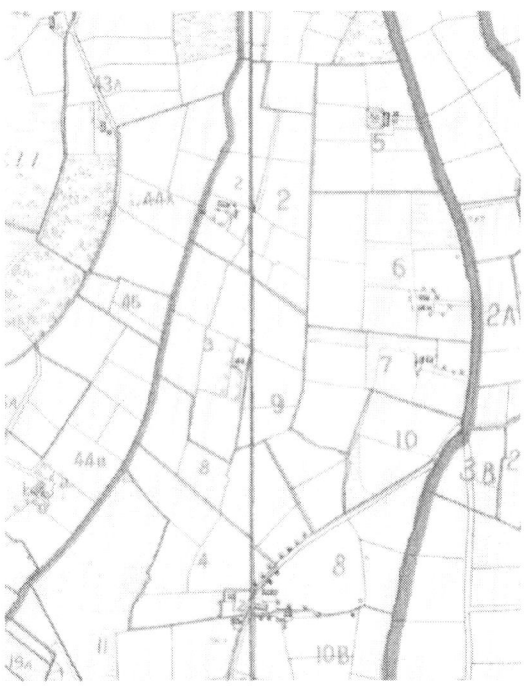

Extract from the Griffith's Valuation map of 1864 showing the location of Reed Hanna properties, marked as 4 and 5 in Aughnaloopy townland.

Reed Hanna had two known sons: James (c.1829) and John (c.1832). According to family history, the eldest son James went to America while the younger son John stayed at home and tended to the family reed farm. Upon their father's death c.1867, James returned home to find that the entire farm had been left to him and nothing at all to his brother John. Pressure was applied from the Elders of Mourne Presbyterian Church to apply some degree of fairness to this situation and as a solution James agreed to delete some acreage and give it to his younger brother John.

The situation explains the details recorded on the Griffiths Revaluations. Reed Hanna's property passes to *'The Reps. of James Hanna'* in 1867. A new house is noted as being built on the site in 1891 although the land is still under the control of 'The Reps. of James Hanna'. In 1894, the property passes to 'John & James Hanna' and so it looks as if this is when the legal situation was finally resolved legally. Until 1894 the Hanna property identified as number 4 and 5 on the Griffith's Valuation was leased from James Moore.

From 1894 it was held 'in fee', i.e. was owned by the Hanna brothers. The later change is likely a consequence of the 1891 Irish land Act.

James Hanna

After returning from America and resolving the issues concerning the family estate, James settled on the Hanna property in Ballinran townland. He remained single and did not have any children. Perhaps as a consequence of the difficulties surrounding his father's legacy, James prepared a very detailed Will on March 18, 1896. This was eleven years before his actual death. He appointed his brother John and his nephew John as executors of his estate. He left the home that he lived in to his nephew John as well as the mountain land in Upper Ballinran, noting that these were owned jointly with his brother John (his nephew's father). His nephew John also inherited his uncle's share in Mills Farm, Wilsons Farm (GV8), the Flanagan farm (GV2), and the farm that his nephew John was presently living in at Aughnaloopy. When James died on August 19, 1907, his effects were valued at over 263 pounds. The site at Ballinran is still owned by a direct descendant of the Hanna family and has been renovated in recent years.

John Hanna and Ellen Jane Annett

Reed Hanna's younger son John married Ellen Jane Annett on May 2, 1861 at Mourne Presbyterian Church. Ellen was the daughter of Alexander Annett and Mary Hutchinson from Moyadd. Ellen's brother John Annett and her sister Maria's husband Thomas Beck were witnesses to the marriage. John states his place of residence at the time of his marriage as Ballinran and it is likely that it was in Ballinran townland that the couple began their married life together, with Reed Hanna occupying the site in Aughnaloopy. The fact that James Hanna was not noted as a witness to the marriage may indicate that he was in America at this time. John eventually built a home on his father's land in Aughnaloopy. John and Ellen Jane had at least three children: James (c.1862) who married Sarah Ann McKnight, John (b. 1866) who married Isabella Scott and Mary Jane (b. 1873) who married Thomas McKee. After John died Ellen went to live with her son John and his family in Ballinran.

The Children of John Hanna and Ellen Jane Annett

James Hanna and Sarah Ann 'Annie' McKnight

John's son James is noted on the 1901 census as living in Aughnaloopy. James married Sarah Ann "Annie" McKnight on January 28, 1890 at Drumlee Presbyterian Church. Sarah was the daughter of John McKnight from Fofanny. The young couple moved into a new home built on land originally held on lease by James's Grandfather 'Reed' Hanna. The couple had five children living at home in 1901: Mary Ellen (c.1891), Jane "Jennie" (b. 1893), James (b. 1896), John (c.1902) and Annie (c.1904). A daughter Annie had died when she was 4-years old in December 1902.

In February 1906, James left Ireland, travelling on the SS Umbria en route to Boston. He arrived in New York on February 19, 1906 and stated that he was going to stay with Jane McKnight on Chestnut Hill in Boston. Jane was Annie McKnight's sister and she had moved out to America in March 1899. Sarah Ann did not follow her husband out to Boston and at the time of the 1911 census, she was still in Aughnaloopy with three of her children: James, John and Annie. James worked for many years in America, before finally returning home to Aughnaloopy. At the time of the 1930 US Federal census, James is lodging at a house on Hale Street, Essex, Massachusetts that was managed by a Frenchman Mussey Marcel and his Swiss wife Margaret. Also lodging in the house were Hugh and Bennett Daugherty and Richard Duffey. James gives his occupation as a teamster for construction workers. The other men all state that they were construction labourers. James gives his age as 68 years. James eventually returns to his family in Ireland in 1939. He appears on a UK Incoming Passenger List for the SS Luconia, part of the Cunard White Star Line. The ship sailed from Boston arriving in Liverpool, England on June 19, 1939. James is listed as being 77-years old and having the occupation of a 'teamster'. James died in Ireland and is buried in the Mourne Presbyterian Church burial grounds. His wife Sarah is buried in the McKnight family grave in Drumlee. Sarah's grandson James (son of James Hanna and Agnes Anderson) used to travel to Drumlee regularly to repaint the gold lettering on the family gravestone every four years or so. He maintained a close relationship with the McKnight side of the family.

Mary Ellen Hanna
James and Sarah Ann's daughter Mary Ellen Hanna left Aughnaloopy when she was 17-years old. She travelled on the SS Caronia with 19-year old Alexander Beck, and 16-year old Leah Spears who were also from Aughnaloopy. They arrived in New York on May 7, 1908. Leah was the daughter of Samuel Spears and Jane McClenaghan and Alexander was the son of Alexander Beck.

Jane 'Jennie' Hanna and Samuel John McCullough
James and Sarah Ann's daughter Jennie had left home by the time of the 1911 census. She had moved to New York, where she married Samuel John McCullough on December 16, 1913 in Manhattan.

Samuel John was the son of William McCullough and was originally from Annalong. He moved to America when he was 19-years old on the SS California, arriving in New York on May 31, 1909. Samuel John gave the address of his cousin R Jones at 260, Brook Avenue, New York. Jennie and Samuel John had three children: Irene, William J and Joan. In 1942, Samuel John completed a WWII Draft Registration Card where he listed his address as 1988 Newbold Avenue, Bronx.

Jennie's son William J McCullough exemplifies the positive role that Aughnaloopy descendants had on their newfound homelands. In his a book entitled *'Minuteman Activist: To Promote the General Welfare'*, William gives a detailed account of his life growing up in the Bronx, New York, as a son of immigrant parents. As a citizen, William achieved a record of public safety service at city, state, federal and international levels that ultimately earned him national recognition as a leading authority in criminal justice. During a thirty-seven-year career as a soldier, he responded to the call of duty on five occasions, serving in three wars and eventually attaining the rank of colonel. During 1945 to 1948 William helped care for more than a million displaced persons and refugees in bomb-destroyed Germany. In his career as a Captain in the New York Police Department, William trained and supervised the faculty of the New York City Police Academy. To enhance police professionalism, William founded Looseleaf Law Publications and produced twenty-eight titles. He also created the NYC Academy Playhouse, where he wrote, produced, directed, and narrated thirty-one playlets, which enjoyed a seven-year run in downtown Manhattan. William and his sister Joan now live in South Carolina, USA.

James Hanna and Agnes Anderson
James married Agnes Anderson from Kilkeel and had the following children: James 'Jim', Rachel, Margaret, William, Juanita 'Nita', Douglas, Jean, Charlotte 'Lottie', Norman, Anna, Thomas 'Tommy', and Maisie. They also adopted and raised a son Everette. Two children also died in infancy. The family first lived at 'The Hollow' in Kilkeel town centre, before moving a short distance to a house at Newcastle Street and later to Hanna's Close where they lived for several years. Following the death of Sarah McKnight Hanna, James and Agnes moved to the family home at Aughnaloopy. Agnes Anderson Hanna died in October 1967 and her husband James in March 1988. Both are buried in the Hanna family grave at Mourne Presbyterian Meeting House graveyard in Kilkeel.

John Hanna
In 1921, John sailed from Liverpool on the SS Carmania and arrived in New York on April 8. He was 21-years old and stated that he was going to join his father James in Manchester, Massachusetts. Travelling with John was his Aunt Rachel McKnight. Rachel was 45-years old, single, and a milliner. She gave her aunt's address as 11823 North 18 Street, Philadelphia. John stayed in America where he married and had two sons John 'Johny' and Patrick. Johny remained single, his brother Patrick married and

had a son John and a daughter Susan.

Annie Hanna
James and Sarah Ann's youngest daughter Annie was born in 1904 and is listed on the 1911 census living at home with her mother. When she was 18-years old, she travelled on the SS Baltic arriving in New York harbour on March 4, 1922. She listed her mother Annie as her next-of-kin in Ireland and said that she was going to stay with her sister Mrs. Samuel McCullough at 618 East 136 Street in New York. Annie travelled with 48-year old Ashley Hanna from neighbouring Aughnahorey. Ashley was returning to America having made a trip home and gave her brother-in-law William McConnell's address as 203 West 148 Street, New York as her destination. Also onboard were Dunnavan girls Mary (age 36) and Elizabeth (age 35) Cunningham who were going to stay with their aunt Mrs. P Trainor in Chicago. Ashley Hanna had first moved out to New York in May 1902, sailing on the SS Oceanic, when she travelled with her sister Adelaide and Ballinran natives Samuel Speers and James Parke. Ashley and Adelaide were the daughters of Thomas Hanna and Agnes 'Nancy' Parke. Annie Hanna worked in New York for about ten years and eventually returned to Kilkeel.

John Hanna and Isabel Scott
John and Ellen's son John Hanna married Isabella Scott at Warrenpoint Presbyterian Church on January 29, 1907. Isabella was the daughter of Samuel Scott and Agnes Hanna from Ballinran. Witnesses to the marriage were neighbour Robert Denny and Agnes's sister Eliza Jane Scott. Agnes was just 16-years old at the time of her marriage, John Hanna was 41-years old. By the time of the 1911 census, John and Isabella were settled in Ballinran townland with two young children, Ellen who was 2-years old and 8-month old Mary Jane. John's mother Ellen Annett Hanna was also living with her son. She stated that she was 69-years old and that she was a widow.

Mary Jane Hanna and Thomas McKee
John and Ellen's only daughter Mary Jane was born on June 11, 1873. She married Thomas McKee from Magheramurphy on October 31, 1897. Mary Jane was 24-years old and Thomas was 32-years old. Thomas was a farmer and the son of William McKee and Mary Mitchell. Witnesses to the wedding were James McKee and Mary Jane Minnis. Her brother James had taken over the Hanna property at Aughnaloopy and her brother John, the Ballinran farm so when Mary Jane married she moved to her husband's home on the Harbour Road. By the time of the 1911 census Mary Jane and Thomas had three children: Mary, John Hanna, and James. Thomas died on June 30, 1928, his effects were valued at £233 17s 6d.

Mary Wightman and George Hanna
There is uncertainty over whether George originated from Aughnahorey or Aughnaloopy but it is known that he is not related to James Hanna 'The Reed'. George was born c. 1785 and married Mary Wightman c.1830. The couple had at least 5 children: George (Feb 6, 1840), Mary Jane ((March 17, 1842), Margaret (August 17, 1844), Samuel (September 24, 1849) and Eliza (January 23, 1852). Their son George married Mary Margaret Hanna on December 29, 1871 at Mourne Presbyterian Church in Kilkeel. George stated that he was the son of George Hanna and that he was from Aughnaloopy and Mary Margaret was the daughter of William Hanna from Aughnahorey. This distinction may be have been to differentiate between the two Hanna families who were now both living in Aughnahorey. George's family may have originated in Aughnaloopy. When Mary Jane marries William McCulla, she says she is from Aughnahorey and when Margaret marries Hugh Beck, she also lists Aughnahorey as her home townland. In George senior's Will dated 1879, he again states that he was from Aughnahorey.

The Griffith's Valuation listing for George is at GV 11 ABCD, (a) Aughnahorey. However, it would appear that George Senior had some connection with Aughnaloopy. Mary and George's daughter Margaret married Hugh Beck on January 24, 1865. Hugh was the son of John Beck and Ellen Edgar. These are names associated with Aughnaloopy but Hugh states that he was from Moyadd. The following year Margaret and Hugh had a daughter Mary Margaret who was baptised on March 8, 1866. Her place of birth was recorded as Aughnaloopy. William John was baptised the following year and again the place of birth was stated as Aughnaloopy. The couple had nine more children: Ellen, George, James, Elizabeth, Annie, Sarah Jane, Joseph, Gilbert McClymont and another Elizabeth. Unfortunately, the place of birth is often recorded as being the parish of Kilkeel with no townland specified.

By 1901 Margaret Hanna and her husband Hugh Beck were living in Maghery, Greencastle with children Joseph, Gilbert and Elizabeth. Also with them were grandchildren: Robert, Elizabeth and George Cousins who were the children of Mary Margaret and John Cousins. When the 1911 census was enumerated, Hugh was a widower but living with him in Maghery was son Joseph, daughter Annie Auchmuty, and grandchildren: Robert Cousins, Hugh and Annie Gervin, Nellie Beck and Robert Beck Auchmuty.

Gilbert McClymont Beck

When he was 18-years old, Gilbert McClymont Beck joined the Royal Field Artillery Regiment of the British Army. After 3 years service, he enlisted in the Royal Irish Constabulary. Just 4 years later he decided to move to Australia where he joined the Queensland Police Force. When Gilbert died in 1939, the following obituary appeared in the Courier-Mail newspaper (Brisbane) on April 27, 1939.

> *Sergeant Gilbert McClymont Beck, one of the best-known members of the Queensland Police Force, died in St. Martin's Hospital on Anzac day age 53 years. Possessor of an exceptionally fine physique, Sergeant Beck was drill in instructor at Petrie Terrace training depot, where he had been stationed for the last five years. He was the first man to train dogs for police work in Queensland, and he held a police medal awarded for courageous conduct in the execution of duty. Sergeant Beck was born at Kilkeel, County Down, Ireland. At 18 years of age he joined the Royal Field Artillery Regiment, with which he served for three years. He was then appointed a member of the Royal Irish Constabulary, officiating as jujitsu instructor and after four years of service decided to come to Australia in 1911, and a year later he became a member of the Queensland Police Force. As an Imperial reservist, he was called up at the outbreak of the Great War, and saw service in Gallipoli, France, and Italy. Sent later to Salonica he contracted malaria, which affected his health in later years. He underwent an operation six months ago. His funeral yesterday was largely attended. Inspector A. A. Bock rep. resented the Commissioner of Police, and other officers present were Inspector C. Watson, Inspector F. M. O'Driscoll, Inspector C. Perrin, Inspector F. B. Kearney (Ipswich), Sub Inspector J, A. D. Bookless, Senior Sergeant C. Price, and representatives from the Criminal Investigation Branch, Water Police, traffic office. Petrie Terrace depot, and South Coast districts. Sergeant Beck is survived by his widow and a son.*

William John Beck and Mary Jane Bingham

George Hanna's grandson, William John Beck married Mary Jane Bingham from Dunavan on June 29, 1886 at Mourne Presbyterian Church in Kilkeel. William's sister Sarah C Hanna and Hugh Wilson were witnesses to the wedding. At the time of their marriage William John was 19-years old and was working as a farmer, Mary Jane was 17-years old. By 1901, William John and Mary Jane were living in Rostrevor with their eight children: George, Margaret, Minnie, Grace, Hugh, Sarah, William and Ann.

Chapter 31

Johnston Family

The earliest record of the Johnston family is the name of Richard, recorded in the 1830 Tithe Applotment Book where it is documented that he paid tithes on 4 acres of land. The name of Richard's wife is not known but the couple had at least five children: Richard, William, George, John, and Sarah 'Sally', all born c.1820 to c.1830.

Richard Johnson and Margaret Allen (GV28 & GV39)

Richard son also named Richard married Margaret Allen on August 22, 1858. The marriage took place at Massforth RC Church in Kilkeel and was witnessed by neighbours John Doran and Mary Fitzpatrick. In 1864, Richard is listed as leasing land at number 38 on the Griffith's Valuation. There is no house on the land but Richard and his wife appear to be living with Margaret's mother Jane Allen in the house at GV39. When Jane dies in 1871, Richard holds the lease to both GV38 and GV39. According to the revaluations of the land, Richard died soon after his mother-in-law and the house and land passes to a John Allen (the husband of Ellen Keown).

William (GV36b & GV37)

Richard's son William leased a small house at number 36b on the Griffith's Valuation and also some land at number 37 from Thomas F Moore. When William died c.1885 his property passed to Margaret Doran the daughter of John Doran and Sarah 'Sally' Johnston. Margaret had several siblings including Catherine, Ellen, John and Annie. Both John and Annie married and settled in Canada. The house was pulled down c.1897 and this coincides with an approximate death date for Margaret. The lease passed to John Cunningham (Catherine 'Kate' Johnston's husband).

John Johnson and Bridget 'Biddy' Bradley

Another sibling John Johnston married Bridget 'Biddy' Bradley on February 6, 1853 at Massforth RC Church in Kilkeel. Witnesses to the marriage were James Quinn and Ellen Keown. The couple had seven known children: William (b. November 27, 1853), James (b. December 24, 1855), Mary (b. March 25, 1858), Patrick (b. November 1, 1861). Bridget (b. January 4, 1865), John (b. January 17, 1867) and Rose Ann (May 6, 1873). In 1873, he acquired the lease of number 34 from James Bradley (his father-in-law). Then in 1878, with his neighbour James Keown, he takes over the lease of additional land at number 29 from John Keown. This was originally leased to William Wright at the time of the original Griffith's Valuation. The following year John Johnston takes over the lease of a house, office and land identified GV33 from James Keown.

At the time of the 1881 UK Census, John is lodging at 59 Paget Street, Liverpool with four of his children: William (age 26), James (age 24), Mary (age 22) and Rose Ann (age 8). John, William and James are all employed as dock labourers and Mary is working as a dress maker. John states that he is married but his wife Biddy and children Patrick, Bridget and John do not appear to have moved to Liverpool with the family.

In 1882, James married 19-year old Julie Ann Han(d)ley and in 1891 the couple are living in Kirkdale, Liverpool. James is working as a dock labourer. James's father John Johnston is living nearby with sons Patrick and John and his daughter Bridget Rogers (who at aged 26 is a widow). Also in the house in Bridget's son William Rogers, 3-month old Mary Ann Johnston and a boarder James Cunningham. the men are all employed at the nearby dockyards.

Julie Ann and James Johnston had twelve children together including: Mary Ann (b. 1884), James (b. 1886), William (b. 1888), Joseph (b. 1890), John (b. 1892), Elizabeth (b. 1894), George (b. 1896), Richard (b. 1898), Rose (b. 1899), Margaret Mary (b. 1902) and Gertrude (b. 1904).

Some time after 1891 John returned to Aughnaloopy and he is listed on the 1901 census at home with his wife Bridget. Also in the house was their daughter Rose Ann was married to Patrick Collins (the son of James Collins) from Maghereagh and their son John Collins. Their daughter Bridget Johnston Rogers had also returned to Ireland and was living there with her sons John and William. 18-year old John Sloan was also living with the family. He was a son of Mary Johnston.

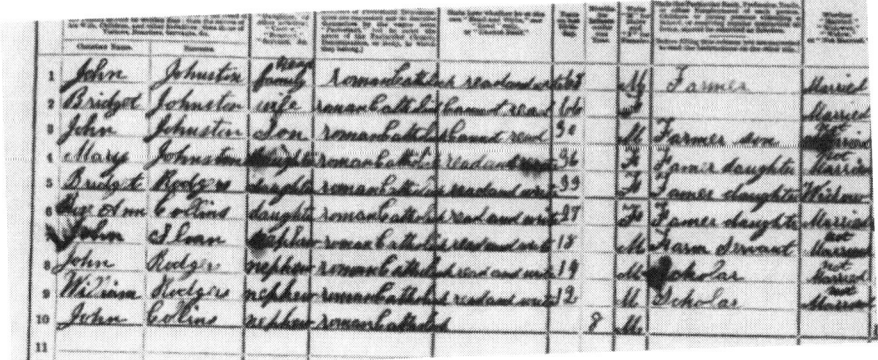

Extract from the 1901 Census showing the family of John Johnston.

Although John and Bridget returned to Ireland, James chose to remain in Liverpool where he raised his family. James's family is listed on the 1901 UK census living at 58, Rimrose Road in Bootle, Lancashire, where he is employed in the nearby docks along with his son James. At the time of the 1911 UK Census, the family has moved to 37, Sea View Road in Bootle. On the census, Julie Ann states that she had twelve children of whom nine were still living and living at home with her. James and William are working with their father at the dockyards. Joseph and John were working as grocer's assistants, George was an errand boy and Elizabeth was employed as a dressmaker.

John Johnston died on March 27, 1912, in Aughnaloopy. His estate and possessions passed to his widow Bridget. Their grandson James Johnson died the same year on December 24.

James and Biddy's other grandsons, William, Joseph, John, George and Richard were all called up to serve during World War 1. Luckily they all survived but George, the youngest suffered from shell shock. Tragedy befell the family when George's son Arnold was called up to serve in World War II and died on his third day fighting in France.

Photograph of James Johnston and his wife Julia Ann Han(d)ley, taken at the marriage of their daughter Elizabeth to William Quinn.

Kindly donated by Bill Quinn of Kilkeel.

John and Biddy's daughter Mary is listed in the papers relating to the 1925 Northern Ireland Land Act and the Estate of Betty Clarke (spinster). In a document published in The Belfast Gazette, dated January 10, 1930, Mary Johnson (spinster) is noted as paying rent of £5 10s 0d to Betty Clarke for over 8 acres of land. Mary raised her son Johnny Sloan in Aughnaloopy but he like many of his generation eventually moved to the United States. The property eventually passed to the Quinn family.

The family maintained their connections with Kilkeel and Elizabeth eventually married William 'Strawberry' Quinn from Aughnaloopy (son of Thomas 'Avenue' Quinn and Mary Fitzpatrick).

George Johnson and Catherine Hagan

Another sibling was George who married Catherine Hagan from Aughnaloopy and the couple had a daughter Catherine 'Kate' who was baptized on September 20, 1846. George is listed on the Griffith's Valuation with a house, office and land at number 36a that he leased from the Moore family. George held the lease until his death c.1885 when it passed to his son-in-law John Cunningham (who was originally from Magheramurphy). Kate Johnston and her husband John Cunningham had five children but just four survived childhood: Thomas, John, Patrick and Joseph. The family is listed on the 1901 census. By 1911 census for Aughnaloopy, just Joseph remains at home with his parents. Thomas, John and Patrick had all moved to Montana, USA.

Sarah 'Sally' Johnson and John Doran

No baptism record has been located for Sally and so it is not possible to confirm that she was a daughter of Richard. Sarah 'Sally' married John Doran c.1855, before the civil registration of marriages. This was a union of two established Aughnaloopy families. As with Johnson, the Doran family is recorded in the 1830 Tithes document and both families are likely to have been in Aughnaloopy for many years prior to this. A baptism record exists for their daughter Margaret dated December 21, 1858, the record lists Aughnaloopy as the place of residence. The couple had at least four other children: Catherine (b. 1864), Ellen (b. 1857), John Jnr. (b. 1869), and Annie (b. 1871). Their son John immigrated to Canada arriving in Halifax, Nova Scotia on April 8, 1988 at just 19-years old. His sister Annie also moved to Canada although the details have not been confirmed. John married Annie Laura Lavigne on January 17, 1905 and Annie married Ellis Lyons on November 12, 1918.

> 'The first adults I recall other than my parents, were my maternal grandfather's siblings, Mary and Johnny Johnston*. They were born towards the end of the famine and lived near my home. Mary was a minor historian. Not only did she relate the background of our neighbours, but also had a good memory of Charles Stewart Parnell, the leader of the Land League Campaign and how her home area was affected. As an example, she recalled how her mother refused an offer of extra land through fear of not being able to pay more rent, which would be demanded.
>
> *In old age, she had lost none of her astuteness. She told how in a period of political unrest, a pompous police inspector called and asked if there were any drilling going on there. "No" she replied, "we have not got the ploughing finished yet". He was of course referring to unlawful military activity.*
>
> *Johnny specialized in storytelling. His stories were always associated with highwaymen, ghosts and of course, the fairies. All were very scary and it was often with relief we got home to our mother. Sometimes we doubted the accuracy of his stories, but we dared not challenge him.'*
>
> Thomas Quinn, Kilkeel.
>
> * These are two of the children of John Johnston and Biddy Bradley.

Chapter 32

Keown Family

The Keown family was established in Aughnaloopy from before the time of the 1830 Tithe Applotment records. During the 1860's, two members of the family are listed in the Griffith's Valuation for Aughnaloopy, Ellen and James. Ellen Keown had a property listed at number 32A and B on the Griffith's Valuation and James had property at GV33.
The family had close ties with the Keowns in Leitrim.

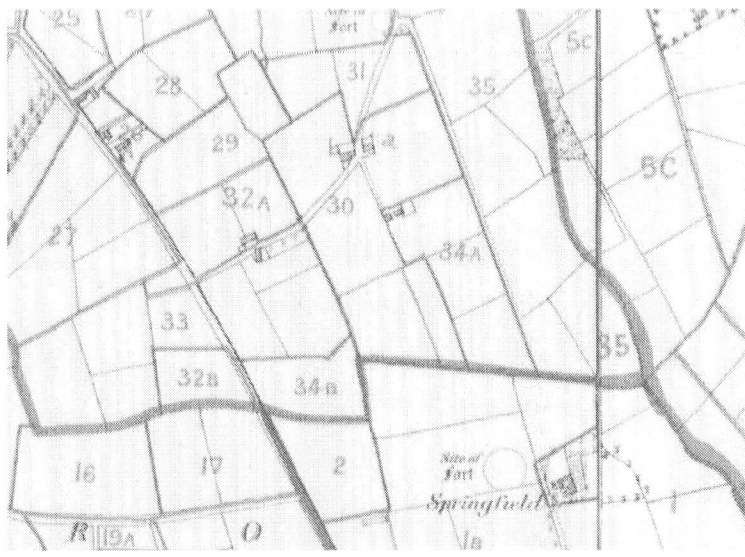

Extract from the Griffith's Valuation map of 1864 showing the location of the Keown properties, marked as 32 A and B and 33 in the south of Aughnaloopy townland.

Ellen and Thomas Keown (GV32)

Ellen (or Elenor) appears to have been the wife of Thomas Keown but her maiden name is unknown. The couple had at least eight children: Robert (b. 1822), John (b. 1825), Ellen (b. 1826), Mary (b. 1830), Thomas (b. 1832), Elizabeth (b. 1833), Hugh (b. 1836) and then a boy Charles born in 1845. Thomas died prior to 1876. A study of the Griffith's revaluation documents shows that Ellen remains in the property identified as number 32 until 1888 whereupon it passed to her second son John.

The children of Ellen and Thomas Keown

Robert Keown and Nancy Mitchell
Thomas and Ellen's oldest son Robert married Ann 'Nancy' Mitchell c.1844. No record of the marriage has been found. The couple had at least seven children: Thomas (b. 1845), Elizabeth Ann (b. 1850), Robert (b. 1852), George (b. 1856), John (b. 1860), Ellen (b. 1862) and William J (b. 1854). Baptismal records for several of their children have been located in Kilkeel Church of Ireland records. The family left Aughnaloopy, and may have spent some time in Stockport, Cheshire before eventually settling in Baxter, Ontario, Canada. This explains why the family homestead passed to his younger brother John. Robert was a farmer by occupation and died on August 28, 1891. He is buried in Muskoka and Parry Sound.

Robert and Nancy's son Thomas is listed on the 1911 census for Canada. He too is a farmer living in Muskoka, Ontario. He is listed with his wife Cynthia Synet Anne Regan and three of their children: William Thomas, Herbert and Frank Nixon.

John Keown and Ann McKnight

John married Ann McKnight from Leitrim (daughter of David McKnight) on January 25, 1866 in Kilkeel Church of Ireland Parish church. Witnesses to the marriage were John's younger brother Hugh and Richard Duncan from nearby Aughrim. The couple had at least one child, Thomas, born on May 30, 1868. John is recorded on the 1901 census with his brother Hugh and sister Ellen. He states that he is a widower. John died on September 15, 1907. His worldly goods passed to his brother Hugh and then to his nephew James Allen (Ellen's son). There is no mention of John's son Thomas in the Will, suggesting that Thomas may have predeceased his father.

Ellen Keown and John Allen

Robert's sister Ellen must have caused quite a stir in Aughnaloopy when she married her Catholic neighbour John Allen on February 15, 1857 at Massforth RC Church in Kilkeel. Their witnesses were Patrick Doran and Margaret Cunningham. The couple settled at the property with John's mother Jane, listed at number 39 on the Griffith's Valuation. Also living at the house was John's sister Margaret.

Margaret Allen married the following year on August 22, 1858 to local boy Richard Johnston. John Doran and Mary Fitzpatrick were witnesses to their marriage. John Allen and his wife Ellen remained in the property until after 1911 and raised seven children there including Annie (c.1860), Thomas (b. 1861), Jane (b. 1868), James (b. 1869) and George (b. 1871). George died in childhood. The children were all baptised at Massforth RC Church in Kilkeel. The marriage details of two of their children are known. Jane married butcher Charles McConville from the Mountain Road, Kilkeel on November 1, 1885 and James married Sarah Mccartan (father Richard), from Moneydarragh on February 17, 1890.

John Allen took over the land of his brother-in-law Richard Johnson c.1872, indicating that Margaret Allen and Richard Johnson did not have any children.

Elizabeth Keown

Elizabeth was born c.1833; she remained single and lived at home in Aughnaloopy. She is recorded on the 1901 census living with her widowed brothers John and Hugh. John states that he belongs to the Church of Ireland, whereas Elizabeth and Hugh are noted as Roman Catholic. Elizabeth is not mentioned in her brother John's Will from 1907 nor is she listed on the 1911 census, indicating that she died between 1901 and 1907. There is a death registration for an Elizabeth Keown in Kilkeel in 1902, aged 73.

Hugh Keown and Ellen Quinn

Hugh Keown married his neighbour Ellen Quinn on May 31, 1876. Patrick Bradley and Mary Small were witnesses to the marriage that took place at Massforth RC Church in Kilkeel. Hugh and Ellen were both approaching 40-years old and both stated that they were of the Roman Catholic faith. Ellen was an orphan, her parents having died just weeks apart from each other in the Spring of 1874. Her brother John was married and settled in Aughrim, her brother Richard was in America, her sisters were all dead and her other brother 'Mark's Pat' was married and settled with Sarah Sloan from Ballymageogh. When her father wrote his Will, Ellen was still living at home caring for her parents and running the home and farm. Mark likely assumed that Ellen would never marry and so he left her everything. The reasons behind this late marriage to Hugh Keown are unknown. It is possible that Ellen was distraught over the loss of her parents and panicked over how she would care for the farm. Perhaps Hugh and Ellen had wished to marry for several years but only felt able to enter into the marriage after her parents

Ellen Quinn - photograph donated by Angela Brannigan of Moneyscalp.

were no longer alive. It is also possible that Hugh saw marriage to Ellen as a way of acquiring land. Whatever the reasons, sadly the union did not last and Ellen did not find happiness in her later years.

Ellen was only 53-years old when she died on April 19, 1895. She is most likely to have been buried in Massforth, but the whereabouts of her grave are unknown. Ellen made a very detailed Will with the help of the local parish priest Dr. Marner. When Ellen wrote her Will she described herself as 'Ellen Keown or Quinn'. Ellen left everything she had been bequeathed by her father to her nephew, Johnnie Quinn.

Johnnie (the eldest son of John Quinn and Margaret O'Neill) was present at Ellen's death and may well have helped her around the farm in the years preceding her death. Johnnie Quinn married Mary 'Nellie' Haughian (daughter of Alexander Francis Haughian and Bridget Teresa Doran), from Brackenagh on November 28, 1901. Three years later the couple had a daughter whom they named Ellen. Tragedy continued to haunt the family, and Ellen died from an accident at home when she was just 30-years old.

Hugh Keown died in 1908 and does not appear to have left a Will.

Charles Keown
Charles was baptized in Kilkeel Church of Ireland Church on June 4, 1845. He was born nine years after his closest brother Hugh when his mother Ellen was in her 40's. Nothing more is known about Charles.

Three James Keowns
There are at least three men of similar age called James Keown living in proximity to Aughnaloopy at the time of the Griffiths Valuation. There is James Keown who leases a house at 37BAb Ballinran from William Hanna, there is James Keown at GV3 in Leitrim who leases a house and a considerable piece of land from the Trustees of the Kilmorey Estate and then James Keown listed at GV33 for Aughnaloopy.

Sally Fegan from Derryogue and James Keown (GV33)
One of the James Keown in the area was the husband of Sarah 'Sally' Fegan from Derryogue, Kilkeel. He was born c.1821 and married c.1846 but unfortunately no baptismal or marriage record has been found. James is listed on the Griffith's Valuation at number 33. James originated from Aughnaloopy as stated on his daughter's Mary Jane's marriage details. The family attended the Church of Ireland Parish Church in Kilkeel. James and Sally had at least seven children: Mary Jane (b. 1846), Elizabeth Sarah (b. 1848), Edward (b. 1850), Matilda (b. 1853), Ann (b. 1855), Thomas (b. 1859) and James (b. 1862). Their daughter Matilda died at 21-years of age on Mary 28 1875. Nothing is known about their youngest son James.

Mary Jane Keown and Charles Higton
Mary Jane married Charles Josiah Higton (son of William Henry Higton a coastguard from Ballymartin and his wife Margaret Donnan) on April 13, 1869 at Kilkeel Church of Ireland Parish Church. The couple had at least four children: William (b. 1870), Matilda (b. 1872), Charles Henry (b. 1875) and Robert (b. 1876).

Charles Josiah tragically died in 1876, when he was just 30-years old, leaving his wife and 4 children under 6-years old. No further information is known about their children William or Matilda. Their son Charles Henry married Anna Martha Walmsley of Leitrim on January 5, 1895 and their son Robert married Jane Newell (daughter of William Newell from the Harbour Road, Kilkeel) on March 3, 1904.

In May 1983, Charles Henry and Anna Martha Higton sailed on the SS Numidian from Londonderry to Quebec, Canada. They had at least three children born in Canada: Mary Jane (b. 1895), Margaret (b. 1895) and Josephine (b. 1897). The family then moved to the United States where a son Robert James was born in 1898.

Anna Martha and their children returned to Kilkeel sometime after 1898. Charles Henry Higton remained in the United States and is listed on the 1910 US Federal Census, living alone in Lorrain, Ohio. He is employed as a ship builder working at the shipyards. Anna Martha is listed on the 1911 Census of Ireland, living on Greencastle Street in Kilkeel with her children.

Robert Higton also appears to have spent some time working in the United States before his marriage to Jane Newell. He is listed on an incoming passenger list for the SS Ethiopia arriving in Londonderry on November 1, 1898. In 1911, Jane Newell Higton is documented on the Census for Ireland living on the Harbour Road with her two children both born in Co. Down, but her husband is not present at the time.

Elizabeth Sarah 'Sarah' Keown and Thomas Robinson
James's daughter Elizabeth Sarah married 21-year old bachelor Thomas Robinson on December 23, 1875 at Kilkeel Church of Ireland Parish Church. Thomas was the son of Andrew Robinson. Elizabeth Sarah had at least two children: James (b. 1877) who married Mary J Bradford and Thomas John (b. 1880) who married Sarah Henderson from Derryogue, Kilkeel. After Elizabeth Sarah's husband Thomas died, she married her cousin William Fegan from Derryogue on November 11, 1890. Elizabeth Sarah, William Fegan and Thomas John Robinson are recorded on the 1901 census of Ireland as living in Derryogue. By the time of the 1911 census, Thomas John had married Sarah Henderson (daughter of Thomas Henderson from Derryogue) and the couple had three young children, William, Thomas and Mary. They were all living in the house at Derryogue with Elizabeth Sarah Keown and her husband William Fegan.

Edward Keown and Margaret Ann Edgar
James and Sally Fegan's son Edward married Aughnaloopy girl Margaret Ann Edgar on January 25, 1876 at Mourne Presbyterian Church in Kilkeel. The couple moved to the United States in 1881 and settled in Camden, New Jersey where they are recorded on the 1900 US Federal Census with their 14-year old daughter Minnie E. Also living in the home on New Street was a nephew James Edgar.

By the time of the 1910 US Federal Census, Minnie E had married Henry Gregg and was living with her husband and parents at the house on New Street. Edward was recorded as being 54-years old and was employed as a labourer at an oilcloth factory. His son-in-law Henry Gregg was working as a blacksmith for the railroad. Neither Margaret nor Minnie were employed outside of the home.

Ann Keown
James Keown and Sally Fegan's youngest daughter Ann married her neighbour Hugh Shields (son of William Shields) at Kilkeel Church of Ireland Parish Church on March 15, 1878. They had at least one son William born in 1880.

Thomas Keown and Margaret Denny
James remained at the family property in Aughnaloopy until his death on March 22, 1903. His son Thomas was living with him along with Thomas' wife Margaret 'Maggie' Denny and their first child Annie. James left a Will in 1903 that stated he left no widow and four lawful issue. Only his son Thomas and daughter Annie are named. It is known that his son Edward had already moved to the United States. Thomas took over farming the family land and is listed on the 1911 census with his wife Margaret and children: Annie (b. 1898), Mary 'Minnie' (b. 1903), James (b. 1905), David (b. 1908), and William Thomas (b. 1910). Margaret states that she had eight children of whom three died in childhood. The names of these children are unknown.

James Keown from GV3 Leitrim and Sarah
The other James Keown living in nearby was born in Leitrim c.1812 and is listed on the Griffith's Valuation at number 3 in Leitrim. His wife was named Sarah but no further

information is known about her. According to the Church of Ireland burial records James died in 1884 at aged 72.

James and Sarah had a son, William, who was baptised November 25, 1837. It was William who appears to have inherited the family homestead in 1884. William died on February 14, 1916 leaving a widow Ellen and no children. He bequeathed his property in Leitrim to his nephew Andrew Graham.

James and Sarah also had a daughter Elizabeth Sarah Keown, who married John Graham on February 28, 1867, at the Meeting House Lane Presbyterian Church. John was the son of Andrew Graham and Nancy Mills from Ballinran. Elizabeth Sarah and John had at least seven children: Nancy (b. 1869), James (b. 1870), Ellen (b. 1872), Mary (b. 1874), John (b. 1876), Andrew (b. 1878) and Elizabeth (b. 1880). It was their son Andrew who inherited the family property in Leitrim. It seems likely that the James Keown mentioned below was also a son of James and Sarah.

James Keown from Leitrim and Jane Spears

The third James Keown married Jane Spears (daughter of Samuel Spears) on November 12, 1857 at the Mourne Presbyterian Church in Kilkeel. James stated that he was from Leitrim and the son of James Keown. Jane was only 16-years old when she married. She too was Presbyterian and was the daughter of Samuel Spears from Aughnahorey. Jane is listed as a widow in the 1901 census, when she is living in Aughnaloopy with her brother Samuel Speers and his wife Jane McClenaghan. It was a busy household with eleven children ranging down in age from 22 to 1 years old living at home (Mary Margaret, John, James, Samuel, Sarah, Robert, Leah, Thomas, Martha, Annie, and William). James Keown and Jane Speers are known to have had three children. Their son James was baptized in Mourne Presbyterian Church on April 24, 1859, Mary Jane was also baptized there on April 14, 1863. A birth record for their son Robert has been found dated May 6, 1867. Nothing further is known about James, Mary Jane or Robert.

No Will has been found for James although it is known that he died prior to the 1901 census.

Chapter 33

Mills Family

Widow Jane Mills

The Widow Jane Mills is listed in the 1830 Tithes Applotment Book for land held in Aughnaloopy and Leitrim. In 1803 a John Mills is noted on the Agricultural Census for Drumcro but whether this is Jane's husband is impossible to determine.

John, Nancy and William Mills

In 1864, John Mills leased a small house and garden from James Moore in the centre of the townland designated as number 12 in the Griffith's Valuation. John was married to Mary Speers from Leitrim and they had a daughter Ann who was born on August 18, 1842 and baptized on September 12, 1842 at Mourne Presbyterian Church in Kilkeel. It does not appear that the couple had any other children and no marriage record for Ann Mills has been located. John remained in Aughnaloopy until 1889 when Alexander Beck took over the lease. There is a burial record for a John Mills in 1892 aged 84.

John may have had a sister Nancy Mills who married Andrew Graham and settled in Ballinran.

There is another potential sibling William who married Eliza Hamilton and had at least two children: James (b. February 4, 1846) and Eliza (b. March 2, 1848). James and Eliza were baptized at Mourne Presbyterian Church in Kilkeel.

By 1901, there are no Mills families listed in Aughnaloopy. Alexander Beck and his wife Sarah Ann (Baird) are living on the site previously occupied by John Mills.

A Mountain View from Aughnaloopy.
by: Shelley Jayne Crawford Maskery (Shelley Jayne Illustration)

Chapter 34

Moore Family

1732 Lease of Land from Robert Nedham
Documents relating to the presents of the Moore family in Aughnaloopy date back to 1732. It was on January 20, 1732, that Robert Nedham Srn. granted a lease of his lands including Aughnaloopy (which was noted as comprising two-hundred and thirteen acres) to William Moore, James Moore, Charles Moore and Joshua Wauchope. William, James and Charles Moore were the sons of William Moore from Ballynahatten; their mother was a member of the influential Wachop family. Joshua Wachop (c.1698) was the son of William Wachop and Margaret Redmond of Cranfield. The Wachop and Moore families were very closely related throughout several generations, with Joshua Wachop's daughter Margaret also marrying into the Moore family.

1778 Men of Mourne
On December 13, 1778, a list of the Committee of the Men of Mourne was published that included four members of the Moore family: John Moore from Aughnaloopy, John from Ballymagart, Stuart and Francis. In a document dated May 24, 1780 John in noted as holding the post of Chair of the recently formed Men of Mourne Volunteer Corps.

1786 Freeholder List
A 1786 Freeholder Lists archived at PRONI includes several members of the Moore family: John (Kilkeel), Charles (Cranfield), Hugh, and Nicholas. At this time, the freehold was registered at Kilkeel Court House. The names John and Charles were common in the Moore family throughout the years and the Charles of Ballynahatten and Charles of Cranfield are grandsons of the original William Moore who was granted the 1732 lease.

1796 Flax Growers List
The 1796 Flax Growers List includes nine members of the Kilkeel Moore family: Charles, Charles Jr., Charles, Sr., Francis James, Jane, John, Margaret and Nicholas. Nicholas had a £50 freehold registered on October 14, 1805 for Aughnaloopy, although he lived in Newry.

1830 Tithes Applotment Book
There are three members of the Moore family listed in the 1830 Tithes Applotment Book; John and Hugh who had over 7 acres of land together as well as the Widow Mary Moore who had just over an acre of land.

Griffith's Valuation
Sir Richard Griffith's instigated the Townland Valuation of Aughnaloopy in 1834. In the valuation book held at PRONI three houses were noted in Aughnaloopy, one belonging to John Moore. The property was initially valued initially at over £3 valuation but was then determined to be under the final £5 valuation and so an annotation has been added 'Under Value'. In the final valuation of 1864, properties GV1 to GV15 (with the exception of a small, unoccupied house owned by Alexander Annett at GV11a) are all leased from James Moore. GV12 to GV16 are also leased from James Moore. John and Hugh Moore are noted as the immediate lessors from properties GV17 to GV21. The sites identified as GV22 and GV23 are occupied by John Moore and leased by Hugh Moore. Thomas F Moore held the leases for properties GV29b to GV39.

1901 Census

By the time of the 1901 Census, just one member of the Moore family is listed as being resident in Aughnaloopy. Lucretia Moore stated her occupation as Farmer and Landowner. Born Lucretia Davidson Moore in nearby Lurganconary, Lucretia was the daughter of Hugh Moore of Aughnaloopy and Lucretia Davidson. She had inherited the land at Aughnaloopy from her uncle John Moore who is designated in early documents as being 'of Aughnaloopy'. Lucretia was living with a female servant Sarah Quinn who was originally from Dunnaval. The property was listed as a second class home, having stone walls, a thatched roof, 7,8 or 9 rooms and 5 windows to the front of the house. The property was to become known as Heath Hall and when Lucretia Davidson Moore wrote her Will in 1915, she references Heath Hall.

Heath Hall Guest House

Heath Hall now operates as a successful Guest House run by owner Eddie McGlue. The McGlue family were originally from Maghereagh. Eddie's father Hugh bought the house in the 1940's. Eddie McGlue has a keen interest in local history and is always willing to help guests with their family research.

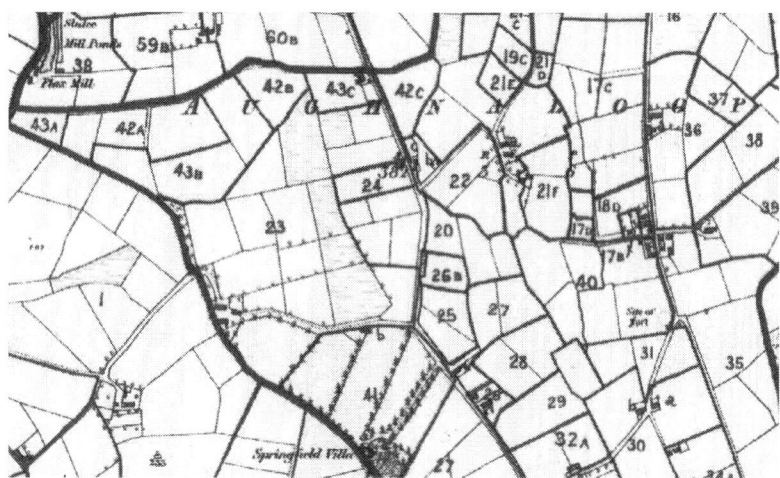

Extract from the 1864 Griffith's Valuation Map showing the location of the land that was leased by John Moore from his brother Hugh Moore (GV22 and 23). John lived in the house situated at GV22 that eventually passed to Lucretia Davidson Moore. The site is now occupied by Heath Hall Guest House.

Chapter 35

Morgan Family

Special thanks to Deirdre McEvoy, Dublin, Ireland, Tony Daly, Dublin, Ireland, and Sister Mary Campion McCarren fcJ, Salford, England.

Despite the Morgan family connection with Springfield Villa in Aughnaloopy and the known commercial success of the Morgan family in Kilkeel, their name does not appear in the 1830 Tithes documents for Aughnaloopy. Nor are they mentioned in the original Griffith's Valuation of 1864 for the townland. It is not until 1884, when James Hamilton Morgan takes over the lease from his mother-in-law Mary Ann Hamilton Morgan Murphy that the family is documented as living in Aughnaloopy.

James Morgan and Mary Clarke

James Morgan was born c.1806 and married Mary Clarke c.1845. The couple had at least six children: John (b. 1847), James Hamilton (b. 1849), Catherine (b. 1854), Mary (c.1850), Susan (c.1850) and Patrick (b. 1853). Mary Clarke Morgan died on August 10, 1872 when she was 47-years old. James Morgan died five years later and the couple are buried at Massforth Graveyard in Kilkeel. A townland is not included on the baptismal records for James and Mary's children, just the parish of Kilkeel is noted.

John Morgan

Their eldest son John was baptised at Massforth RC Church in Kilkeel on April 8, 1847. He remained unmarried and died close to his fortieth birthday on April 8, 1887.

James Hamilton Morgan and Mary Ann 'Minnie' Murphy

Their second son James Hamilton Morgan was baptised on June 30, 1849. He was a hard-working, successful man and despite his relative wealth worked his way up through the ranks of his trade. In 1871 he left Aughnaloopy and worked in Liverpool as a grocers assistant. Having established himself he returned to Kilkeel where he married Mary Ann 'Minnie' Murphy in 1878 and they started their life together in Aughnaloopy. The couple had a child born a year later but the boy, named James Joseph Morgan, died at just 6-months old. They were to have five further children together all born in Springfield House, Aughnaloopy: Mary Josephine 'Geneva' (who married Edward Sloan), Gertrude (who joined the Faithful Companions of Jesus), John Patrick, Joseph Hamilton (who married Ellen Josephine 'Nellie' Mageean), and James Francis.

James Hamilton Morgan travelled a lot with his work as a merchant and he trained his sons John Patrick, Joseph Hamilton and James Francis to work as shop assistants in the family shop on Bridge Street, Kilkeel. This was a tradition in the family as it had been James Hamilton Morgan that had taken over his father's business interests. His wife Minnie Murphy was from a wealthy family and was likely a great help in managing the family affairs. Her family was well connected to the business families of Kilkeel and Newry. Minnie Murphy Morgan died on October 22, 1896 when her youngest son James Francis was just 8-years old.

About four years after his first wife died, James Hamilton Morgan married Imelda McMullan in the Belfast RC Church at Knockbreda, Belfast. Imelda was from 'Churchfield House', Hollywood, and her father Matthew was also a wealthy merchant. When James died on June 16, 1902 the value of his estate was calculated as £10,824 3s 7d. He appointed John and William Hughes, merchants from Liverpool, as his executors. No family connection has been found between the Hughes family and the Morgan family. To his wife Imelda, James Hamilton left 250 pounds and stipulated his desire for her to live with his children at Springfield House. However, he stated:

> '.......in case they do not agree to her doing so I will that my wife shall occupy for her life or until her marriage the house and garden in Aughnaloopy occupied by Mrs. Gonsalves'.

Imelda does not appear to have stayed in Aughnaloopy following the death of James Hamilton Morgan as she is not listed on the 1911 census. There is some indication that she may have moved to Dublin.

In his Will, James Hamilton Morgan stated that his daughters Mary Josephine and Gertrude were to be given one thousand pounds each on reaching the age of 24 or on marrying. He specified that this money was to be '...*free of the control of any husband'*. Both girls moved to England after their father died. Mary Josephine married Edward Sloan in 1906. Although originally from Ireland, Edward had established himself in Kirkdale, Liverpool in the grocery business. He is documented on the 1901 census living at 58, Commercial Street with his cousins John, Henry and Mary all whom assisted in the business. After their marriage Mary Josephine and Edward Sloan moved to new premises at 1, Hongonment Grove, Waterloo, Liverpool. This address has not been located on a modern map of Liverpool. The couple had at least three children: Mary Josephine, Ann Gertrude and Edward Eugene. Tragically their infant girls died within a day of each other in 1907. Tragedy stuck again in 1911, when Edward died, leaving Mary Josephine to cope with her 1-year old child. At the time of the 1911 UK census, Mary Josephine was living with her son Edward Eugene and a servant Mary Ann Stevens. Mary Josephine continued to run the grocery business.

In 1905, three years after her father's death Gertrude became a member of the Faithful Companions of Jesus, taking the name Mother Eugenia in religion.

> *The Faithful Companions of Jesus are a teaching order of French origin..... In and near Manchester they conduct several flourishing schools, viz., Manchester, St. Austin's; Salford, St. John's; Salford, St. Peter's; Salford, Mount Carmel; and Pendleton. They also teach Liverpool, St. Patrick's; Birkenhead, St. Mary's; Preston, St. Austin's; and Chester, St. Wedhurgh's. It is understood that boarding schools where girls of the richer classes may obtain a good education form their first care; but they have been induced by charitable motives to add the charge of schools for the poor to this special work, and as they confine themselves entirely to education, and enjoy the advantage of being a numerous body under one superior-general, they seem destined to become of great service as accomplished teachers of elementary schools.'*
> (From: Terra incognita, or the convents of the United Kingdom, by John Nicholas Murphy)

Sister Mary Campion McCarren, British Province Archivist for the Faithful Companions of Jesus, kindly provided information that gives us an insight into Mother Eugenia's life. She initially spent a year in training at Sedgley Park in Salford and was then transferred to Holt Hill, Birkenhead. The move was prompted by ill health and it was hoped that:

> '...the change of air would restore her former health.'

Despite her illness, Mother Eugenia was most anxious to work and feared that she was a disappointment to her Reverend Mother Provincial, and the Mistress of Novices, who had taken such pains to make her a good and useful member. More than once she is reported to have said, '...*but I have not worked.'* She refused to give in to her frailty and insisted on getting up each morning to attend Mass and receive Holy Communion. It is recorded in the Holt Hill Annals that on December 8, 1908,

> '...her strength giving way, she was obliged to abandon the thought of getting up any more.'

It further notes:

> 'Our dear Mother further distinguished herself by her great spirit of prayer and her constant cheerfulness during her illness. Her own desire was to be really perfect. She was anxious to learn the Prayers for the Dying by heart, so that to the last she would be able to follow them.'

Mother Eugenia died on February 26, 1909.

> 'On the day she died, the 26th of February, she prayed the whole day; the chaplain was with her from five o'clock until 6:30 p.m. saying the rosary, and giving her the last Absolution between every decade. Our dear invalid was conscious to the very end. At about 6:30 her pure soul took its flight to her Divine Spouse, whom she had faithfully served during her short life, and we trust, to take her place amongst those of our dear Society who already enjoy the Beatific Vision. R.I.P.'

Her passing was reported in The Intermountain Catholic, a newspaper based in Salt Lake City, Utah, on April 3, 1909.

John Patrick assisted his father running the grocery businesses in Kilkeel and is listed on the 1901 census as working in the Morgan property on Bridge Street. Following his father's death John Patrick appears to have left Kilkeel.

James Hamilton Morgan and Minnie's son Joseph Hamilton Morgan married on August 29, 1905, at St. Malachy's RC Church in Belfast. Witnesses were Daniel Mageean and Mary Marner. Joseph's occupation was listed as gentleman. Ellen Josephine 'Nellie' Mageean was born on February 14, 1875 at Darragh Cross, Saintfield. She was the daughter of Daniel Mageean and Susan Marner. Joseph and Nellie had at least three children: Joseph, Daniel and Ellen. On July 31, 1910, the family departed from Londonderry on the SS Furnessia arriving in New York on August 8, 1910. Joseph gave his aunt Mary Davis as his next of kin and stated his occupation as Auctioneer. They gave their final destination as Los Angeles. They did not stay there long as at the time of the 1911 census, the family is listed as living in Aughnahorey. Joseph now states his occupation as horse dealer. In July 1914, he sailed again from Londonderry, this time on the SS Columbia, arriving in New York on August 3, 1914 for passage on to Los Angeles. He now states his occupation as butcher and his next-of-kin as his wife Mrs. Nellie Morgan at 24, Lavinia Square, Belfast. Lavinia Square is a continuation of Agincourt Avenue – the address listed on Mary Davis power of attorney document (see below).

The Mageean Family
Nellie Morgan's brother Daniel Mageean joined the Priesthood, being ordained on June 17, 1906. He was appointed to Glenavy Parish on July 10, 1907 and transferred to St Malachy's College in September of the same year. Daniel was appointed as the 28th Bishop of Down and Connor in on August 25, 1929. He is recognised as a champion of Catholic rights and succeeded in getting the anti-Catholic nature of much of Northern Ireland life raised in the House of Commons at Westminster.

In 1939 he coined the much-quoted phrase: *'A Protestant Parliament for a Protestant People'*, attributing it to his opponent the Prime Minister Lord Craigavon, but it was a slight misquotation.

Daniel was not the first member of the family to join the Church. His uncle was the Reverend Richard Marner who was the parish priest in Kilkeel for 33 years. In fact, at the time of the 1901 census, Nellie Josephine was staying with her uncle in Ballymageough, where she was working as a schoolteacher. It is likely while staying in Kilkeel that she met Joseph Hamilton Morgan. Richard Marner was the grand nephew of the Reverend Richard Curoe who was a Parish Priest in Dunsford and then Kilkeel. It was Richard Curoe who was responsible for the building of St. Colman's Roman Catholic Church (Massforth) in Ballymageough, where he was Parish Priest for 33 years.

Catherine

Catherine Morgan was baptised on November 28, 1854. Nothing is known about Catherine and she has not been located on the 1901 or 1911 census.

Mary Morgan and John Davis

James Hamilton Morgan and Mary Clarke's daughter Mary married John Davis on January 16, 1875 at Massforth Roman Catholic Church. John was a 40-year old widower when they married. At the time of their marriage John was a Naval Chief Officer stationed at Cranfield Point. John Davis appears to have entered the Coast Guard Service on the March 2, 1857, having been nominated from HMS Arrogant, with a first posting to Ventnor on the Isle of Wight. Although a few years after the Crimean War, Tony Daly who manages the Coastguards of Yesteryear website at www.coastguardsofyesteryear.org thought it worth checking the medal roll for HMS Arrogant and found that John Davis, Captain of the Main Top, Ships No. 5, was awarded the Baltic medal, which was sent to Ventnor CG Station in 1857.

On February 11, 1860 John Davis requested a transfer, and was posted to Castletown, where, on November 4, 1861 he was promoted to Commissioned Boatman. He remained at Castletown until October 6, 1871 when he was removed to Leestone as Chief Boatman, and then on April 6, 1874 he moved to Cranfield as Acting Chief Officer. During his time at Cranfield he had a number of title changes, but was finally confirmed as Chief Officer in January 1875. There remains some uncertainty as to the year of his birth as he variously gives it as 1827 and 1829. However, he consistently gives the Cove of Cork as his place of birth. John was awarded the Royal Naval Long Service Good Conduct Medal in October 1878. John's exact date of death is unknown and no Will has been found. Mary was a widow at the time of the 1901 census and states her occupation as retired grocer. She is living in Dunnaman with a 10-year girl Nellie McGrath who states she was born in Belfast. Mary remained living in Kilkeel until her death on April 13, 1913.

Susan Morgan

Nothing is known about Susan other than that she was a witness at her sister Mary's wedding to John Davis.

Patrick Morgan

Patrick was baptised on March 9, 1853. When he was about 20-years old he moved to America and settled in San Francisco. He does not appear to have married. When his sister Mary died on April 13, 1913, her property consisted of just stocks and shares in Belfast & Co. Down Railways and in the District Water Commission totalling £141. She was a widow with no children or grandchildren so her younger brother Patrick was her lawful next of kin. Patrick was living at 161A Henry Street, in San Francisco at the time. It appears that he had little interest in returning to Ireland so he appointed his nephew Joseph Hamilton Morgan to act on his behalf. Joseph Hamilton Morgan was the son of James Hamilton Morgan and Minnie Murphy. The paperwork instructing the transfer of authority was prepared by solicitor James Murphy of Newry and was witnessed at Stockton, California on December 28, 1914.

Chapter 36

Quinn Family

Mourne historian and writer J S Doran believed that the Quinn family originated from the headquarters of the clan in East County Derry. However, by 1830, they were certainly well established in Aughnaloopy with Edward Quinn and William Quinn paying tithes on almost 14 acres of land.

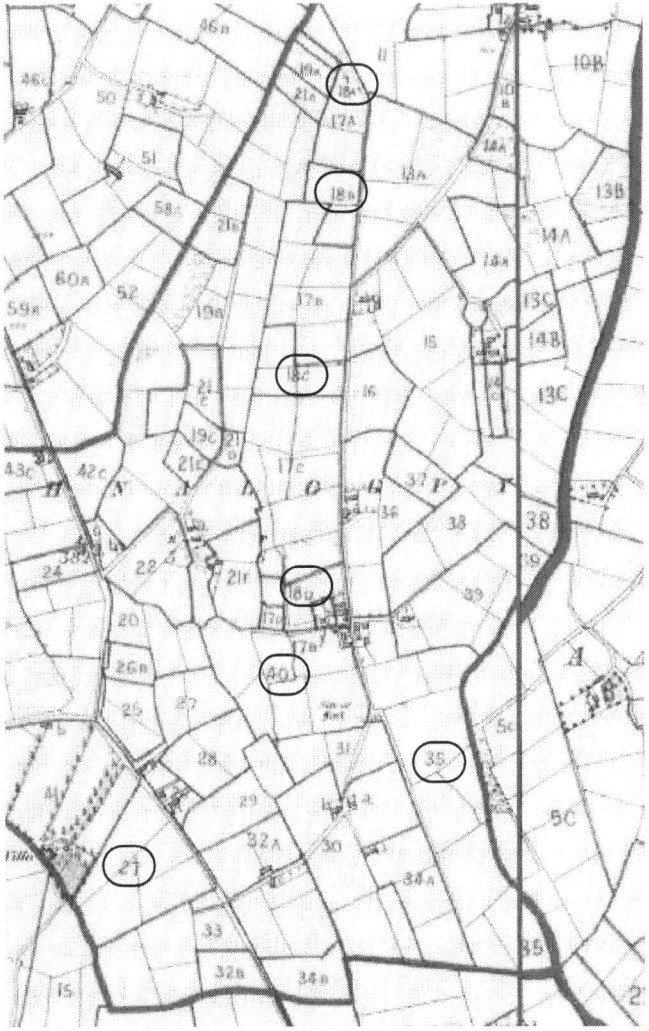

When the 1864 Griffith's Valuation, was completed, Edward Quinn is documented at GV18 with approximately 5 acres, Mark Quinn is listed at GV27 with 10 acres, James Quinn at GV35 with approximately 16 acres and Thomas at GV40 with over 8 acres.

Research into the Quinn family is complicated due to the fact that several members of the family had property and business interests in multiple townlands including Aughrim, Leitrim, Ballymageogh and Drummalane. There was a tendency towards large families and Christian names were often repeated through the generations.

Extract of the 1864 Griffith's Valuation map showing the location of Quinn properties in Aughnaloopy - GV18ABCD, GV27, GV35 and GV40.

Any relationship between Edward at GV18, Mark at GV27, Thomas (who married Margaret Donaldson), and James Quinn is unconfirmed. Further information on each branch of the family is given below.

Edward Quinn (GV18ABCD)

Very little is known about Edward other than that he was born c.1800 and lived until c. 1883. An Edward Quinn is noted in the 1830 Tithes Applotment Books and it is possible that this is the same Edward living at the GV18 location. The name of his parents or his wife are unknown. Edward is listed on the 1864 Griffith's Valuation with separate holdings identified as 18ABCD that he leased from John and Hugh Moore.

In 1864, his property amounted to just under 6 acres. It ran down the west side of the Aughnaloopy Road and was interspersed by land farmed by Patrick Fitzpatrick noted as GV17ABCD. The distribution of land suggests that Patrick Fitzpatrick and Edward Quinn may have been related through marriage but no conclusive evidence has been found to support this.

Edward Quinn's family home appears to have been situated at 18D on the Aughnaloopy Road, with the other locations used as farming land. Edward had at least four children, James, John, Mary and Catherine and it is possible that there were others.

James Quinn (GV18ABCD)
Edward's son James took over the family property and is listed in the 1901 and 1911 census. In 1901 he gives his age as 68, lists his occupation as farmer and has a servant 64-year old Mary Cunningham living in the house with him. In 1911, he gives his age as 84-years old and states that he is single. He died on April 7, 1911 leaving no widow or lawful children. His Estate passed to his nephews Patrick Quinn, Edward Quinn and James Doran.

John Quinn and Catherine 'Kate' Feron
John was born c.1836 and married Catherine 'Kate' Feron (Fearon, Ferrin) on November 9, 1873. Kate was the daughter of Patrick Feron from Moyadd. Peter Feron and Mary Ann Quinn were witnesses to the marriage. The couple had at least four children: Edward (b. 1876), Mary Ann (b. 1878), John (b. 1879) and James (b. 1881) and settled in Moyadd townland.

Mary Quinn and Denis Doran
Edward's daughter Mary married Denis Doran from GV15, Aughnaloopy on February 19, 1860. Mary Doran and Mary Fitzpatrick were witnesses to the marriage (further evidence for a Quinn/Fitzpatrick connection). The couple moved to Moneydarragh Beg where they raised at least five children: Mary (b. 1861), Arthur (b. 1865), John (b. 1866), Catherine (b. 1868) and James (b. 1870). At the time of the 1901 census, Denis was deceased and Mary was living in Moneydarragh with her children Mary, John and James. When Mary's brother James Quinn died on April 7, 1911, Mary inherited 5 pounds and her son James Doran a third of his uncle's estate in Aughnaloopy. No provision was made in James's Will for his nephew's Arthur or John or for his niece Catherine and they are not living at home at the time of the 1911 census.

Catherine Quinn
Edward's daughter Catherine remain unmarried and lived in Aughnaloopy her entire life. It is possible but unconfirmed that Catherine had a son Patrick who was baptised on March 10, 1867.

Mark Quinn (GV 27)
By Angela Quinn Brannigan, Moneyscalp.

Always having a keen interest in my family history, I had a desire to find out how long my Quinn family home had been in Aughrim and the names of the people that lived there. Listening to stories told, I knew it had been there for at least 150 years or more and I had always assumed that generations of Quinn's had always lived there.

I already knew that my Great Grandfather was called John Quinn, and that he was married to Margaret O'Neill. With this information, I was quickly able to find their marriage details from the Ulster Historical Foundation based in Belfast. This search contain information most unexpected, it appeared that that John Quinn had in fact, came from Springfield, in the townland of Aughnaloopy. Margaret's place of residence was not stated, they were married in 1862. Now I was left to ascertain why John Quinn was living up in Aughrim. A visit to the Public Records Office of Northern Ireland (PRONI) in Belfast and a search in the Griffith's Revaluation Books soon confirmed that prior to John Quinn being tenant of number 19 in Aughrim, the property was in the name of Bernard and Rose O'Neill, Margaret's parents. Before Bernard was his father Toal O'Neill in 1803, that was as far back as I could search, with records to confirm.

John Quinn's father was noted on his marriage certificate as Mark Quinn. Luckily, there were not to many Mark Quinns in the area and I was able to identify that my Great Great Grandfather Mark Quinn lived in at GV27 in Aughnaloopy. Mark Quinn was a farmer married to Margaret Mackin and they raised their family of three boys and two girls in a little house just at the entrance to where McGlue Brothers sheds are now. The old house was knocked down many years ago, but the old two-story barn is still there to this day.

After a brief conversation with Eddie McGlue of Springfield, I was most delighted that he kindly let me have a copy of a photograph he had taken in the early 1970's, which showed the old Quinn homestead there and it was a lovely ending to my project on my Quinn family history.

This photograph shows the old house that Mark and Margaret Quinn (nee Mackin) reared their five children in. The house is to the left of the picture, and shows that all the windows have been removed. Shortly after this photo was taken, the house was completely demolished, to make way for the new owners.

Close to the old house you will see an old barn with a little window in the gable. This old barn is still there to this day and is all that remains of the old Quinn Homestead. The fields behind the home and also on the opposite side of the Moyadd Road were owned and farmed by Mark Quinn and his sons.

Margaret Mackin and Mark Quinn (GV 27)

Mark Quinn's wife was Margaret Mackin. There is some uncertainty over Margaret's surname before she was married. It has been speculated by Vincey Quinn of Kilkeel, that the name was originally O'Loughlin or McLoughlin but that the family changed it to Mackin '....*for political reasons*'. Certainly on her daughter Mary Anne's birth certificate, Margaret's surname was clearly noted as Mackin.

There is also some conjecture that Margaret came from Ballyvalley townland near Clonallon, Rostrevor. However, when Mark Quinn prepared his Will in 1873 he appointed Patrick Mackin from Dunnaval as an executor. This was likely Patrick Mackin, husband of Alexandrea 'Ally' Marmion and son of Nicholas Mackin. This would suggest a close connection to the Mackins of Dunnaval and perhaps Margaret was indeed from that townland. Patrick Mackin had several siblings, including Mary Ann who married James 'Hamilton' Quinn from Aughnaloopy (who is believed to be a brother of Mark Quinn), Sarah 'Sally' Mackin who married William Clarke and possibly an Ellen Mackin who married Thomas Cunningham. If there is a link to Ballyvalley and a family name change, it may be from the previous generation.

Margaret and her husband Mark Quinn seem to have been financially comfortable. They owned two houses in Newry Street, Kilkeel that were rented out. They had the house in Aughnaloopy where they raised their family and they had another house that was rented to James Cunningham Taylor.

Margaret and Mark Quinn had at least seven children: John (b. 1836), Ellen (b. 1837), Richard (c.1838), Margaret (b. 1841), Mary Ann (b. 1847), Sarah Ann (b. 1850), and Patrick 'Mark's Pat' (b. 1851). Nothing is known about Mark and Margaret's daughters Margaret or Sarah Ann. Mary Ann predeceased her parents dying at as an infant.

John Quinn and Margaret O'Neill

Mark's oldest son John married Margaret O'Neill from Aughrim on January 1, 1862 at Massforth RC Church in Kilkeel. Margaret was the daughter of Bernard 'Barney' O'Neill and his wife Rose who are listed at number 19 on the 1864 Griffith's Valuation. John appears to have moved over to Aughrim and in 1883 is named as being responsible for the site. John and Margaret reared a large family including Johnny (b. 1865) who married Mary 'Nellie' Haughian and settled in Aughnaloopy, Mary (b. 1866) who married John J Rourke and settled in albany, New York, Mark (b. 1868), Margaret (c.1868), James (b. 1869), Ellen (b. 1872) who married Benjamin J Rigaud and also settled in Albany, New York, Rose (b. 1874), Catherine (b. 1876) who married James 'Jim' Cunningham and settled in Carginagh, and Hugh (b. 1878) who married Sarah Trainor and stayed in Aughrim. At least five of the siblings: James, Mary, Margaret, Ellen and Rose moved out to the United States and settled in Albany, New York.

Ellen Quinn and Hugh Keown

Margaret and Mark's daughter Ellen was born in 1837. She married Hugh Keown on May 31 1876 and settled in Aughnaloopy. Ellen cared for her parents in their later years and was present at their deaths. Further information on Ellen is given in the chapter on the Keown family.

Richard Quinn

Like many of his generation Richard moved out to America and never returned home. He is mentioned in his father's Will who states that the house that was rented out to James Cunningham Taylor should be given to Richard should he return home.

Patrick Quinn 'Mark's Pat' and Sarah Sloan

Patrick was born in 1851 and married Sarah Sloan on May 4, 1867. Sarah was the daughter of Michael Sloan from Ballymageough. Witnesses to the marriage were Ellen Mackin and James Sloan. Patrick listed his occupation as farmer and

Sarah stated that she was a sewer. The couple had two sons, Joseph (b. April 7, 1871) and Richard (b. April 14, 1868). Like his uncle of the same name, Richard went to Montana to work about 1915 and never returned home. The other son Joseph stayed at home, he never married and had a reputation of being an extremely intelligent man. Joseph was regarded by the local population as being *'as good as a solicitor'* and despite working the family farm his entire life, he always made time to help those that came to he with legal problems. Apparently, Joseph prevented at least one neighbour from being evicted and losing his home. Joseph asked the man to show him the letter he had received, he read it and told his neighbour when they come to evict you, send for me. So as requested when the bailiffs arrived with the eviction order, Joe was called on. Joe looked at the notice and declared that they could not put the man out of his home, as they had spelt his name wrong. He told them to go and read the law in relation to this, which they did, the man was allowed to live in his home and the charge was dropped. Joe eventually lost his leg due to illness, and so he started working as a carpenter, a skill he taught himself. He made himself a wooden leg, and had a good trade in making coffins. So with his carpentry and legal skills he was certainly a great asset to the local community.

Margaret Mackin Quinn died at the age of 66 on the March 13, 1874, from bronchitis just three weeks after her husband Mark who died on February 22, 1874 of general debility.

William Quinn – Linen Merchant

Another branch of the Quinn family was headed by William Quinn, William Quinn was born c.1740 and became a successful linen merchant. There is a William Quinn listed in the 1830 Tithes Applotment Books for Aughnaloopy, but it is impossible to confirm the location of this land in townland, Whether William was born in the Kilkeel area or moved there in adulthood is unknown. William apparently reared ten sons, the seventh being named Thomas. No information is available on the other children.

Thomas Quinn and Margaret Donaldson

William's son Thomas lived in Aughnaloopy where he worked as a farmer. On November 30, 1830 in Newry, Thomas married Margaret Donaldson, a daughter of William Donaldson, who was a wholesale baker and confectioner from Greencastle Street in Kilkeel. Thomas and Margaret had a large family including a son Henry who died in infancy, Margaret (c. 1831), Jane (c.1833), Matilda (c.1834), Ann (May 1, 1839), Arthur (c. 1842), Henry 'Harry' (December 25, 1843), Elizabeth (December 19, 1845), Thomas (February 2, 1849) and Charlotte (January 8, 1853). No further information is known about Arthur, Elizabeth or Charlotte.

The Children of Thomas Quinn and Margaret Donaldson

Margaret Quinn and Arthur Cunningham

Thomas Quinn and Margaret Donaldson had a daughter Margaret. A marriage record has been located for a Margaret Quinn to Arthur Cunningham dated February 7, 1855. Witnesses to the marriage were Daniel Kinny and Elizabeth 'Betty' Cunningham. Unfortunately the parents names have not been recorded and so it is impossible to confirm at this point whether this is Thomas Quinn's daughter. Arthur Cunningham and Margaret Quinn had at least two children Ann (b. February 13, 1869) and Arthur (b. December 27, 1870).

Matilda Quinn and Terence McCartan

Thomas's daughter Matilda was born in 1846. She married Terence McCartan from the Longstone on December 5, 1866; witnesses to the marriage were Matilda's brother Henry and Mary Sloan. The couple settled in Lower Mourne where they had at least ten children: Terence (baptized May 19, 1863 sponsors were R McCartan and B Cunningham), Mary Anne (baptized September 25, 1870 sponsors were Alex Spears and Eliza McKibben), Arthur (b. August 10, 1872), Bridget (baptized October 27, 1872 sponsors were William McKibben and Anne McCartan), Thomas (b. 1876),

Patrick (baptized July 27,1877 sponsors Pat Higgins and Matilda McKeown), Edward (b. 1878), Margaret (baptized October 29, 1879 sponsors William and Anne McCartan), Sarah Jane (b. 28 Nov. 1879), and Henry (b. 1883). Matilda remained in Moneydarragh until her death on September 6, 1911. Her son Thomas and his wife Sarah Ann Rooney (from Brackenagh) took over the farmstead.

Ann Quinn and 'Dancing Tom' McCartan

Ann married Terence's brother Thomas McCartan from the Moneydarragh on November 2, 1857 December 5, 1866; witnesses to the marriage were Francis McCartan and Ellen Sloan. Thomas McCartan was a great Irish dancer and earned the title of 'Dancing Tom'. He is referred to in the publication 'An Old-Timer Talking - Reminiscences and Stories', narrated by Hugh Marks of Kilkeel to local author W J Fitzpatrick:

> *GREENCASTLE FAIR*
>
> *'..... An' I suppose ye heard tell o' Greencastle Fair? A never was at it but A was talkin' to them that was. There was a song about it. Me mother knowed it, God rest her. "Who has had the luck to see Greencastle Fair? A Mourne man all in his glory was there". "That's all A know of it, but A think the Mourne man mentioned in the song was a man called Dancin' Tam McCartan from the Longstone. He was a champion step-dancer, none to touch him. The last fair at Greencastle was about 70 years ago. It was always held on the 12th August, and on that mornin' the roads wud be black wi' people from all airts and parts and say wud be black as well wi' all kin's o' wee boats and yawls filled wi' people from Cooley and roun' there. There wud be great fun wi' the boatmen, wan tryin' to outdo the other in sailin. "There wur no end o' tents and caravans. It was mostly in the tents that the dancin' took place and ye may be sure the music wud ha' been worth a listenin' to - pipers and fiddlers and fifers. There wur prizes for the best step-dancers and they wud ha' danced jigs and reels and hornpipes and Irish set dances. There wud ha' been all kinds o' 'kereckters' at the fair, jugglers and spey-men and spey-weemin, and men sellin' all kin's o' things lek churns and tubs and other wudden veshils that's not used nowadays, and cloggers sellin' clogs, for nearly ivery man, woman and wean in Mourne wore clogs in them days, and then there wur woollen waivers sellin' pleadin' and banyins; nearly all the men wore banyans in them days. In troth ye cud ha' bought everything from a needle to an anchor at Greencastle Fair. An' there was lashins and leavin's o' all kin's o' atin and drinkin'. Whiskey at 3d or 4d a glass and porter at 1½d or 2d a bottle. The stir lasted to the early hours o' the morning and many an ould horse or donkey made their way home themselves wi' their owners lyin' stocious' in the carts. Och, them was the days. It's mebbe just as well drink's not as chape nowadays or there'd be whole lots wud never be sober, troth naw.'*

Further light was shed on the Greencastle fair by Mr. James Cunningham, manager of the Bridge Bar, Kilkeel, who remembers his grandmother telling him of the blind fiddler who came across from Cooley every year to play at the fair. This fiddler, who had been blind from birth, attended all the festivals throughout Ireland, and also taught people to play the violin.

> *'I heard my grandmother say,'* recalled Mr. Cunningham, *'that one year when he was fiddling for the dancing competitions he said ".....if Dancing Tom McCartan's alive that's him I'm playing for now...." And so it was.'*

Ann Quinn and her husband 'Dancing Tom' settled in Moneydarragh where they had at least eleven children including: Thomas (baptized March 6, 1859 sponsors were Henry McCartan and Kate Digney), William (baptized May 8, 1861 sponsors Patrick Collins and Martha Quinn), Hugh (baptized August 3, 1862 sponsors Terence McCartan and Margaret Quinn), Annie (b. 1865), Bernard (b. 1867), William (baptized September 23, 1867 sponsors John McVey and Mary Doran), Elizabeth (b. 1868), James (b. 1870), Arthur (b. 1873) and Charlotte (b. 1874). There may also have been a daughter Margaret.

Thomas McCartan died on October 27, 1893. The Aughnaloopy and the Quinn connection was maintained through their son Hugh's marriage to Mary Ann Clarke on September 24, 1895. Mary Ann Clarke was the daughter of Charles Clarke and Ellen Quinn (who was the daughter of James 'Hamilton' Quinn). Hugh and Mary Ann settled in Moneydarragh, where they had at least two children, Hugh (b. 1898) and Charles (b. 1901).

From the Liverpool Dockyards to a Californian Ranch
Ann and Tom McCartan's daughter Annie married William Marmion from the Grange, Kilkeel. William was one of ten children of John Marmion and Elizabeth 'Betty' Sloan. William spent time in the dock area of Liverpool with his brothers John, Patrick and Peter. The oldest brother John eventually took over the firm of Sir Thomas Houston and with his brothers largely controlled the Liverpool dock area, employing many men from their native Mourne. William Marmion, his wife Annie McCartan Marmion and their children, John Thomas (b. 1885), William Henry (b. 1894) and James Sloan (b. 1897) left Liverpool and traveled out to California where he worked on Henry Quinn's ranch in Kern. William eventually returned to Kilkeel where he died on March 3, 1940.

The Poet
Ann and Tom's youngest daughter Charlotte McCartan married Daniel Fitzpatrick (son of Daniel Fitzpatrick and Sarah Hughes) from Moneydarragh on September 12, 1901. John Fitzpatrick (Daniel's brother) and Maggie McCartan were witnesses to the marriage. The couple had three children William John 'W J', also known as 'The Poet', Sarah Ann and John.

A Californian Pioneer - Henry 'Harry' Quinn
Many in Mourne will know tales of Harry Quinn, the great pioneer of California. Harry was born on Christmas Day in 1843, the son of Thomas Quinn and Margaret Donaldson. Harry was purported the seventh son of Thomas who was also a seventh son. Harry spent his childhood in a small thatched-roofed cottage, 'Springfield', on the Kiln Road in Aughnaloopy where his father worked as a farmer. (The Kiln Road has not been located on a modern day map of Aughnaloopy). It is during his early days that Harry gained a love of farming and acquired valuable knowledge that would help him later in life. Research into Harry Quinn was aided by the immense impact he had on his adopted homeland of California and the efforts of his descendants to record his life. Harry's route to his eventual fortune was not a direct one. He left Aughnaloopy c.1859 at just 16-years old bound initially for the gold mines of Australia.

Deported for Poaching a Hare
The land in Mourne during Harry's childhood was not intensively cultivated or profitable. The gorse, rocks and rushes of the moors stretched right through Aughnaloopy down to Drumcro townland. Roads were few, money was scarce and food was in short supply. Game was plentiful but the estate agents and keepers kept a sharp eye for young boys like Harry that may have been on the hunt to supplement the family food supply. Many rumours surround Harry's move to Australia, including far-fetched tales of being deported for poaching a hare, but it is most likely that Harry was just a young man who felt the need to seek adventure and find his place in the World. It is known that Harry was not the only Quinn from Aughnaloopy to make the passage to the New World. Nicholas and James Quinn from Aughnaloopy (possibly cousins of Harry) are documented as travelling on the SS Tudor to Australia in July 1859, their brother William also emigrated; as did an older relative Henry Quinn (likely an uncle who also emigrated around this time).

On Harry's arrival in Australia it is purported that he first went to the mines of the Melbourne colony and subsequently to the mining districts of Adelaide. This certainly ties in with the notion that he met up with Kilkeel natives Nicholas, William and James Quinn. They are known to have worked in the Australian Goldfields at Ballarat and Bendigo and then with the discovery of gold in Otago, New Zealand, moved Gabriel's Gully in 1861.

Off to California

Harry's passion lay not in mining but in farming and sheep rearing. He secured a position on a large sheep ranch working as a common labourer for several years, where he zealously learnt the details of running a large ranch. Sometime around 1868 he had gained the knowledge he needed and had saved enough money to embark on his next adventure. This time he set sail for California, landing in San Francisco. There is some speculation that he also paid for three companions to travel with him and that one of these may have been Jack Shannon from Kilkeel.

After working on various ranches, Harry made acquaintance with Archibald Leitch, a successful sheep-raiser and landowner who was working in Stanislaus County in the Central Valley of California. Leitch was a native of Robinson County, North Carolina, born September 24, 1822, his parents being John and Isabella (McCorgle) Leitch, both from the Highlands of Scotland. Harry began working for Leitch in 1873 and his boss was quickly impressed with Harry's energy and farming skills. Leitch sent him into Kern County as a pilot for his flocks, and at the end of two years took him into partnership. Harry also developed skills as a successful businessman, he purchased a half interest in twenty-two hundred head of sheep and he took up a pre-emption claim of one hundred and sixty acres of land. He also purchased railroad land and acquired large tracts from homesteaders who were unable to prove up on their claims. In 1886, Harry who was an adventurer at heart took an extended tour passing through twenty-two states of America. While in North Carolina he met his partner Mr. Leitch's niece, Katherine 'Kitty' Robertson. They were married on December 15, 1886 and returned to homestead on the Rag Gulch Ranch where they raised seven children: Margaret (b. 1887), John Robertson (b. 1889), Thomas Walker (b. 1892), Archibald Giles (b. 1894), Cletus Edward (b. 1896), Mary A. (b. 1898), and Mildred Kathryn (b. 1900).

During the early days in the history of Kern County the Quinn farm was the only place for miles where a traveller could obtain food and water and hence immigrants headed for the ranch from every direction; watering their stock and resting while enjoying the hospitality and welcome of Harry Quinn and his wife Kitty Robertson. News of Harry's success spread through Mourne and many men travelled to California to work alongside him. From ranch records some of the Mourne men listed as being employed by Harry include: John Crangle, Tom McGivern, Jim Donnan, Pete O'Hagan, Pat White, Robert and Fred Morris, Peter Doran, Tom McConville, Charles Orr, Robert Reilly, Joseph Bartley, Henry Huston, John Henderson and several of the McCartans from Lower Mourne. William Marmion (b. 1863) also spent time working at Harry Quinn's ranch. He later married Annie McCartan who was Harry's niece.

Harry was not without his share of misfortune. During the drought of 1877 he was forced to seek new ranges for his sheep. With a flock of eighteen thousand six hundred and sixty sheep he went into Nevada and at first found abundant pasturage, but while at Fish Lake valley he was caught in a severe snowstorm and fifteen thousand sheep perished at one time. On his return to Kern he had only twenty seven hundred head of sheep and was $5,000 in debt. Undismayed by a catastrophe that would have discouraged most men, he continued working to enlarge his flock and in a few years had paid off his debt.

For many years he was engaged in raising thoroughbred French merinos, which were shipped throughout the United States and to Mexico and South Africa for breeding. In 1911 he sold the last of his stock and devoted his attention to raising Shorthorn Durham cattle.

Harry died in 1932, age 89-years in Tulare County, California and Kitty died 2-years later. The myths and facts surrounding Harry Quinn are at times difficult to separate but there is consensus that he was a hardworking man who provided welcomed employment to many of his compatriots from Mourne.

Harry's life has been put into song by his great grandson Tom Richardson who plays with the California-based band The Farallons. The song is available on the Internet at: http://thefarallons.com/music.html

QUINN'S JOURNEY

Please to meet you I'm Harry Quinn.
I come from Kilkeel in County Down.
I sail from my home in Ireland,
the seventh son of the seventh son.

I sailed from Newcastle in '63.
Round Tierra del Fuego to the Melbourne quay,
where stars and stripes did catch my eye.
I said "That's me flag boys," Australia good-bye

I'm going to the Golden State
Make me my fortune before it's too late
Land of plenty, or so they say
California, I'm on my way.

Across the Pacific our sails did fly
As we trained our eyes on the eastern sky
and sighted a country my dreams had belied
'Jesus, Mary and Joseph!' I cried.

So I toiled and toughened and made my way
and built my fortune and family.
From Rag Gulch it stretches out far and wide,
on up to Val Verde on the eastern side.

I'm going to the Golden State
Make me my fortune before it's too late
Land of plenty, or so they say
California, I'm on my way.

A hundred years later my great grandson
borne of the valley and raised in the sun,
did travel to Ireland to the County Down
and married a lassie in Belfast town.

A great grand-daughter of Maeve the Queen,
and the seventh son of the San Joaquin.
Two daughters begotten - so proud and strong
and gave them the power to carry on.

I'm going to the Golden State
Make me my fortune before it's too late
Land of plenty, or so they say
California, I'm on my way.

Lyrics and photograph kindly donated by Tom Richardson

Jane Quinn and John Lloyd
Henry Quinn's sister Jane (c.1826) also moved to the United States. She married John Lloyd and the couple settled in Centerville, Alameda, California. It does not appear that the couple had any children. They are documented on the 1880 US Federal census, where John, age 62-years is noted as a labourer and Jane age 54-years old is keeping house. John is also listed on the California Voters Lists where he states that he was originally from Ireland and that he became a naturalised United States citizen on August 31, 1875 in San Francisco.

Thomas Quinn and Susan Doran
Thomas Quinn and Margaret Donaldson had a son Thomas born in February 1849. Thomas married Susan Doran from Moneydarragh on November 25, 1880. Susan was the daughter of John Doran and Eliza Clarke. Thomas took over his father's property in Aughnaloopy and the couple remained there until their death. They did not have any children. Susan Doran Quinn died in 1911 and Thomas in 1921.

Mary Ann Mackin and James 'Hamilton' Quinn

James 'Hamilton' Quinn leased several sites in Leitrim and Aughrim at the time of the Griffith's Valuation. Whether he held land in Aughnaloopy is unclear but certainly there are several references linking him to the Quinn family of Aughnaloopy. There is a James Quinn listed on the 1864 Griffith's Valuation, leasing a 14-acre site with home and outbuildings from Thomas F Moore, recorded as GV35, but it can not be confirmed that this is James 'Hamilton' Quinn. The middle name Hamilton was supplied by Vincey Quinn of Kilkeel. It is not known if James was baptised with the name or whether it was a name used to identify him from the other James Quinns in the area.

It has been speculated, but is difficult to confirm that James 'Hamilton' Quinn was a brother or more likely a cousin of Thomas Quinn who married Margaret Donaldson. Certainly the families knew each other and Harry Quinn is believed to have spent time in Australia with James 'Hamilton' Quinn's sons. His mother is thought to be from the Hamilton family but no evidence has been found to verify this.

In addition to his Aughnaloopy connections, James 'Hamilton' Quinn had leases on property in GV37 Aughrim, and GV37 and GV38 in Leitrim. The site referenced as GV38a in Leitrim was a flax mill known as Larry's Mill (a derivation of Laragh's Mill). It bordered Francis Rogers and Patrick Doran's land in Aughnaloopy.

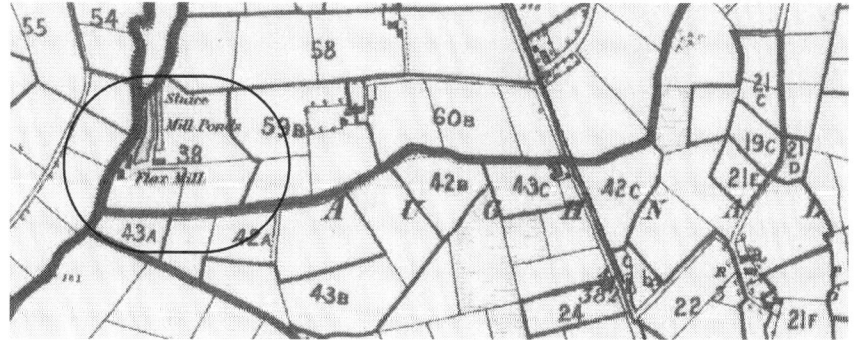

James 'Hamilton' married Mary Ann Mackin c. 1825. Based on naming patterns and other circumstantial evidence Mary Ann is thought to be a sister of Patrick Mackin who was married to Alexandrea 'Ally' Marmion, and also Margaret Mackin who married Mark Quinn. Their father is believed to be Nicholas Mackin.

James 'Hamilton' and Mary Ann Mackin had a large family including: Nicholas (who married Mary Cunningham in 1857), William (who married Katie Duggan in 1884), Ellen (who married Charles Clarke in 1867), James, Patrick (who married Margaret Quinn c. 1863), Ann (who married James Doyle in 1861), John, Henry, Margaret (who married Edward Murney in 1872), Mary (who married James Cunningham in 1873), Thomas (who married Mary Fitzpatrick in 1895) and possibly a daughter Sarah. James 'Hamilton' Quinn died in 1889 and Mary Ann Mackin Quinn died in 1892. No Wills have been located for either James 'Hamilton' or Mary Ann.

The Children of James 'Hamilton' Quinn and Mary Ann Mackin

Nicholas Quinn and Mary Cunningham

Nicholas was born in July 1829, the son of James 'Hamilton' Quinn and Mary Ann Mackin. On July 12, 1857, he married Aughrim native Mary Cunningham (the daughter of Peter Cunningham and Sarah Kenny). The following year Mary gave birth to a daughter Ann, baptized August 6, 1858, who would be their only child. When Ann was still an infant Nicholas left Ireland with his brother William, moving first to Australia in July 1859 on the SS Tudor and then on to New Zealand.

In 1860, Nicholas purchased 'Bellevue Farm' at Makikihi, and it would seem that he then sent for his wife and daughter to join him. Nicholas was listed on the Roll of Electors for Canterbury, 1869; and was recorded as the owner of 862 acres of land at Makikihi (valued at £6,586), he also had land in Waimate Borough (valued at £200) and in Timaru (valued at £7,000 in 1882). Nicholas was instrumental in establishing an Irish Catholic Community in Waimate and the surrounding areas.

On September 8, 1884 his daughter Ann married Cork native Humphrey Geaney, who was a successful butcher in the area In the newspaper announcement Nicholas states Drummalain (sic) as his home in Co. Down, suggesting that he had moved there after his marriage to Mary Cunningham.

PUBLISHED SEPTEMBER 11, 1884
GEANEY - QUINN. On the 8th September, at the Roman Catholic Church, Waimate, by the Rev. Father Goutenoire, assisted by the Rev. Father Devoy, Humphrey, second son of Michael Geaney, of Cork, Ireland, to Annie, only daughter of Nicholas and Mary Quinn, of Makikihi, formerly of Drummonlain, County Down, Ireland.

When Nicholas died in 1903, the value of his estate was approximately £23,000. He left a detailed Will that helped established his family connections in New Zealand and Ireland. Money and land bequeathed by Nicholas enabled the building of the first church in Makikhi on a five-acre site. The church that cost £900 was built of brick from his brother William's brickyard and had room for 200 worshippers. Nicholas also left specific instructions for the procurement of a peal of bells for the use of the Catholic Cathedral at Christchurch in the Provincial District of Canterbury. Bishop John Grimes placed the matter of the bells in the hands of a Belgian trading firm, *Comptoir Commercial Anversois*, who in turn commissioned Monsieur A Causard in Tellin to cast them. The bells were dispatched to Lyttelton on the SS Greisenau on the November 6, 1904 and arrived just in time to be ready for the grand opening of the completed Cathedral on the February 12, 1905. The combined weight of the bells was 3660 kilograms and the cost of £463NZ.

In September 2010 and again in February 2011, Christchurch Basilica was horrendously damaged by earthquakes that rocked the city. The earthquake cracked pillars, twisted walls, shattered stained glass, collapsed buttresses, and fractured masonry throughout the building. The bells were silenced! Bell recovery is part of the current painstaking job of assessing the damage throughout the cathedral but it is hoped that the bells bequeathed by Nicholas Quinn of Aughnaloopy will indeed ring out again across the city.

Our Lady turns towards the City

A dome and part of the tower that supported it tumbled from Christchurch's Cathedral of the Blessed Sacrament in the February 22, 2011 earthquake. A statue of Our Lady that stood a ledge inside the tower remained standing and

WAIMATE.

(From our own correspondent.)

October 13.

A short time ago a suggestion was made to erect a new church at Makikihi. The matter was submitted to his Lordship Bishop Grimes, and, much to the delight of those who had moved in the matter, approval of the scheme was received. The question of a site, a most important item, was not allowed to stand in the way, as Mr N. Quinn, of Makikihi made a generous offer of five acres of land facing the main road about a quarter of a mile on the south side of the Makikihi hotel ; and to cap this liberal offer, he further gave the substantial donation of £200. Needless to say this handsome offer had the effect of spurring on others to do their utmost. Without delay plans and specifications were prepared, and the tender of Mr E. Foden, of Timaru, for labor only, was accepted. A few figures regarding the dimensions might prove of interest. The main building is to be 20ft by 40ft, sanctuary 15ft by 16ft, sacristy 10ft x 9½ft, porch 7ft x 6ft. The building is to be erected in brick, and is of very neat design. There are six lead lights on either side, and in front a lead light on either side of the door, with an ornamental circular lead light over the door, all being of cathedral glass. The plans and specifications were prepared free of charge by Mr O'Connell (Christchurch), father of the Rev. Father O'Connell, late of Waimate. The total cost of the building is estimated at between £700 and £800. In connection with the solemn ceremony of laying the foundation stone, the arrangements were very complete. His Lordship Bishop Grimes, accompanied by Dean Foley and Rev. Fathers Regnault, Aubry, Tubman, and Le Petit left the Waimate presbytery about two o'clock on Sunday, proceeding to Makikihi to perform the ceremony. Drags conveying the members of St Patrick's Church choir, and the Waimate brass band followed. Upon arrival at the ground, the band, under Mr C. J. Goldstone, played several suitable selections, much to the enjoyment of fully 300 persons. The Rev. Father Regnault intimated that Mr James Meehan, of Makikihi, had a few words to say, and then he called upon that gentleman. Mr Meehan then read the following address to his Lordship Bishop Grimes, and which was signed on behalf of the Catholics of Makikihi by Messrs Nicholas Quinn, William Quinn, James Meehan, and Patrick Quinn :—

T I M A R U.

(From an occasional Correspondent.)

DEATH has again visited this parish and has taken a kind and familiar face from amongst us. On Wednesday, the 9th inst, Mrs Humphrey Geaney died at the early age of 34 years, leaving a family of three young children, her husband, and her father and mother to mourn her premature death. The greatest sympathy is felt throughout the district for Mr Geaney by his numerous friends, and also for Mr and Mrs Nicholas Quinn, the parents of the deceased. Mrs Geaney was educated at the Christchurch and Dunedin convents and has resided in Timaru since the date of her marriage in 1884. She has at all times previous to her illness taken an active and prominent part in parochial matters, and has always responded with true generosity to the various calls made for charitable or deserving objects. Her truly kind and charitable nature, gentle and unobtrusive manners won for her a large circle of friends, who sincerely regret her early death. The last few months of her illness were months of suffering, which she bore with great fortitude, being attended by her mother, who nursed her unceasingly and with an amount of unwearied attention and care, which only a fond mother can bestow. Living a truly pious and Catholic life, she died a calm and peaceful death surrounded by her family and fortified by all the rites of the Church. The Rev Fathers Hurlin and Tubman were frequent visitors at the sick room, ministering the consolations of holy religion to the dying patient. On Friday the body was removed to the church of the Sacred Heart, where a solemn *Requiem* Mass was celebrated by Father Tubman, Father Regnault (Waimate), being deacon, and Father Le Petit (Temuka), sub-deacon. At two o'clock the funeral left for the cemetery—the organ playing the Dead March in "Saul" as the body was being removed from the church. The members of the Hibernian Society marched in regalia at the funeral, which was a remarkably large one, friends of deceased being present from Waimate, Makikihi, Temuka, and the surrounding districts. Father Hurlin officiated at the grave, the responses being given by Fathers Tubman and Regnault. The coffin was strewn with choice floral wreaths and crosses, the last tribute of respect to one who during her life made no enemies but many friends.—R I P.

A GRAIN SHED ON FIRE.

When the train from Oamaru passed Studholme yesterday morning, the passengers had an usual and regrettable addition to the scenery in the shape of a destructive fire, Mr Nicholas Quinn's large grain shed, containing many thousand sacks of wheat, being ablaze. The fire was first discovered about 5.30 in the morning; the alarm soon spread, and a large gang of men were quickly on the spot. The store is situate to the north of the Junction Hotel, and at the time of the outbreak contained about 25,000 sacks of grain. The seat of the fire was well in the centre of the shed, which is built of timber and iron, and after an engine and seed cleaning plant at the western end of the building had been got out of danger, all efforts were centred on removing grain and getting at the seat of the fire. Ere this was done, however, an effort was made to extinguish the fire with the small supply of water in the tanks, and a short length of hose. Messengers were also sent to get the Waimate Fire Brigade's hand plant. All northern doors having been sealed to prevent the wind from that quarter keeping the fire from spreading, the southern doors were opened, and while men dragged the grain through these, drays carted it away to safe spots in the paddocks adjoining. A huge hole was also cut in the side of the building where the smoke was densest, and by the time the Waimate Fire Brigade arrived all was in readiness for the attempt to quench the fire. Fortunately this attempt was successful, and before noon, the building and most of its contents were saved and the fire put out. A great quantity of grain, a rough estimate being from 4000 to 5000 sacks, was damaged by fire, smoke and water, and piles of sacks were dragged out and dumped anyhow in a safe place. The grain is the property of Messrs Quinn, Meehan, and others, and up to dark last night damaged portions of it were still being got out. In some cases bags had burst by the fire charring them, and in other cases bags were singed by fire, blackened by smoke or sodden with water. The men who worked at the fire deserve the greatest credit and that their efforts were in a measure highly satisfactory must be most gratifying to them. We understand that the building and contents were insured, but to what amount we were unable to learn last evening. Probably by to-day the full extent of the damage, which in any case must be considerable, will be known.

Timaru

(From our own correspondent.)

The church building fund received a substantial increase through the late Mr. Nicholas Quinn, of Makikihi. Mr. Quinn belonged to the Waimate parish, yet he has bequeathed £600 to the proposed new church in Timaru— £300 of that amount to be expended on a peal of bells, also £700 to the Christchurch Cathedral. He has left £400 to the Waimate church, and £200 to the Makikihi church. The convents at Waimate, Christchurch, and Timaru receive £50 each, and to other institutions and other church purposes he has left bequests making in all about £3000.

remained unharmed. Oddly, before the quake, the statue faced inwards, where bell ringers could see it as they tolled the bells. After the quake, it faces outwards. The bells are silent now and the ringers are wondering what message lies in Our Lady's 180-degree turn.

The Church benefited considerably from money bequeathed by Nicholas.

DIOCESE OF CHRISTCHURCH September 14, 1903
The Very Rev. Dean Foley, who remained on the West Coast labouring in the interests of the Cathedral and diocese, has telegraphed to the Bishop to the effect that he had succeeded in securing a site and was arranging for the building of a church in the locality where one does not exist but is urgently needed. Sunday last being the feast of the Holy Name of Mary and paternal feast of the Marist Order, his Lordship the Bishop preached on Sunday evening at Vespers an occasional sermon at St. Mary's, Manchester Street. Speaking at the complimentary conversation on last Tuesday evening, his Lordship the Bishop said that despite the numerous calls recently made on the people of the West Coast, and the appeal made by himself for the Cathedral building fund was the third for that object, he had received over £600 during the visitation. In carrying out the expressed desire of the late Mr. Quinn an iron arch and lamp have been erected over the gateway of St. Joseph's Church, Temuka, the cost being borne by the estate of the deceased gentleman.

Nicholas was not the only benefactor to the Cathedral and just as the building is a wondrous architectural statement, perhaps even more wondrous is that a small congregation of mainly working-class Irish immigrants funded the entire project.

William Quinn and Catherine 'Katie' Duggan
William was born in Aughnaloopy in 1828, the son of James 'Hamilton' Quinn and Mary Ann Mackin. He left Ireland with his brother Nicholas and the two men achieve success mining in Australia and New Zealand. William invested his earnings in land at Makikihi where he built a home that he named 'Annalong'. He is listed on the Roll of Electors for Canterbury in 1869 and in 1882 is recorded as the owner of 2514 acres in Waimate County valued at £12,696 and of land in Waimate Borough valued at £400.

William married Catherine 'Katie' Duggan, from Tralee, County Kerry on January 22, 1884 at the Church of the Most Blessed Sacrament, in Christchurch. Katie was the daughter of Denis Duggan and Deborah O'Sullivan. Her parents stayed in Ireland but some of her nine siblings moved to New Zealand including Patrick, James, John, Mary and Bessie. Several worked for their brother-in-law William Quinn.

William and Katie had four sons: James Patrick (b. 1885), William Aloysius (b. 1887), John Joseph (b. 1888), and Henry Augustus (b. 1892) and a daughter Kathleen (b. 1894) who died in infancy. There was an artistic tendency in the family. William turned his creative skills into developing a brickworks, designing a shopping arcade and building a homestead in Makikihi. By 1894 he was running the brickworks and owned three threshing mills. His son William Aloysius was interested in photography. James was a keen artist and travelled to London to study painting and exhibit his work. Henry was interested in astrology and purchased a telescope so that he could study the stars. William Aloysius died tragically when he was just 26-years of age as the result of a road accident.

KILLED BY MOTOR-CAR MAN LYING ON THE ROAD WAIMATE
A young man named William Quinn was run over by a motor-car near Makikihi at about 12 o'clock last night, and died shortly after. A party was returning home from Waimate, and the car ran over Quinn, who was lying on the road between Makikihi and his home.

KILLED BY A MOTOR YOUNG FARMER'S DEATH. TIMARU, 17th June.
An inquest was held today concerning the death of William Quinn, a young

farmer of Makikihi, who was found unconscious and with a leg broken and injuries to the head and shoulders, on the main road near Makikihi on the night 10th June. He died after removal to his home. The principal evidence was given by a party of four, who were returning from Waimate to Timaru in a hired car. The driver stated that he saw something lying flat on the road. He took it to be a shadow till he was close up to it; then he supposed it was a bag of coal, and swerved the car, but a front wheel bumped over something, which he supposed was a lump of coal from the bag. The others behind him in the car felt no bump. The driver, knowing another car was following, said he would stop and shift the bag of coal. He pulled up, and on going back found it was a man. He concluded he had run over a leg. When he got back another witness, a neighbour named Martin, who had been walking along the road, had reached the body and was moving it. The car went back to Waimate for a doctor. There was evidence on the road that the body had been dragged, but the car driver was sure his car had dragged nothing. The Coroner found that deceased died from shock, the result of injuries through being run down by a motor-car. There was no evidence to show who was the driver of the car which caused the injuries.

William's sons James and Henry were reclusive in nature and they remain bachelors. John Joseph appears on the WW1 Service Personnel & Reserves List where he states his occupation as framer. He was the only one of the brothers to have married but unfortunately died at just 55-years old. John Joseph and his wife Mary Josephine Dossett had a daughter Maureen and a son John Emmet, who settled in Pleasant Point near Timaru.

William Quinn died on July 1, 1914 at age 80-years old from heart failure at his residence 'Annalong', Makikihi. His estate valued at £28,500NZ, passed to his wife Catherine and their sons. Catherine died in 1946. James and Henry eventually spent all the family money causing 'Annalong' to be sold in 1968. When the property changed hands, the new owner discovered six statues which were made for the New Zealand International Exhibition, held in Christchurch during 1906 and 1907. The group of figures were sculptured by Mr. J McDonald of Wellington and cast in Carrera plaster and bronzed. They stood in the Exhibition's Main Corridor. At the conclusion of the exhibition the group of Māori statues was acquired by William Quinn and were then stored in a shed on his farm for about 60 years. Only one statue was salvageable. It was put up for auction and then donated to the Waimate Historical Society. Photographs of the statues can be viewed at:
http://www.nzmuseums.co.nz/account/3188/object/1286
http://www.nzmuseums.co.nz/account/3188/object/50545/Māori_Statues

Arcadia Theatre - Waimate's Unique Arcade

This classic brick building stands linking Grigson Street and High Street in Waimate. The Category II registered historic building was constructed in 1906 by Mr William Quinn, following the conclusion of the Christchurch Exhibition. William bought a great deal of dismantled equipment and transported it all to Waimate by rail. The 296,970 bricks needed for the building were all made at his Makikihi brickworks and transported to Waimate by traction engine. Initially the building was comprised of an arcade with an attractive symmetrical brick frontage, which had a large glass dome-like arch and a matching glass canopied veranda. Inside the arcade on each side were 12 small shops with four internal staircases.

As a viable business venture the arcade only lasted a decade and in 1916 was remodelled into *'The Arcadia Theatre and Billiard Room'*. The theatre had a dress circle with 175 seats and stalls with 550 seats. Before Waimate was served with hydropower, a big gas engine drove the generator at Arcadia. After ten thirty at night, the gas-lit streets would often black out, so unless the lamplighter re-lit them, theatre goers would go home in the dark! A newspaper article from the Evening Post, dated August 30, 1920 gives an idea of some of the performances put on at the theatre.

Albert Steele, at the Arcadia Theatre, Waimate, completed 106 hours 15 minutes' continuous piano playing, winding up freshly after midnight on Saturday night.

The Arcadia also has claim to showing the first 'talkies' were there in 1930.

Disaster struck in 1955 when fire broke out and destroyed the theatre. The billiard rooms remained and it was here that Tommy Yesberg learned his sport and won the National titles in 1960, 1964 and 1975. He represented New Zealand in the World Championships held in Auckland in 1975.

Pro-Ject Waimate has recently successfully purchased the Arcadia with the intent to restore this magnificent old building to its former glory. Information is available online at http://www.quinnsarcade.co.nz/

Patrick Quinn and Margaret Quinn
James 'Hamilton' and his wife Mary Ann Mackin had a son Patrick who also moved to New Zealand. Patrick was born 1833 and married Margaret Quinn c. 1864. Patrick and Margaret had at least eight children (Mary b. 1867, who died in infancy, Joseph (b. 1868), Patrick (b. 1869), James (b. 1874), Thomas (b. 1874), another Mary (b. 1877), William (b. 1878), and Henry (b. 1882) all born in Ireland and also a daughter Ellen Josephine who was born in New Zealand in 1884. The family moved to New Zealand c.1883 and Patrick purchased 'Beach Farm' in Makikihi close to his brother Nicholas.

Patrick and Margaret's son Patrick married Mary Catherine Tober in Waimate and the couple had a daughter in 1903 named Margaret after her grandmother. Patrick died when his daughter was just 9-years old from a ruptured appendix. His estate was valued at £682NZ.

Tragedy befell the family in 1906 when Patrick and Margaret's son Henry was killed in an accident.

New Zealand Tablet, February 22, 1906
The North Otago Times reports that Mr. Henry Quinn was killed at Makikihi on Thursday. Mr. Quinn was cutting crop, and his brother, who was working near at hand, heard the machine revolving very rapidly and rushed over, he found his brother lying near by dead, the only words he was able to utter being ' Good-bye'. Dr. Barclay was summoned from Waimate. It is supposed that the horses started off while deceased was attending to a part of the machine that had gone wrong. His head was badly crushed through being struck by an arm of the packers.

Patrick and Margaret's son James married Teresa Kelly and worked as a farmer. He died in 1940, aged 90.

Their daughter Mary married Patrick O'Neill and their daughter Ellen Josephine married Limerick man Edward O'Neill. Edward's parents were John O'Neill and Bridget Heron but whether he was related to Patrick O'Neill is unknown.

Patrick and Margaret Quinn's son William married Gertrude Storey in New Zealand. William had the distinction of being the first in Makikihi to purchase a motorcar. In 1911 William purchased the Makikihi Hotel, which was destroyed by fire on March 19, 1929. The hotel was rebuilt and he took over the license again, until he sold the hotel in 1936 and retired to Timaru. William died in June 1957 and his wife Gertrude died in December 1968. They had six children together: William Henry Leonard (b. 1908), Tomas James (b. 1910), Gertrude Elizabeth (b. 1912), Nicholas (b. 1914), Margaret (c.1915) and Patrick (c. 1916).

TELEGRAPH WIRES SEVERED BY HOTEL FIRE CHRISTCHURCH
Evening Post, March 20, 1929. All telegraphic and telephonic communication between Christchurch and Dunedin was severed last night by a fire, which occurred at Makikihi 20 miles south of Timaru, at 8 o'clock. The fire occurred in Makikihi Hotel, on the main South road, alongside of which runs the telephone and telegraph wires. So fierce was the heat that the lines, which were only separated from the building by a narrow footpath, were destroyed for some distance. At least one of the poles that held them also destroyed. All communication was lost at 8.20 p.m., but was restored at 1 a.m.

Patrick died in September 1903. At the time of his death his estate was valued at £2,570NZ. His widow Margaret died in October 1912. Her estate was valued at under £400NZ; most of the family money and land having already passed to the couple's children.

Henry Quinn
Patrick, William and Nicholas had a brother Henry who also spent time with them in New Zealand. Henry was baptized on November 1849 making him considerably younger than his siblings. It is reputed that his wife and child died as a consequence of childbirth but no documentation has been found. Most of the information on Henry comes from the probate documents associated with his estate. He wrote two Wills, one in 1912 and one in 1916. At some point prior to 1912 he returned to Ireland. He died on January 19, 1920 in Springfield, Aughnaloopy and is buried in the family plot at Massforth RC Graveyard in Kilkeel.

Probate of Henry QUINN late of Springfield, Augnaloopy, Kilkeel in the County of Down, Farmer (located at Archives NZ, Peterborough Street, Christchurch).

First Will, signed 14 Oct 1912
I appoint Thomas QUINN, resident at Aughnaloopy, to manage my land in New Zealand, formerly the property of Nicholas QUINN deceased, to act in relation to my estate and property in new Zealand and to the premises as fully and effectually as I myself could do.

Second Will, signed 05 Jul 1916
Henry QUINN of Springfield, Kilkeel. I appoint my brother Thomas QUINN and Thomas O'NEILL of Dunnavan as my executors and trustees.
All property to trustees in trust for my said brother Thomas QUINN for his life and after his death for the use of William Henry QUINN, son of my said brother, Thomas QUINN.

Witnesses: Patrick H. DONNELLY, Grocer, Kilkeel. P. T. COLLINS, Solicitor, Newry.

Affidavits:
Thomas QUINN of Studholme Junction in the Dominion of New Zealand.
'I have acted as Agent for the deceased for some years prior to and up to his death in respect of his property.' Deceased was born in Ireland and of British Nationality. Estate under 5000 pounds - sworn at Temuka 5 May 1923.

Francis Arthur JOYNT - of Temuka - stated that Thomas QUINN of Studholme Junction and Thomas QUINN of Springfield were both born in Ireland.

District Registry of Belfast
Henry QUINN, late of Springfield, died 19 Jan 1920 at Springfield. Administration granted to Thomas QUINN of Springfield, brother of deceased.

Thomas Quinn 'Avenue Thomas' and Mary Fitzpatrick

Thomas was born in Leitrim on August 8, 1851, the youngest son of James Hamilton Quinn and Mary Ann Mackin. He was jus 8-years old when his brothers Nicholas and William left for Australia and eventual passage on to New Zealand. Thomas followed his brothers out to New Zealand but returned to Ireland before 1895 where he married Mary Fitzpatrick on February 26, 1895. Mary was the eldest daughter of Patrick Fitzpatrick and Catherine Murphy from Leitrim. Witnesses to the marriage were James O'Neill and Rose Fitzpatrick. The couple stayed in Ireland where they reared their seven children: William Henry 'Strawberry Willie' (b. 1896), Ann Teresa (b. 1897), Mary (b. 1898), Catherine (b. 1902), James (b. 1902), Thomas (b. 1907) and Mary 'Minnie' (b. 1908). Thomas was a shrewd businessman and seemed to take a lead role in managing the family finances. At the time of his death in 1929 he owned the home farm in Springfield, a three-acre farm at Drumcro, a field at Heath Hall on the east side of the county road, a wrack bed on Millbay shore (bought from Patrick Cunningham), and a house in Kilkeel (bought from Hugh Hanna). He also owned property in New Zealand. Thomas appears to have made no provision for his daughters in his Will, with his property being divided between his two sons, William Henry and Thomas. His son James had died in infancy.

Ann Quinn and James Doyle

It was through research on Ann Quinn, that this project on Aughnaloopy began. There are birth records for an Ann Quinn on May 1, 1839 and January 17, 1840, but no parents names are given. It is impossible to determine which is the correct record for the daughter of James 'Hamilton' Quinn and Mary Ann Mackin. The other record is likely for Ann, the daughter of Thomas Quinn and Margaret Donaldson. Fortunately Ann's marriage record has been located. She married James Doyle from Newcastle Street, Kilkeel on October 9, 1861 at Massforth RC church in Kilkeel. Witnesses to the marriage were Peter Doyle and Mary Rogers.

By the mid 1880's Ann's husband James Doyle was a wealthy merchant, running a bakery, a general store on Newcastle Street, Kilkeel and transporting granite and coal across the Irish Sea. Ann's father James was a wealthy farmer and flax mill owner with property in Aughnaloopy, Leitrim and Aughrim and so this made for a most suitable marriage. The couple had eight children together: Mary 'Minnie' (c.1863), Margaret (b. 1865), William John 'Willie' (b. 1867), James 'Dudley' (b. 1869), Thomas 'Tommy' (b. 1872), Sarah Ann (b. 1876), Henry Joseph 'Harry Joe' (b. 1878) and Albert Patrick (b. 1882).

Ann appears to have played a significant role in managing James's business affairs and the family prospered throughout the late nineteenth century. However, life was not without it's share of misfortune. Their daughter Sarah Ann died as a young child c.1877. Then in 1888, disaster struck when James was forced to abandon his vessel, the inaptly named Prosperity at Ballyquin Point.

Their son Willie was the first to marry. His wedding to Catherine Cunningham (daughter of James Cunningham and Ann Higgins, of the Moor) took place in Lower Mourne on November 14, 1895. Willie was a farmer and settled on land given to him by his father James at the Moor.

On November 10, 1897, Margaret Doyle married John 'Klondyke' Rooney from Old Town, Moneydarragh. John Rooney had worked in America and had arrived back in Kilkeel a very wealthy man. He purchased the Royal Hotel and operated as a spirit merchant. He also owned the first movie theatre in Kilkeel. Margaret and John did not have any children of their own but they raised Willie's daughters Winifred 'Winnie' and Mary Margaret 'Daisy' after their mother died in 1907.

James 'Dudley' Doyle married Mary Ellen 'Ellie' Maguire on February 8, 1899 in Castlewellan. Mary Ellen was the daughter of Dominic Maguire a schoolteacher from County Donegal and Harriet Teresa Kennedy from Annsborough. In 1901, James was working in the fishing industry while Ellie ran a drapery shop on Bridge Street, Kilkeel. The couple had four girls, three whom survived infancy: Harriet Teresa 'Etta' (b. 1901), Rose Eithne (b. 1903) and Margaret Eileen (b. 1906).

Mary 'Minnie' Doyle married a widower Terence Magee on October 14, 1903. Terence was originally from County Monaghan. His first wife was Annie Maguire from Cootehill in County Cavan. Terence and Annie had eleven children together before her death in 1901. The children were: Mary Catherine (b. 1882), Bridget Agnes (b. 1884), Francis Peter (b. 1885), Patrick Joseph (b. 1886), Terence (b. 1888), John Matthew (b. 1891), Thomas (b. 1894), Charles Henry (b. 1896), Anna (b. 1897), Michael Stephen (1898), and Leonitia Christina (b. 1900)

At the time of the 1911 census, Terence and his children were living on Upper North Street in Newry, whereas Minnie Doyle Magee continued to live in Kilkeel with her mother Ann who was running the family business.

Ann's husband, James Doyle died July 16, 1906. Ann continued to run the shop on Newcastle Street, Kilkeel until her death on October 21, 1916.

James and Ann's son Henry Joseph 'Harry Joe' Doyle had an adventurous spirit. He is known to have spent time in New Zealand with his maternal uncles Nicholas, Patrick and William. Nicholas was very fond of Harry Joe and had hoped that he would settle in New Zealand. However, it was not to be. Harry Joe moved on to South Africa, where another branch of the Doyle family were established. He was apparently appalled by the racism he witnessed there and returned to Kilkeel. Adventure called once more to Harry Joe, and he set sail, this time headed for Butte, Montana. He arrived in New York in August 1900 and traveled by railroad across country where he hoped to make his fortune in the copper mines. On September 12, 1918, Harry Joe was obliged to complete a Draft Card as part of the Third Registration. This was for men aged eighteen to twenty-one and thirty-one to forty-five. Fortunately the War was over within two months with the ceasefire being declared on November 11, 1918. As the world welcomed 1919, the War was over but peace did not come to Butte. This was the year that Prohibition was instigated and saloon raids began on January 1. Declining demand for copper brought a wage cut of $1 a day for Harry Joe and his colleagues. Butte responded in the only way it knew how – by calling a strike! To break the strike the Governor called in the 44th US Infantry. February 10, 1919 was a bloody day in Butte as the soldiers bayonet nine strikers. Enough was enough! Harry Joe and his compatriots had to leave Butte. In convoy, they managed to escape Montana and sailed home on a troop ship from the port of San Francisco. During his time in America, Harry Joe had traveled from *sea to shining sea,* arriving in New York harbour and departing from San Francisco Bay. On December 30, 1919, he married Sarah Elizabeth Rogers from the Old Town, Moneydarragh. Sarah was the daughter of John Rogers and Ellen Maginn. Witnesses to the marriage were Arthur Rooney and Catherine Rogers. The couple settled on Newcastle Street in Kilkeel where they raised a family of eight children. Harry Joe's time in Montana has been turned into a play entitled *'From the Mountains of Mourne to the mines of Montana'* by American playwright and actress Lisa Hayes. The play debuted at the Ulster Folk and Transport Museum in 2007 and has also been performed in Michigan under the direction of Sue Rogers (who is related to the Rogers family of the Old Town, Moneydarragh).

James and Ann's sons Albert and Tommy both remained single. They worked in the fishing industry with their brother James. Tommy died in 1918.

James 'Hamilton' and his wife Mary Ann Mackin had a son James and a son John but nothing is known about their life. They had a daughter Ellen who married Charles Clarke (son of Hugh Clarke and Catherine McCrink) from Moneydarragh Beg, on January 18, 1867. Witnesses to the marriage were Patrick Quinn and Margaret Quinn. Ellen and Charles had at least two children: Mary Ann (b. 1868) and James (b. 1869). Mary Ann married Hugh McCartan (son of Thomas McCartan and Ann Quinn) on September 24, 1895 and the couple had at least two sons: Hugh and Charles.

James 'Hamilton' and Mary Ann had a daughter Margaret who married Edward 'Ned' Murney from Ballincurry, Kilbroney on January 14, 1872. There are several transcriptions errors in the documentation relating to this family will Murray, Moynihan and Murney all being recorded in official documents. Ned was the son of Peter Murney and Rose Maginnis and was born on January 25, 1840. Ned and Margaret had at least 8 children including Mary 'Cissie' (b. 1873), Peter (b. 1875), John (b. 1877), James (b. 1878), Rose (b. 1880), Annie Kate (b. 1880), Edward (b. 1882) and William (b. 1886).

Mary Quinn was born to James 'Hamilton' and Mary Ann Quinn c. 1851. On October 1, 1873, she married 34-year old James Cunningham from the Moor. Witnesses to the marriages were henry Quinn and Ellen Cunningham. James Cunningham gave his father's name as Ivor and stated that he was deceased. Mary Quinn and James Cunningham settled at the Moor where they had at least 6 children: John (b. 1875), James (b. 1877), Ephraim (b. 1882), Thomas (b. 1883), Patrick (1885) and William (b. 1887). James, Thomas and Patrick all moved out to New Zealand and settled close to their maternal uncles.

Richard Quinn

Information on Richard is limited and his relationship to the Quinn family of Aughnaloopy is unclear. He died on October 12, 1889 and his possessions passed to his daughter Ann who was married to Dennis Murray of Killaghy, County Armagh. He also named a son John in his Will stating that he was living in America.

James Quinn (GV 35)

James Quinn is listed on the 1864 Griffith's Valuation as leasing a 14-acre site with home and outbuilding from Thomas F Moore. The farmland was located in the south of the townland on the Aughnahorey border. His home was situated on the west side of his land in the Aughnaloopy Road and intersected with GV40 (Thomas Quinn), GV17B (Patrick Fitzpatrick) and GV18D (Edward Quinn).

In 1865, the property passed over to Ann Quinn and then in 1874 to James Quinn. In 1893, it passed to Patrick Bradley (the son of Hugh Bradley and Ann Quinn). Two years later on June 11, 1895 Patrick married Abigail 'Abby' Callaghan from Ballinran and the couple had at least three children: James (b. May 22, 1896), Ann Mary (b. March 25, 1899) and Sarah (c.1902). Witnesses to the baptism of James were Rose Ann Johnson and Matthew Rogers. Witnesses at Ann Mary's baptism were John Johnston and Ellen Flanagan. Patrick Bradley died on February 12, 1924.

When Ann Quinn Bradley died on February 22, 1896, the Inland Revenue Affidavit stated that she was a widow and that she had three lawful children. In addition to Patrick, there was a daughter Sarah who was married to one of the McVeighs. and the other child was likely called Hugh. Ann left her house and belongings to her daughter Sarah McVeigh and stated that her granddaughter Sarah Bradley should always have a home there.

Chapter 37

Rogers Family

Francis, James and Patrick Rogers are listed in the 1830 Tithes Applotment Book for Aughnaloopy paying tithes on over 14 acres of land.

On the Griffith's Valuation in 1864, Francis leased a house, office and a small plot of land just off the Moyadd Road from John and Hugh Moore. A larger plot of farming land on the Leitrim border was also leased to Francis Rogers by William Orr. This may be the same Francis but interestingly, the land identified as number 42 passes to the representatives of Francis Rogers in 1874 and then passes to a Patrick Rogers in 1879. The site of the house is listed to Francis Rogers until 1890 when it passes to James Morgan. A search of the death records for Kilkeel would suggest that there were two Francis Rogers in the area of a similar age. One death record notes that 70-year old Francis Rogers died in 1889. This must therefore be the Francis who lived in the house that was taken over by James Morgan. Another record is for 85-year old Francis Rogers who died in 1873. This would appear to be the Francis whose land passed to Patrick Rogers.

Thus, there were two Francis Rogers with links to Aughnaloopy, one born in 1788 who died in 1873 and the other born in 1819 and died in 1889. It is possible that these were father and son and the elder is likely the Francis listed in the Tithes Book of 1830.

Patrick Rogers took over the land held by the older Francis in 1879 and it then passed to Edward Rogers in 1892.

One of the Francis Rogers had a daughter Mary Ann who married Bernard Doran from Aughnaloopy on June 6, 1862. A witness to the marriage was John Quinn. Bernard and Mary Ann had a son Patrick who was baptised on April 2, 1863. Nothing further is known about this family and it is speculated that they may have emigrated as several of the Doran families from the area moved to Canada.

At the time of the 1901 census Bridget Rogers was living with her parents John Johnson and Bridget 'Biddy' Bradley. Bridget had married John Rogers from Aughnaloopy in 1886 in West Derby, Lancashire but was widowed prior to 1901 and was living at home with her two children, John and William. Her son John's baptism is recorded in Kilkeel as December 5, 1886 and his Godfather was named as George Rogers – likely a brother of John. No record has been found for William but on the 1911 census he stated that he was born in Liverpool. Bridget and her 3-year old son William are listed on the 1891 UK census as living in Kirkdale, Liverpool. At 26-years old, she is already widowed but her son John is not recorded in the household. She appears to have returned to Aughnaloopy between 1892 and 1900. Bridget's sister Rose Ann was married to Patrick Collins on September 14, 1899. Rose Ann and her son John were also living at home in Aughnaloopy in 1901. Also living in the house was Mary Johnson and her son John Sloan. On March 11, 1904 John immigrated to America on the SS Celtic where he went to work in Miles City, Montana.

Bridget Johnson and John Roger's son William was the only Rogers left in Aughnaloopy townland at the time of the 1911 census. He was living with his grandparents and his aunt Mary Johnson. The land eventually passed to the Quinn family.

Chapter 38

Speers Family

The surname Speers and variants including Spears, Spiers, Speirs, came into Ulster in the 18th century from both Scotland and England.

Samuel, William and John Speers

In 1830, Samuel Speers is documented as paying tithes on two plots of land in Aughnaloopy (a 6-acre and a 10-acre site). By the mid-eighteen sixties, three families with the name Speers were living in Aughnaloopy townland. Samuel Speers occupied a farm of over 10 acres identified as number 6 on the Griffith's Valuation in 1864, William Speers farmed over 6 acres of land identified as GV3 and John Speers had a house and over 11 acres of land at GV8. It is likely, but not possible to confirm, that Samuel, William and John were related and probably brothers.

No marriage records have been located for Samuel or William, although it is known that they both married and had children. On the details of John's marriage to Elizabeth Doran on June 14, 1846, his father's name is listed as William Speers and the townland is noted as nearby Leitrim. There are several Speers families in Leitrim including a Samuel and a William named in the 1830 Tithe Applotment Books, and it is likely that the Speers from Aughnaloopy are related to the Aughnaloopy Speers.

Samuel Speers, who lived at GV6, had a daughter Jane (b. 1841) who married into the Keown family of Aughnaloopy and a son Samuel (b. 1848) who married Jane McClenaghan from Aughnahorey.

William from GV3 was married to Margaret Hanna and had at least four children: Samuel (b. 1843), Margaret (b. 1849), Hugh (b. 1850) and Mary Margaret (b. 1851).

John, from GV8, married Elizabeth Doran June 14, 1846 at Kilkeel Church of Ireland Church. Elizabeth was a widow when she married John Speers and was a daughter of Patrick Doran. Her first husband is unknown. John and Elizabeth had at least eight children: Ann (b. 1843), James (b. 1844), Alexander (b. 1848), Margaret (b. 1849), John (c.1850), Mary (b. 1851), Eliza (b. 1854), and Jane (b. 1857).

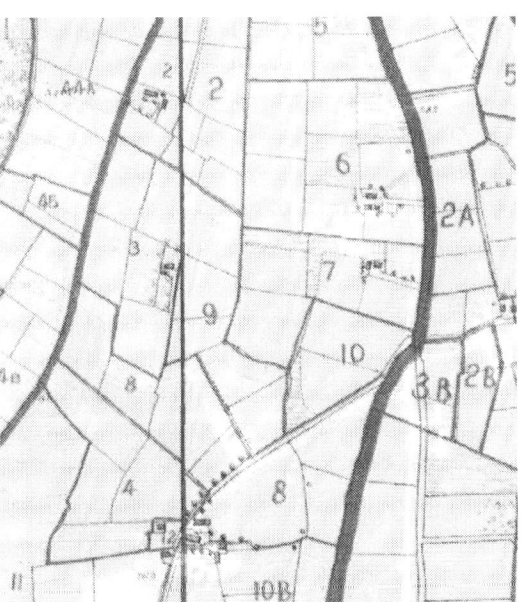

This extract from the 1864 Griffith's Valuation shows the location of the Speers property at numbers 3, 6 and 8.

William Speers and Margaret Hanna (GV3)

Margaret Speers and Samuel Speers

On June 2, 1870 Margaret Speers, the daughter of Margaret Hanna and William Speers, married Samuel Speers, the son of Alexander and Ann Speers, in Lennox and Addington, Ontario, Canada. Samuel documents that he was born in Amherst Island. The following year the couple are recorded on the Canadian census with their 2-month old son

Alexander. Samuel now states that he is of Irish origins and that he is a farmer. By 1881, the family has grown to include several children: Rachel, William F, Margaret H, Alexander and Isaac. The first-born son must have died in infancy as this Alexander is listed as being 2-years old. The family name is recorded as Spiers and the family is living close to Margaret's sister Mary Margaret and her husband James McMath. At the time of the 1891 census the family has grown further with the addition of children Nelson, Deborah and Beatrice. Samuel's parents are known to be Ann and Alexander Speers but their place of origin is unknown. It is certainly possible that they too originated in Aughnaloopy or a nearby townland.

Mary Margaret Speers and James McMath
Mary Margaret Speers was born to William Speers and Margaret Hanna of Aughnaloopy on October 12, 1851. Mary Margaret left her homeland and moved to Amherst Island in Canada where she met and married Canadian farmer James McMath. The marriage took place on March 15, 1876 when bride and groom stated that they were both 25-years old. In 1881, the couple are listed on the Canadian census with their three children: William, Jane and Herman. By 1891, the family had grown and seven children are listed: William, Eva, Herman, Elizabeth, Maud, Anna and Joseph. James was still farming but they had moved from Lenox to Chatham. Their daughter Elizabeth died on August 28, 1900 and is therefore not recorded on the 1901 census. Other than the loss of their daughter, life for the McMath family does not appear to have changed much in the ten years since the previous census. When Herman reached 21-years of age he married May Anderson on November 1, 1906. His mother Mary Margaret died the following year on October 31, 1907 followed by James McMath on September 30, 1910. Herman settled in the area with his wife and four children until his death on August 24, 1950. Most of the family stayed in the Chatham area including William J. who died in 1933, Mary Jane 'Eva' who died in 1961, and Ida Elizabeth who lived until 1990. In 1915, Annie Matilda moved across the border to Detroit where she lived with her husband Charles Garner until 1951. Maud Louise McMath also moved to the United States, settling in Detroit where she died in 1961.

Samuel Speers and Elizabeth
It is thought that William and Margaret's son Samuel may have spent time in Amherst Island, Canada with his sisters Margaret Mary and Mary before moving south to Troy in New York. In 1880 he is listed on the US federal census, with his wife Elizabeth and children: William J (age 5), Mary J (age 4) and Ellen (age 11 months). The family is living at 32 Fourth Street in Troy, Rensselaer near Albany, in New York State. Samuel documents that he is working in a steel works and that he has been unemployed for two months during the previous year. It was not uncommon for workers in the iron and steel industry to spend some time each year out of work. Also living in the household is Margaret Perry and Mary Shaughnessy. Samuel and Elizabeth document that they were born in Ireland and that the children were all born in New York.

By 1900, Samuel is widowed but still has his children living at home with him. The family has moved a couple of blocks over to 445 Second Street in Troy, Rensselaer, New York. Samuel is working as a labourer, William as a collar cutter, Mary as a housekeeper and Ellen as a stitcher. The family name is recorded as Spiers and Samuel states that he has been in the United States for 32 years. The property is a two-storey home with the other floor occupied by brother and sister Anna and John Kinsella.

By the time of the 1910 US federal census, William had left home but Samuel still had his daughters Mary J and Ellen living with him on Second Street. The family name was now recorded as Spears. Samuel was working as a labourer for the gas company, Mary was keeping house and Ellen was working at the collar factory. In the other part of the house lived William and Jesse Clifton and their young nieces Helen and Carmen Graham.

By 1930, the spelling of the name was back to Speers. Samuel was now 74-years old but he was still employed at the Gas Company and Mary J stayed at home keeping house. John Fitzgerald, his wife Anna and their three young children John, Gerald and Mary now occupied the other part of the building.

> **Collar City**
> *Troy was the centre of the collar-making industry in the United States and so it is not surprising that William, Ellen and many of their neighbours were employed as collar cutters and stitchers. The industry provided employment for thousands of working women, most of whom were Irish. To its residents, Troy was and still is called 'Collar City'. Collar workers laboured for long hours, often under trying conditions. The sewers stitched the collars by hand or machine, and worked at home and in the large collar factories of the area. After the collars were made, they were passed into the hands of laundresses who prepared the collars for sale to retailers. They were employed in independently owned laundries or in the laundering departments of large collar factories. Laundresses' working conditions were particularly harsh involving boiling water, caustic starches, dangerous detergents, and hot, heavy irons.*

Hugh Speers and Charlotte Cousins

William and Margaret's son Hugh stayed in Aughnaloopy at the family homestead, identified as GV3. At the time of his marriage to Charlotte Cousins from Brackenagh on May 10, 1898 at Rostrevor Presbyterian Church he was a widower and had a son also called Hugh who was born c.1886. The name of his first wife is not known. By the time of the 1911 census, Hugh was living in Aughnaloopy with his second wife Charlotte Cousins, also in the home was his son Hugh who was now married to Annie Elizabeth Orr from Ballymartin (daughter of Jocelyn Orr and Jane McKibbin). The name Hugh Speers was to continue with the birth of a son on September 8, 1911. A second child named Jocelyn after his maternal grandfather was born the following year. Sadly Hugh senior was not to meet his second grandson as he died on August 16, 1912 just two months before his arrival. Just two years later Hugh Jnr. died at 27-years old. His Will stated that he left a widow, two lawful children and '*two more remote lawful issue*'. Whom this statement refers to is unknown. His Will documents that his father William Speers's land and that '...*known as Patrick Bradley's*' should pass to his second son Jocelyn. One farm in Aughnaloopy was estimated to be 4 acres and was held in Fee Simple subject to the terminable annuity of £1 1s 4d payable to the Irish Land Commission. It was valued for probate at £67 18s 10d   The other was estimated at over 16 acres and valued at £396 3s 4d.

Samuel Speers and Jane McClenaghan (GV6)

Samuel Speers was born in 1848, at the property identified as number 6 on the Griffith's Valuation, located on the Aughnahorey Road. He was likely the first-born son as he was named after his father. On February 15, 1877, he married Jane McClenaghan at the Mourne Presbyterian Church in Kilkeel. Jane was the daughter of Jane Scott and Robert McClenaghan from nearby Aughnahorey townland. Jane had a sister Mary who married Alexander Speers on March 7, 1878 and two weeks later their brother James married Eliza Speers on March 21, 1878. Alexander and Eliza were the children of John and Elizabeth Speers.

Samuel and Jane had at least sixteen children including: Mary Margaret (b. 1877), John (b. 1879), James (b. 1880), Samuel (b. 1881), Agnes 'Nannie' (b. 1883), Elizabeth Jane "Lizzie" (b. 1885), Sarah (b. 1877), Robert (b. 1889), Elizabeth Leah 'Leah' (b. 1891), Thomas (b. 1893), Martha (b. 1895), Annie (b. 1898), William (b. 1899), Hugh (b. 1902) and Albert Joseph (b. 1904). The children were all baptised at Mourne Presbyterian Church in Kilkeel.

The family is recorded on the 1901 census for Aughnaloopy. Living at home was Samuel, his wife Jane and their children Mary Margaret, who was working as a sewer, John and James who were employed as set makers, Sarah, Robert, Leah, Thomas, and Martha who were all at school and 3-year old Annie and 1-month old William. Samuel's sister Jane Keown was also living with the family. She was a widow and was working as a seamstress.

By the time of the 1911 census, 32-year old Mary Margaret was the only daughter still at home. The older boys John, James and Samuel had also left home and Robert and Thomas were now helping their father to run the farm. The younger boys William, Hugh and Albert Joseph were still at home and attending school. Also living with the family was a granddaughter; 3-year old Ivy Speers. Ivy's place of birth is recorded, as being the Cape Colony and it is believed that she may be the daughter of one of the Speers boys that moved to South Africa in search of work. Sadly, Gladys Ivy died in 1914.

Agnes 'Nannie', Elizabeth Jane 'Lizzie', Sarah, Leah, Martha and Annie all left Aughnaloopy between 1901 and 1911 and eventually settled in the Bronx area of New York within walking distance of each other. The girls kept close ties to Ireland, with Agnes and Leah both marrying Mourne men. Leah's husband John Burden was instrumental in many young men from Annalong moving to New York where they found employment as stone cutters and masons.

Agnes Speers and Arthur Pue from Annalong

In 1920 Agnes 'Nannie' is settled on Eighth Avenue, New York with her husband Arthur Pue and their children: James (age 8), Elizabeth (age 7), Alfred (age 3) and baby Martha. Nannie and Arthur stated that they moved to the United States in 1909. All of their children were born in New York. Arthur worked as a stonemason and Nannie as an embroiderer of fine dresses. A ship manifest has been located for Arthur Pue showing that he emigrated from Ireland in April 1909. Arthur confirms his occupation as a stonecutter and gives his place of birth as Annalong. He documents that he is married but his wife is not on the ship with him. He gives his father's name as Arthur and states that he has a brother John who lives on Eight Avenue, New York. Nannie joined her husband in the following month travelling on the SS The Lusitania. She gives her place of birth as Aughnaloopy and lists her father as S Speers. It appears that Arthur and Nannie had spent some time in South Africa prior to moving to the United States. A record has also been found for John and Nancy Pue travelling together from Durban, South Africa to Southampton, England on the SS German, landing in Southampton on July 1, 1908. Several of Nannie's brothers are also believed to have worked in South Africa and there is some speculation that Samuel Speers moved out to South Africa and eventually died there. Certainly, there is evidence that the family had South African connections with Ivy Speers who was born in the Cape Colony living with the family at the time of the 1911 census. Nannie's husband Arthur Pue was also from a large family. His father, also called Arthur, and his mother Elizabeth Skillen had at least eleven children: Thomas (b. 1879), Arthur (b. 1883), Samuel (b. 1886), John (b. 1888), Alexander (b. 1890), Elizabeth (b. 1892), James (b. 1894), Robert (b. 1897), Francis (b. 1899), Annie (b. 1901) and Sarah (b. 1903).

Arthur Pue's parents, Arthur Pue and Elizabeth Skillen married on June 8, 1876 at Annalong Presbyterian Church. On the 1901 census they are listed as being 'Brethren' and in 1911 'Brethren' is noted along with the statement 'information refused'. Arthur is remembered as being a pious man who kept his bible on hand and as being able to quote from the scriptures as the occasion required.

Elizabeth 'Lizzie' Speers and Albert Biggs

In 1920, Lizzie and her husband Albert are living with their children: Marjorie, twins Ethel and Dorothy, Ivy, Charlotte and Albert on West 135th Street, New York City. Albert is employed by the gas company as a chauffeur. At the time of the 1930 US federal census, Lizzie is listed as living on Lancaster Avenue in the Bronx with her husband Albert and their children: Marjorie, twins Ethel and Dorothy, Charlotte, Albert and Walter. Albert is still working as a chauffeur. Lizzie states that she came to the United States in 1905.

On February 9, 1943, Lizzie and Albert's son Walter enlisted in the US Army. He stated that he had completed two years of high school and that he had worked in semi-skilled warehousing, storekeeping and related occupations. He entered the army in the rank of private and noted that he was single without dependents. He fought in France as part of the 346th Infantry 87th Division but tragically died in combat on December 14, 1944. He was awarded the Purple Heart Medal for bravery.

Sarah Spears and George Paules
Sarah was baptised on May 5, 1887. She left Aughnaloopy and travelled to New York on the SS Campania travelling with Charles Perry, Peter Burns, Thomas Murphy, Robert Newell and Isabella Anderson. The compatriots arrived in New York Harbour on April 13, 1907. Sarah was 20-years old. On July 31, 1918 she married George Paules who was originally from Pennsylvania. The couple are listed on the 1920 US Federal Census living in New York with their 8-month old son George. By 1930, the couple have a daughter Ethel who was born in 1924. George Paules worked in the clothing industry and is listed as an inspector of silk in 1930.

Isabella Leah 'Leah' Speers and John Burden
Samuel and Jane (McClenaghan) Speers daughter Isabella Leah 'Leah' was born on June 20, 1891. She left Aughnaloopy when she was just 16-years old. She travelled with neighbours Mary Ellen Hanna who was 17-years old, and 19-year old Alexander Beck. The friends travelled on the SS Caronia and arrived in New York on May 7, 1908. Alexander was the son of Alexander Beck and Mary Ellen was the daughter of James Hanna and Sarah Ann 'Annie' McKnight. Leah said that she was going to stay with her sister Lizzie.

A ship manifest for the SS Baltic, documents John Burden arriving in New York on April 16, 1906. There was quite a contingent of Annalong folk on board including: Robert Gordon, George Hill, Henry and Robert Aitkins, Andrew Nugent and Hugh Chambers; all whom planned to worked as stonemasons in New York. 20-year old Ellen Newell accompanied the men. She planned to work as a servant and gave the name of her cousin Samuel Jones who was already in New York. The following year John is documented as landing in New York on April 12, 1907 aboard the SS Furnessia. Again he states his occupation as a stonecutter. John Burden was born in Moneydarragh in 1883. He was the son of James Burden and Elizabeth 'Betty' Newell and was one of eight children. Leah and John knew each other for many years before they married. Marge Bosselman, who has assisted in the research of the family recounts that every time John saved up some money, Leah thought he was going to buy an engagement ring and propose marriage. Instead he made a trip back to Ireland and brought someone else from Mourne back to America with him. The Ellis Island immigration records support this story. John is named on a ship manifest for the SS Furnessia, arriving in New York on June 15, 1909. John lists his father's address as the Old Town Road, Moneydarragh. Travelling with him is Walter Mayhew and George Graham, both stonecutters from Annalong. The following year John makes another trip to Ireland and returns to New York on the SS Columbia, arriving at Ellis Island on April 24, 1910. Once again in 1912, he takes a trip back to see his family and returns to America on the SS Celtic arriving on March 23, 1912. On this trip, his sister-in-law Martha Spears travels back to New York with him, as does 20-year old Annie Mayhew from Annalong. In 1914, John makes yet another trip home. This time he returns from Londonderry on the SS Columbia arriving in New York on April 14, 1914. 28-year old George Mayhew from Annalong accompanies him on the trip. George Mayhew was the brother of Annie Mayhew; their parents were George Mayhew and Margaret McBurney.

An Irish Jig Down the Length of the Sigsbee Road
At the time of the 1920 US Federal census, Leah and John Burden are renting a home in New York City on West 156 Street. They have a daughter Ethel and a son Jack. Living with the young family is Leah's sister Martha and her husband Bernhardt Guth. By 1930, John and Leah are settled on Second Avenue in the Bronx with their 13-year old daughter Ethel and 1-year old Eleanor. Sadly, Jack died when he was just 14-years old from a blood disorder and is therefore not listed on the census. Also living in the home was 40-year old James Purdy. After Jack died, Leah had another son named James who was born in Mattituck, New York where the family had a summer home. When her sister Martha heard that Leah had given birth to a little boy, it is reputed that she *'...did an Irish Jig down the length of the Sigsbee Road'*. Their daughter Ethel died when she was 20-years old from a hearth condition that developed as a result of rheumatic fever. Eleanor

is alive and well and living in New Hampshire. She married Jack Chambers (the son of Annie and Alex Chambers) who was also from Mourne.

Martha Speers and Bernhardt Guth

Martha was baptised on June 18, 1895. When she was just 17-years old she travelled to New York on the SS Celtic with her sister Leah's husband John Burden, arriving at Ellis Island on March 23, 1912.

Six years after her arrival in the United States, Martha married Bernhardt 'Ben' Guth on March 14, 1918. Martha and her husband lived with their in-laws Leah and John Burden for a short time. By the time of the 1930 US Federal Census Martha has had a son Jerome 'Jerry' Guth and they have moved to West 177th Street in New York City. Bernhardt stated that he was born in New York and that his father was from Germany and his mother from Austria. He was employed as a travelling salesman in the jewellery business. Bernhardt complete draft documents for WWI and WWII and on both occasions he stated his date of birth as November 14, 1891 and place of birth as New York.

This photograph of Martha Speers Guth and her husband Bernhadt was kindly donated by her granddaughter Marge Bosselman.

Annie Speers and Joseph Edward 'Eddie' Ryan

Annie, the youngest of the Speers girls, was born in 1898. She followed in the tradition of her sisters moving to New York when she was 18-years old. She sailed out of Glasgow on the SS Cameronia with her friend Margaret Scott. The friends arrived in New York on December 7, 1915. Margaret was the daughter of Duncan Scott and Susanna Baird from Moneydarragh. On January 16, 1920 Annie married Joseph Ryan and the couple had just one son named Walter.

Thomas Speers

Thomas was born in August 1893 in Aughnaloopy. He answered the call to military service during World War I and is listed on the Presbyterian Church Extract for the Congregation of Mourne 1914 to 1918 Roll of Honour where he is noted as holding the rank of Private.

William Speers

William was born in Aughnaloopy in October 1899. He left Belfast in March 1926 on the SS Doric sailing to Halifax, Nova Scotia. He listed his mother Jane Speers in Aughnaloopy as his next of kin. The Canadian Government supplemented the cost of his passage and he gave his address as the Government Hotel, in Toronto, Ontario. He was in possession of four pounds. William eventually settled in Minnesota and had a daughter Mary Katherine.

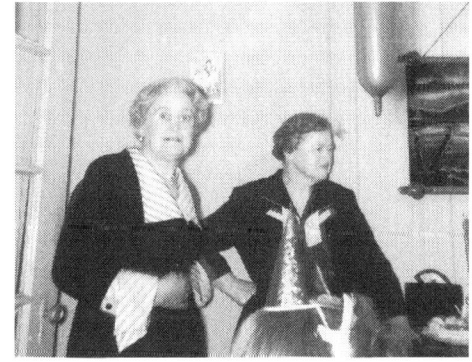

This photograph of Sarah Speers Paules with her sister Elizabeth Leah Burden was kindly donated by Marge Bosselman.

Samuel Speers

Samuel moved to Canada and married a girl called Isabelle.

The other brothers all stayed in Ireland as did the oldest girl Mary Margaret.

Mary Margaret Speers and Robert Forsyth

Mary Margaret Speers was baptized on March 19, 1877. She was the eldest daughter of Samuel Speers and his wife Jane McClenaghan. She is listed on both the 1901 and 1911 census documents as living at home with her family. She assisted the family financially by taking in sewing work. On October 23, 1913, when she was 36-years old, she married Robert Forsyth whose family were originally from Ballinran.

Robert's father Samuel had moved to Frizington in Cumberland (now Cumbria) where he was employed as an iron ore miner. Samuel and his wife Ann Jane had a son George who was born in Kilkeel in 1881, they then moved to England where their sons Robert and John James and daughter Ellen were born. When his wife died Samuel returned to Ballinran with his young children and eventually remarried Elizabeth McKnight on July 8, 1893.

Elizabeth Doran and John Speers (GV8)

John, from GV8, married Elizabeth Doran on June 14, 1846 at the Church of Ireland Church in Kilkeel. Elizabeth was the daughter of Patrick Doran and was a widow when she married John Speers. Her first husband is unknown. At the time of their marriage both Elizabeth and John stated that they were from Leitrim and so they may have moved to Aughnaloopy after their wedding. John stated that his father's name was William and it is possible that he was the son of the William noted as paying tithes on land in Leitrim in 1830. Elizabeth and John had at least eight children: Ann (b. 1843), James (b. 1844), Alexander (c.1848), Margaret (b. 1849), John (c.1850), Mary (b. 1851), Eliza (b. 1854) and Jane (b. 1857), and the family lived at the site in Aughnaloopy identified by number 8 on the Griffith Valuation.

On John Speer's land was a small site and property that was leased to John Wilson but no relationship between the Wilson and the Speers or Doran family has been found.

No further information is known about their daughters Ann or Margaret. Mary and Jane remained unmarried and stayed at home when their brother Alexander took over the family farm.

Alexander Speers and Mary McClenaghan

Elizabeth and John's son Alexander was born in 1848. He married Mary McClenaghan on March 7, 1878 at Mourne Presbyterian Church in Kilkeel and the couple settled on the family homestead in Aughnaloopy. Mary was born in 1857, the daughter of Robert McClenaghan and Jane Scott. Her sister Jane had married Samuel Speers, likely a cousin of Alexander, the previous year. Alexander and Mary had at least nine children, two of whom died in childhood. At the time of the 1901 census daughters Annie, Ellen, Maggie, and Mary Jane were living at home along with sons John, Alexander and Samuel. Also in the house were Alexander's mother Elizabeth, his sisters Mary and Jane and a nephew David Beck.

John Speers and Margaret Scott

John, the son of Elizabeth Doran and John Speers was born c.1850. He married Margaret Scott, the daughter of Robert Scott from Ballinran on January 20, 1871 at Mourne Presbyterian Church in Kilkeel. The couple had at least two children: John (b. 1871) and Robert (b. 1878) and settled in Ballinran townland. At the time of the 1901 census, Robert was living with his aunt Jane Scott and nieces Dinea Scott, Eliza, Martha and Agnes Speers.

My Grandmother Martha Speers Guth

Martha's granddaughter Marge Bosselman, Jerome's daughter, remembers Martha Speers fondly and has kindly contributed the following memories.

My grandmother Martha Speers Guth was an amazing woman, as were her sisters who came to America: Lizzie Speers Biggs, Sarah Speers Paules, Nannie Speers Pue, Leah Speers Burden, and Annie Speers Ryan. The one thing I would like to make perfectly clear is that they were very loyal to one another and an extremely close-knit family; no one came between those sisters. They were always there for one another, no questions asked. They were extremely fun loving and happy they always saw the bright side. I remember a story my grandmother told me about Aunt Sarah's husband apparently he was having an affair, well the sisters got together and chased him down the street hitting him on the head with their pocketbooks, that was the end of his affair! My grandmother was a card player.... poker was her game of choice, just about every Saturday night she either had a card game at her house or took a cab over to the Bronx to one of her friends. I might add she was always dressed to the nines complete with diamonds and pearls. I would go with her sometimes and she would give me 5 cents when she won a hand, I always came home thinking I was rich! I might add it was usually about 3 o'clock in the morning when we finally rolled in. Growing up there was no place I'd rather be than with my Grandmother. My Aunt Leah lived around the corner from my grandmother we would go there often for tea. A friend from the old country used to stop by and she would always read our tea leaves when she left my Aunts and Grandmother would get "a big bang out of her", in other words a big laugh as they used to say. My Grandmother never forgot her roots, I remember Sunday afternoon playing cards with her just the two of us and she would tell me about the Mourne Mountains, and all about growing up in Kilkeel. She told me about Minnie McKnight and Hugh Fullems, the Kilmorys, the big house were she worked as a maid, and her sister Mary Margaret Speers Forsythe all she left behind, but never forgot. My Grandmother was everybody's 'Aunt' I guess because she had a lot of nieces and nephews. I really don't know why, it may well have been just an endearment, I can easily say I was very lucky to have not only known her but very lucky to have one of Kilkeel's own, who I very proudly called Grandma. I had to wait until I was 60 to visit Grandma's beautiful town of Kilkeel. It was just like she said it would be, with the Irish Sea and the beautiful Mourne Mountains. We were welcomed with open arms; I never imagined my sister Carol and I have so many relatives. We visited the house where my grandmother was born, it had been just one room but now with several additions on it, it is a lovely cottage in Aughnaloopy. It's hard to imagine 17 children growing up there and some of them coming to America to lead rich full lives.

She was the absolute best, my friend, my confident, my heart, Martha Speers Guth, Grandma.

'…….no one came between those sisters.'

This photograph donated by Marge Bosselman shows, Elizabeth (Lizzie) Speers Biggs, Annie Speers Ryan, Martha Speers Guth seated in the back and Lizzie's daughter Ethel Capria and granddaughter Mary Scott in the front.

Chapter 39

Trainor Family

Special thanks to Gabriel Greene, Kilkeel

The name occurs with several variants including Trainor and Traynor within the same family.

Thomas Trainor and Bridget 'Biddy' Cunningham (Bradley)

The origins of the Trainor family in Aughnaloopy begin in Ballymageough townland. On March 23, 1858, Thomas Trainor married Bridget 'Biddy' Cunningham at Massforth RC Church in Kilkeel. Witnesses to the marriage were John Maguire and Mary Quinn. Ballymageough is listed as the townland for Thomas but nothing is noted for Biddy. The couple must have moved to Aughnaloopy shortly after their wedding because when their daughter Margaret was baptised on January 1, 1859, Aughnaloopy was noted as their place of residence. This would suggest that Biddy had a previous connection to the townland. The couple had at least five more children: Ellen (b. 1860), Ann (b. 1862), Thomas (b. 1864), James (who died in infancy), and James (b. 1872). There is a possibility that Biddy had been married previously and so it can not be confirmed that Cunningham was her original family name. The speculation of a previous marriage comes from a reference in Thomas Trainor's Will to two step daughters, Catherine Rogers and Mary McVeigh of Maghereagh. There is a Mrs. Mary McVeigh (wife of Thomas McVeigh) living in Maghereagh at the time of the 1901 census, who is of the appropriate age. This Mary documents that her father was Patrick Bradley from Aughnaloopy and gives an approximate date of birth as 1856. On her marriage to Thomas McVeigh on January 18, 1889, Mary states that her father was deceased and lists Annie Trainor as her witness, further supporting the idea that she was the step daughter of Thomas Trainor.

The property that Thomas Trainor leased from the Moore family in the 1860's consisted of over 10 acres of land and is identified as 30a on the Griffith's Valuation. There were two farmhouses on the land positioned on opposite sides of the Aughnaloopy Road identified as GV30a and GV30b. The one house was occupied by Thomas Trainor and his family and the other was the home of Ann Bradley. Ann Bradley (nee Quinn) was the wife of Hugh Bradley (deceased) and she also held a 3-acre site adjoining Thomas Trainor's property. Hugh Bradley is thought to have had three brothers: James, Felix and Patrick. This could be the Patrick Bradley that was married to Biddy before her marriage to Thomas Trainor.

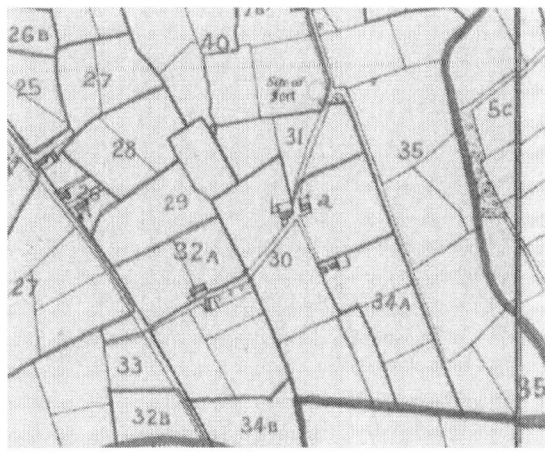

Extract from the Griffith's Valuation map of 1864 showing the location of the farm house lived in by Thomas Trainor marked as 30a and Ann Bradley's home at 30b. The farmhouses are in the south of Aughnaloopy townland and were leased from the Moore family.

Margaret Trainor and Arthur Morgan
Thomas and Biddy's eldest daughter Margaret married Arthur Morgan from nearby Cranfield on January 21, 1882. Witnesses to the marriage were Mary Bradley and Thomas McVeigh. This is likely the couple that settled in Maghereagh. Margaret and Arthur had a daughter Mary Catherine 'Mary Kate' born in 1883 but Margaret died shortly after her birth leaving Arthur with an infant to care for.

Ellen Trainor
Nothing is known about Ellen and she does not appear on the 1901 census.

Ann Trainor and Daniel Canavan
Thomas and Biddy's daughter Ann was baptised at Massforth RC Church in Kilkeel on June 19, 1862. On November 27, 1890 she married Daniel Canavan (the son of John Canavan and Ellen Cunningham). Martha Rooney and Arthur Cunningham were witnesses to the marriage. Daniel stated that he was a farmer and that he was from Leitrim. The couple settled in Leitrim where they had at least four children: Thomas John (b. 1892), Mary Ellen (b. 1894), James (b. 1897), and Annie C (b. 1900).

Thomas Trainor
Thomas inherited the family homestead from his father. Gabriel Greene reports that Thomas was thought to be 6 foot 6 inches tall. He remained single and lived in Aughnaloopy until his death. He is listed on the documents relating to the 1925 Northern Ireland Land Act and the Estate of Betty Clarke (spinster). In a document published in The Belfast Gazette, dated January 10, 1930, Thomas Trainor is noted as paying rent of £5 10s 0d to Betty Clarke for over 9 acres of land.

James Trainor
Nothing is known about James other than that he inherited 30 pounds from his father's estate. He is resident in Aughnaloopy at the time of the 1901 census but is no longer at home in 1911.

Mary Catherine 'Mary Kate' Morgan
At the time of the 1901 census, 18-year old Mary Catherine Morgan was living in Aughnaloopy townland. Mary Kate (as she was known) was living with her grandmother Bridgit Trainor (nee Cunningham/Bradley) and her maternal uncles Thomas and James Trainor. Bridgit Trainor was the widow of Thomas Trainor who was originally from Ballymageogh townland. Mary Kate's mother had died when Mary Kate was only a baby and it is likely that she was reared by her grandmother in Springfield, Aughnaloopy. There were no other known siblings. Her Grandfather Thomas Trainor made provision for Mary Kate in his Will dated 1892, leaving her £10 on '....*the condition that she remains with my family until her 21st year.*'

Arthur Morgan and his wife Charlotte Rogers outside their home in Cranfield. The home is still occupied by a descendant of the family. This photograph was kindly donated by Pat O'Brien who has conducted research on Arthur and Charlotte's son Hugh.

Mary Kate's father, Arthur Morgan (baptised July 31, 1853) was the son of Hugh Morgan from Cranfield and Mary McVeigh. He had at least five siblings, Edward (c.1845), Mary (baptised November 25, 1845), Patrick (baptised July 15, 1848), Hugh (baptised January 20, 1851) and Sarah (baptised May 4, 1861). On February 18, 1896, twelve years after his first wife died, Arthur Morgan married Charlotte Rogers, the daughter of Edward Rogers from Ballymartin and Mary Ann Gibben. Arthur's brother Edward Morgan and Annie McVeigh were witnesses to the wedding.

In 1901 Arthur was living in Cranfield, with his new wife and their two sons James and Hugh.

Mary Kate Morgan married John Patrick Greene, from Maghereagh on January 20, 1910. She gave her place of residence as Springfield. John Patrick Greene was the son of Michael Greene and Anne McKay (daughter of Patrick McKay from Drumcro townland). Lizzie Rooney and Hugh Greene were witnesses to the marriage, officiated by the Reverend F. Burns. Although settled in Maghereagh, Mary Kate retained her family connections with Aughnaloopy and on the night that the 1911 census was conducted she was staying at her maternal Uncle Thomas Trainor's home. Thomas didn't marry and it's likely that Mary Kate visited on a Sunday, attending church at Massforth and helping Thomas with housework. Her husband, John Patrick Greene is recorded on the 1911 census living with his family in Maghereagh. He died on October 11, 1949. The Greene family remain in the property today, which is situated on the Leestone Road.

Photographs of Mary Kate Morgan from Springfield, Aughnaloopy and John Patrick Greene, kindly donated by Gabriel Greene.

Cranfield Connections

In 1911, Mary Kate's father was still living in Cranfield. The family had expanded and there were now five children: James (b. 1898), Hugh (b. 1900), Sarah (b. 1903), Arthur Joseph (b. 1905) and John Francis (b. 1908). Also living in the home was 66-year Edward Morgan, who was Arthur's brother, and 30-year old John Morgan. Edward stated that he was married and John that he was single. Both men stated their occupation as labourer and it is likely that they assisted Arthur running the family farm.

Move to Chicago

Charlotte and Arthur Morgan's children Hugh, Arthur Joseph, Sarah and John Francis all eventually moved to Chicago, Illinois. James remained in Cranfield.

Hugh was the first of the family to emigrate. He travelled to Halifax, Nova Scotia, Canada and then moved on to Sault Sainte Marie, Michigan, United States. When he was 30-years old, he married Donegal-native Catherine Connaghan and the couple raised their family in Cook County, Illinois. Their children included: Arthur P, John F, Charleen, Cornelius J and Hugh C Morgan. Hugh was a member of the International Union of Operating Engineers. He died on February 27, 1970 and an announcement was placed in the Chicago Tribune.

> **Morgan**
> Hugh Morgan, Feb. 25, beloved husband of Catherine Connaghan Morgan; loving father of Arthur P. (Marianne), Cornelius J. (Elizabeth), Hugh C., John F. (Joan), and sister Charlene, O. P.; grandfather of 11; fond brother of Sarah Murtaugh, Arthur, John, and the late James. Funeral Saturday, 9:15 a. m., from Donnellan Funeral Home, 10525 S. Western avenue, to Visitation church, Mass 10 a. m. Interment Holy Sepulchre. Member of International Union of Operating Engineers, local 399. Native of Kilkeel, County Down, Ireland. BE 8-0075.

Arthur Joseph married Ellen Catherine 'Nellie' Doran from Rostrevor on June 19, 1928. The following year, he sailed on the SS Regina, arriving in New York Harbour on February 10, 1929, leaving his wife and infant daughter Mary Charlotte in Rostrevor. He stated on the ship manifest that this was a permanent move and that he would be staying with his brother Hugh at 817 West 51st. Street in Chicago. His wife Ellen Catherine joined him in 1933, sailing on the SS Cameronia, along with their 4-year old daughter Mary Charlotte. Her husband Arthur was listed as now living at 7601 Seeley Street, Chicago. Mary Catherine's contact Ireland was listed as Mrs. Annie O'Hanlon of Church Street, Rostrevor. The couple had two additional children, Patricia and Arthur (b. 1934) both born in Chicago. Mary Charlotte married Edward Victor Zelko and she remained in Chicago until her death in 1991. Edward died in 2003. Patricia married James Dempsey on January 19, 1960 in Chicago. Arthur married Joan Therese Moody on June 16, 1959 and died in Naperville, Illinois in 2007. Arthur Joseph died on April 22, 2007 and an announcement was placed in the Chicago Tribune.

> **Morgan**
> Arthur J. Morgan, beloved husband of Nellie, nee Doran; fond father of Mary (Edward) Zelko, Arthur (Joan) and Patricia (James) Dempsey; loving grandfather of 12; brother of Sarah Murtaugh, the late James, Hugh and John. Funeral Thursday, 8:45 a. m., from Egan Funeral Home, 3700 W. 63d St., to the Church of St. Mary Star of the Sea. Interment Holy Sepulchre. Visitation after 5 p. m. Tuesday. LU 2-2000.

Arthur and Charlotte's youngest son John Francis was born in Cranfield on March 18, 1908. He moved to Chicago in 1930 when he was 22-years old. He travelled with his older sister Sarah (who listed her occupation as a cook) and Mary Margaret Greene on the SS Caledonia, arriving in New York Harbour on April 28. The siblings gave their brothers Hugh and Arthur as their contact in the United States listed the address as 5546 Ingleside Avenue, Chicago. John Francis became a naturalised citizen of the United States November 18, 1937. He was enlisted into the United States Military on August 8, 1942. His civil occupation was stated as 'Semiskilled occupations in slaughtering and in preparation of meat products'. On April 24, 1943 John Francis married Mayo-born Mary Josephine Quinn (daughter of Thomas Quinn and Bridget Rice). The couple had at least four children: Ann, John, Emmet and Brian.

> *John Francis was drafted into the United States forces during World War II and found himself sent to Cranfield. He survived the War but when his three sons were visiting Gabriel Greene's parents on the Leestone Road in the early 1970's, they received word that they had been drafted into the United States forces and they were being sent to Vietnam. I remember them all in tears.*
>
> Gabriel Greene

Chapter 40

Wilson Family

Alexander Wilson

Alexander Wilson is listed in the 1830 Tithes Applotment Book but he had died prior to 1864 Griffith's Valuation. Alexander's wife in unknown but the couple had at least four children: Margaret (c.1815), Ann 'Nancy' (c.1820), John (c.1830) and Alexander (c.1830).

Margaret married Aughnaloopy native James Beck and remained in the townland. Nancy married Nicholas Hagan and after his death married John Skillen from Glenloughan. John married Margaret Hagan and settled in Aughnaloopy. Nothing is known about the son Alexander.

Margaret Wilson and James Beck (GV12)

Alexander's daughter Margaret married James Beck c.1836. Their first son Alexander named after his grandfather was born in 1838. The couple had at least eight more children: Thomas (b. 1841), Margaret (b. 1843), Elizabeth (b. 1845), Ann (b. 1851), Hugh (b. 1852), Jane (b. 1854), Tesetta/Teresa (b. 1856) and Sarah (b. 1858). When Thomas and Margaret were baptised, their place of residence was listed as Aughnahorey, Elizabeth's was listed as Aughnaloopy and for Sarah, Moyadd was listed. When he married Sarah Ann Baird, from Aughrim, at Mourne Presbyterian Church on April 22, 1864, Alexander gave his place of residence as Aughnaloopy. By the time of the 1901 census, Alexander Beck and Sarah Ann Baird were living in Aughnaloopy in a home built on land previously occupied until 1889 by John Mills and his wife Mary Spears. In 1891, the old house that had been on the site was pulled down. Alexander and Sarah Ann raised at least seven children in the house: Ellen (b. 1866), James (b. 1868), Thomas (b. 1865), Hugh (b. 1880), Teresa (b. 1871), Alexander (b. 1873) and Jane (b. 1877).

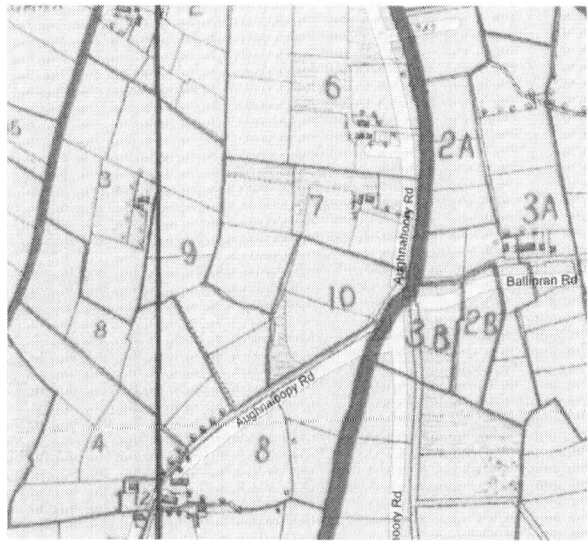

Extract from the Griffith's Valuation map of 1864 showing the location of the properties lived in by the Wilson family.

John Wilson had a small property identified as 8b and also 5 acres of farmland identified as site 9.

The 11-acre site at 8a was occupied by the Speers family.

Nancy Wilson lived at the site identified as GV7. It consisted of over 6 acres.

John Wilson and Margaret Hagan (GV9)

Alexander's son John Wilson married Margaret Hagan on January 11, 1856 at the Meeting House Lane Presbyterian Church in Kilkeel. Margaret was the daughter of William Hagan from Aughnaloopy, who was likely a brother of Nicholas Hagan who was married to John's sister Nancy. There is some speculation John's family may have originated from Drumgrath but this is unconfirmed.

John and Margaret had at least three children: Mary Margaret baptised on December 17, 1861, Teresa born on December 26, 1865 and Ellen born on April 30, 1868.

John Wilson and his family settled at the property identified as number 8b and 9 on the Griffith's Valuation. By 1881, the property had passed to the Hanna family.

Nancy Wilson and Nicholas Hagan (GV7)

Nancy married Nicholas Hagan c.1842 and the couple had at least four children together: Samuel, John, Ann and another child named Samuel. Information on the children is detailed in the earlier chapter on the Hagen family. Nicholas died prior to 1857.

Nancy Wilson and John Skillen (GV7)

Nancy married for a second time on June 11, 1857. Her husband was bachelor John Skillen and it is Skillen's name that is documented on the 1864 Griffiths Valuation for the six acre property identified as number 7 (the site previously occupied by Alexander Wilson). Skillen was not a known Aughnaloopy name and further research revealed that John was originally from Glenloughan. It does not appear that Nancy and John Skillen had any children.

By 1872, the house that was on this site occupied by John Skillen and his wife Margaret Wilson was taken down and the land was taken over by Nancy's brother Alexander Wilson for a couple of years. From then up until the time of the 1911 census, it remained as farming land only and was leased by Alexander Beck of Aughnaloopy. Alexander Beck was the son of Margaret Wilson and James Beck.

An Unrelated Wilson

An unrelated Wilson was also living in the townland. This was Elizabeth Wilson, the daughter of William Wilson, from Blackwatertown. Elizabeth was married to the Rev. George Nesbitt who was the minister at the local church from September 1831 and also the Presbyterian chaplain at Kilkeel Union Workhouse. The couple had two daughters: Bessie Ann (who married George William Thompson) and Sarah (who married Rev. William Jordan). George Nesbitt retired in 1874 and died on May 11, 1880.

Chapter 41

An Orphan's Tale

Special thanks to by Marilyn Wilson nee Bingham, Brisbane, Australia.

Four orphan girls are listed on the 1901 census for Magheramurphy, Kilkeel: Elizabeth Leith (age 11), Agnes Leith (age 8), Mary Elizabeth Douglas (age 10) and Emma Douglas (age 8). The girls are living in the care of a widow, Elizabeth Ann McDowell, who has two daughters of her own Susan (age 18) and Eliza Jane (age 17). The family are all noted as being members of the Mourne Presbyterian Church. Elizabeth Ann McDowell was the widow of Henry McDowell and her property was located on the Harbour Road. Elizabeth Ann was originally from Brackenagh and the daughter of Henry Cousins. She also had a son called Henry who was living with her brother Henry Cousins in 1901 helping out on the farm in Brackenagh. By 1911 Henry Cousins had married Mary Margaret Hanna and was living in Ballinran with their three children: Eileen, Robert and James Henry.

The Leith Family of Ballypalady

Further research into Elizabeth and Agnes Leith revealed that they were the daughters of Joseph and Margaret Barber Leith from Ballypalady, near Templepatrick, County Antrim. This is in contrast to family folklore which maintained that Agnes was originally from Scotland. Agnes's maternal Grandmother, Jane (nee Hood) Barber of Ballypalady, was present at Agnes's birth on September 9, 1893. Agnes was the third of three daughters, born to Joseph (c.1855 – 1893) and Margaret Barber Leith (1855 – 1897). Agnes's father died in the year of her birth and her mother died four years later. It is possible that the Presbyterian Church helped make arrangements for the young girls to be placed in homes when their parents died. Whatever the details, in 1901, 8-year old Agnes and 11-year old Elizabeth, were living in Kilkeel with widow Elizabeth Ann McDowell.

Sadly, Agnes lost her sister Elizabeth Leith in 1905 when she died at just 14-years old. Agnes maintained contact with her other sister Jane and by 1911, Agnes had moved to Belfast where she was working as a general domestic servant for George McKinny, near to the residence where Jane (known as Jean), was employed.

The Douglas Family from County Durham

Research into the orphan girls Mary Elizabeth and Emma Douglas revealed that their family originated in South Shields, County Durham, England. Their paternal grandparents James Douglas and Mary Renwick married in South Shields in 1853. James and Mary had at least six children: David Renwick (b. 1855) and Emma (b. 1857) both born in England and Elizabeth (b. 1862), Mary Renwick (b. 1869), James (c. 1870) and Sarah (b. 1871), all born in Dublin.

James and Mary's son James married Rebecca Hanna on October 27, 1890 in the North Strand Church in Dublin. Rebecca was the daughter of Joseph Hanna, a carpenter from 16, New Street in Newry. They had two known daughters, Mary Elizabeth (b. 1891 in Dundalk, County Louth) and Emma Renwick (b. 1893 in Belfast, County Antrim). It appears that James and Rebecca both died prior to 1901 and hence the girls went to live with Elizabeth Ann McDowell on the Harbour Road in Kilkeel. There does not appear to be any family connection between the girls' parents and Mrs. McDowell and the reason why they went to live with her is unknown. In 1901, the girls' grandparents James Douglas and Mary Renwick were still alive and were living in Duncairn Gardens, County Antrim. James gave his age as 72 and noted his occupation as Tug Boat Owner; his wife Mary was 68-years old. Also in the home were their two daughters: 38-year old Elizabeth and 30-year old Sarah, who were both working as governesses. By the time of the 1911 census, Mary Elizabeth and Emma Douglas had moved into a house on the Cavehill Road in Clifton, County Antrim with their aunts Sarah and Elizabeth. Mary Elizabeth, now 19-years old was working as a National School Teacher, while 17-year old Emma was still at school. It appears that their grandparents had died some time between 1901 and 1911.

James Douglas and Mary Renwick's daughter Emma was born in England in 1857. Emma married William Richard Bradshaw on August 28, 1877 at St. Thomas Church of Ireland church in Dublin. William was an insurance agent and he gave his father William's occupation as a linen factory superintendent. The family moved to the United States in 1882 and settled in Queens, New York, where they raised a large family.

David Renwick Douglas was born in 1855 and the birth registration occurred in Tynemouth, Northumberland. On July 25, 1881, he married Fanny Poynton in Liverpool. Fanny was a widow and eleven years his senior. Her maiden name was Fanny Francis and she was the daughter of James Francis. Fanny died in 1908 and in 1909 David married again, to Elizabeth Renwick (likely his cousin) in Dublin. The couple are listed on the 1911 census as living on Barlow Terrace in Merchant's Quay, Dublin, with Elizabeth's brother William and his wife Maud. David was employed as a Marine Engineer.

Mary Renwick Douglas was born in 1869 in Dublin. Mary died in 1874 in Belfast.

McDowell Sisters marry Denny Brothers

Agnes Leith remained in contact with the McDowell sisters that she grew up with. Susan McDowell married William Denny (b. July 13, 1883) on August 25, 1908 at Rostrevor Presbyterian Church. Susan gave her occupation as a dressmaker and William stated that he was a soldier. Elizabeth Jane "Jenny" McDowell married William's brother Samuel Denny (b. May 5, 1881) on the same day and at the same church. William and Samuel were the sons of Robert Denney and Elizabeth Hamilton. They had a sister Nancy (b. December 25, 1879) and a brother Robert (b. March 13, 1885) and were from Ballinran townland. Jenny Denny corresponded with Agnes Leith all her life.

Jean Leith marries George Henderson

Agnes and Jean had moved back to Kilkeel by 1912 and when Agnes signed the Ulster Declaration, she stated her place of residence as Aughnahoory. On July 16, 1912, her sister Jean married George Henderson, from Cranfield, at Rostrevor Presbyterian Church. George's father was also called George. Witnesses to the marriage were Susan Peoples and William Henderson. George listed his occupation as a mining contractor. The couple eventually moved to New Zealand.

Agnes Leith marries William Bingham

The connection to Aughnaloopy occurs when Agnes married William Bingham in 1921. Their marriage certificate clearly states that both were residing in Aughnaloopy, on April 5, 1921. Williams's occupation was given as labourer. At first, it was thought that this may be an error and that it had been mistranscribed from Aughnahorey. However, viewing the actual marriage certificate clearly shows that Aughnaloopy was written for both Bride and Groom.

William Bingham was born on January 2, 1896, in Aughnahoory townland, the third son, and seventh of eight children. His parents were William Bingham (1857–1940) and Mary Norris Bingham (1856–1946). He was baptised in the Mourne Presbyterian Church, Kilkeel on March 1, 1896. His father was a miller and agricultural labourer, and resided on farmland, near Hanna's Close. Until his marriage William junior lived in Aughnahoory, with his family. He is documented on the 1901 census, the 1911 census records and also on the 1912 Ulster Covenant and in all cases stated Aughnahoory as his place of residence.

Agnes and William's first son, John was born October 20 1922 in Aughnahoory. For unknown reasons Agnes, William and their son migrated to Lower Hutt, near Wellington New Zealand, departing from Southampton on February 3, 1928, aboard the RMS Corinthic. They had another son, Leith Henderson Bingham, who was born in New Zealand in 1930. Agnes died in Lower Hutt, on September 27, 1961. William worked as a Market Gardener, all his New Zealand working life. In his later years he lived with family in Christchurch, New Zealand. He died June 14, 1983 and is buried with Agnes.

Memories of My Gran Agnes Bingham
by Marilyn Wilson nee Bingham

There was a 55-year age difference, between my Paternal Gran, Agnes Bingham, nee Leith, and I. Agnes died when I was twelve; therefore, my memories are childhood ones.

My family moved from Wellington New Zealand, where we had lived only a short car journey from my Grandparent's Lower Hutt home, to Christchurch, when I was six years old. In the late 1950s, a visit from Wellington to Christchurch, in New Zealand's South Island, meant an overnight voyage in a ship. I only have memories of my Grandparents visiting us once in Christchurch, and we only visited them a couple of times. Despite seeing little of my Gran Agnes, after my sixth birthday, I do recall her vividly, having stayed with her, for several weeks, when my two younger sisters were born.

Agnes and William Bingham with their three grandchildren. This photograph was kindly donated by Marilyn Wilson (standing centre) and was taken c. 1958. Agnes died in 1961 and William in 1983.

The Agnes I knew was always frail and old, with thin grey hair in a horizontal roll, kept in place with a fine hair net. Her legs were clad in thick lisle stockings and the only shoes I think she owned were black lace ups. Floral dresses were tightly clasped at her neck with an insignificant brooch. Every Sunday, Agnes swapped her dowdy clothes for her Salvation Army smart black uniform and bonnet.

The Salvation Army had saved Agnes and her family from homelessness, when my Granddad William was unable to work for several months, due to illness. This caused Agnes to leave the Presbyterian Church and join Captain Booth's Army. Agnes had a miserable home life (I was told later by my parents) with an overbearing, grumpy husband. In her Salvation Army faith, she found comfort and companionship. While other grandparents told their grandchildren nursery stories and rhymes, Agnes sang me hymns and told me Bible Stories.

The few female friends I remember visiting Agnes and William's home wore Salvation Army garb. Agnes's elder sister Jean, to whom she was very fond of, lived about 55 miles away, having also migrated to New Zealand from Kilkeel. Agnes, I'm told, didn't remain in contact with many of her Northern Ireland friends, but did write regularly to Mrs. Jenny Denny. Jenny (nee Elizabeth Jane McDowell) had been Agnes's foster sister and the pair wrote to each other until Agnes died in 1961.

Gran Agnes was a kind, loving Grandmother, as warm and comforting as her delicious, freshly baked ginger cake, served with a cup a steaming Milo (hot chocolate drink).

Chapter 42

Springfield Villa

Difficulty into the research of 'Springfield' is confounded by references to Springfield Villa, Springfield House and a small area within Aughnaloopy townland referred to as Springfield.

Springfield Villa is identified as number 41 on the 1864 Griffith's Valuation and subsequent valuations. It lies on the Moyadd Road, on the boundary of Aughnaloopy and Drumcro townlands.

The first Griffith's Valuation was performed during December 1834 to January 1835 in the Kilkeel area. A note is made for Aughnaloopy stating that *'No House in this Townland worth £5 per annum'*. So it would appear that Springfield Villa was built sometime after this date. A smaller home may have existed on the site beforehand but this would not be recorded in the 1834 valuation.

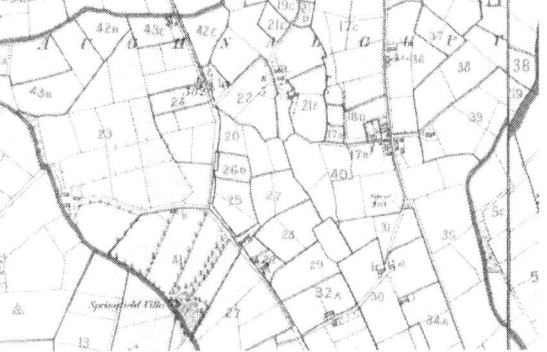

Extract from the Griffith's Valuation map of 1864 showing the location of Springfield Villa at the site identified as number 41. There were two houses on the site in 1864 marked as a and b. 41a was unoccupied and 41b was occupied by James Campbell.

In the 1856 Slater's Commercial Directory, Springfield Villa is listed as being the residence of James Hamilton Esq. and the Rev. George Nesbitt. It appears that the Hamilton family were not, however resident in Aughnaloopy and that they rented Springfield Villa to the Rev. Nesbitt. George Nesbitt was the Presbyterian minister at the local church and also chaplain at the Kilkeel Union Workhouse. He was married and had two daughters, Bessie Ann who married George H Thompson and Sarah who married the Rev. William Jordan.

James Hamilton Esq. died in October 1856 and Springfield Villa passed to his daughter Margaret who was by then married to Francis Carvill, a successful iron, timber and shipping merchant from Newry. Although Margaret lived until 1891, she remained in Killowen and it seems that it was her son James Lewis Carvill who took over the lease of Springfield Villa. It is unlikely that he lived in Aughnaloopy as his work as a merchant and as French Consular Agent for shipping was based in Newry town.

In October 1861, some land revaluations were made prior to the final version of the Griffiths Valuation being issued. Notably, James Murphy, a minor at the time, took over leases previously held by James Lewis Carvill who died in October 1864. James Murphy was the son of John Murphy and Mary Ann Hamilton and a grandson of James Hamilton Esq. He was a first cousin of James Lewis Carvill through the marriage of his mother's sister Margaret Hamilton to Francis Carvill. James was an invalid and died in February 1872.

In 1869, the Griffith's Revaluations note Mary Murphy as the occupier. This could refer to Mary Ann "Minnie" Murphy (James's sister) or to their mother. Possibly James was ill during these years because in April 1869 he wrote a Will stating that he was *'...of sound mind and understanding'*, bequeathing his property to his mother and on her death to pass to his sister. James states that he was *'..of Newry, Co. Armagh'* confirming the notion that he was not resident at Springfield Villa. His sister does appear to have lived in the house and in January 1878 on her marriage to James Morgan she states Springfield as her residence. In 1884, the Griffith's Revaluation states that James Morgan was the occupier of Springfield. No death date for his mother-in-law Mary Hamilton Murphy has been found but perhaps it was on her death that it passed to the Morgan family.

Mary Ann Morgan Murphy died in October 1896 and her husband James Morgan died in June 1901 (having remarried Imelda McMullan from Churchfield House, Hollywood, Belfast). The property is listed as being held by the 'Representatives of James H Morgan' until 1909 when it became the property of Thomas Quinn who lived on the neighbouring property. The property remains in the Quinn family to this day.

From Down to Downunder

From Down to Downunder
I can but wonder
What might have enticed them
Away from Kilkeel.

Who mourned their departure?
Were they so heart sure
That what they were doing
Could only be right?

It was in 1840.
Was their leaving so fraught he
Couldn't bear to record it?
We may never know.

Charlotte and William
Left all behind them
For the promise of life
In a bright southern land.

They named their place Springfield.
Was it after the green fields
They had known and loved,
So far away now?

Their sons grew and became men
Daughters too but then
They were orphaned, too early.
A high price to pay.

Their descendants admire
Their courage, their desire
To better their lives,
To risk all, come what may.

A challenge we face
In this daily rat race
Is to stop and remember
To thank them each day.

by Gaye Cleeland

The following lines were written by John Doran in a diary that he started when aboard the SS Carthalagen in March 1888, en route to the United States. It seems appropriate to duplicate them here. He was 19-years old at the time.

JOHNEY DORAN is my name
And in this book I write the same
The grass is green, the rose is red
This is my name when I am dead

When I am dead and in my grave
And all my bones is rotten
I hope this little book will tell my name
When I am quite forgotten

Mourne Miners

Publications

Made in the USA
Charleston, SC
06 July 2012